Voices *of* Wisdom

HAWAIIAN ELDERS SPEAK

MJ Harden

Photography by Steve Brinkman

COVER PHOTO:

Eddie Pu

BACK COVER PHOTOS:

Puanani Van Dorpe

George Nāʻope

Margaret Machado

Kawika Kaʻalakea

PAGE 1 PHOTO:

John Lake

Copyright © 1999 by MJ Harden
All rights reserved. No part of this book may be reproduced or transmitted in any form or by any means, electronic or mechanical, including photocopying, recording, or by any information storage and retrieval system, without permission in writing from the publisher.

Publisher

Aka Press

103 Johnson Road

Kula, HI 96790

808-878-2126

email : mjh@hawaii.rr.com

Photography by Steve Brinkman.

Tree image used throughout *Voices of Wisdom* drawn by Eric Sato.

Photo of Nainoa Thompson on page 214 by Eric Sato.

Library of Congress Catalog Card Number:
98-96762

ISBN: 0-944134-01-7

Library of Congress Cataloging-in-Publication Data

Voices of Wisdom: Hawaiian Elders Speak
MJ Harden

1. Culture—Hawaiian 2. Travel—Hawaiʻi
3. Hawaiians—Biography 4. Hawaiians—Portraits

Printed in China
10 9 8 7 6

In memory of Eric Sato

There were three of us who started this project,

then Eric left us for other realms.

He always said: "Expect change."

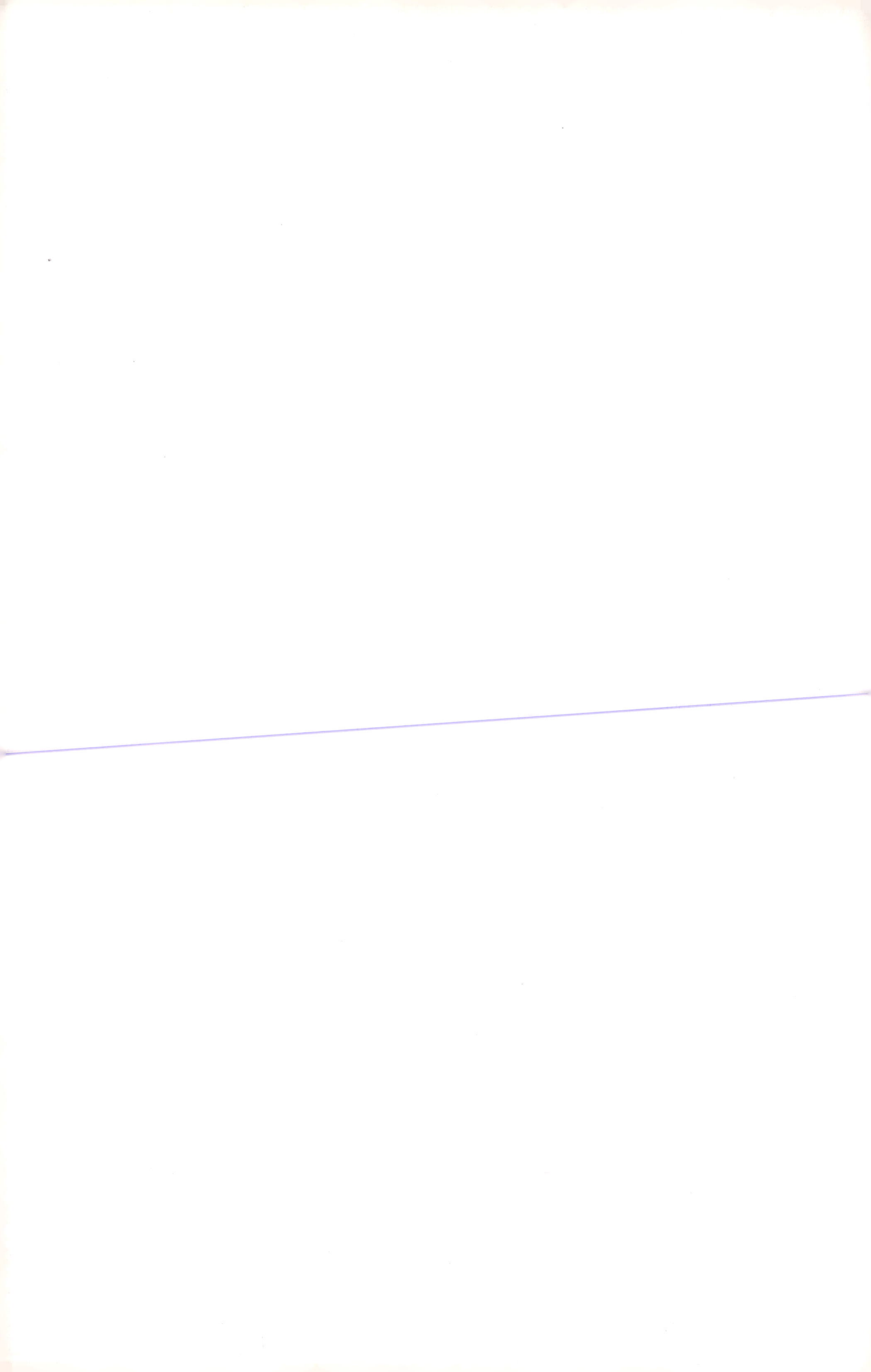

CONTENTS

INTRODUCTION		9
NATURE		13
Mary Kaauamo	*taro* farmer	15
Isabella Abbott, Ph.D.	professor of ethnobotany, seaweed expert	23
Eddie Pu	national park ranger	33
SPIRITUALITY AND HEALING		41
Margaret Machado	*lomilomi* massage master	45
Lanakila Brandt	priest of Lono	53
Kawika Ka'alakea	minister, herbal medicine practitioner	63
PRESERVATION AND HISTORY		71
Lydia Namahana Mai'oho	*kahu* of Royal Mausoleum	75
Charley Keau	archaeologist	85
ACTIVISM		93
Winona Beamer	Hawaiian Studies teacher, *hula* master	95
Kekuni Blaisdell, M.D.	physician, sovereignty advocate	103
Kapeka Chandler	community organizer	113
Elaine Kaopuiki	community activist, *hula* master	119
DANCE, CHANT, GENEALOGY, MUSIC		126
George Nā'ope	*hula* master	129
John Lake	chanter, *hula* master, Hawaiian Studies teacher	139
Edith McKinzie	genealogy expert, professor of Hawaiian Studies	149
Kindy Sproat	falsetto singer	157
ARTS AND CRAFTS		166
Puanani Van Dorpe	master *kapa* cloth maker	169
Marie McDonald	*lei* making expert, author	179
Elizabeth Lee	master *lau hala* weaver	187
CANOE		195
Jo-Anne Kahanamoku Sterling	crew member of *Hōkūle'a*, feather artist	197
Leon Paoa Sterling	captain of *Hōkūle'a*, man of the sea	197
Herb Kāne	artist, historian	205
NEXT GENERATION		213
Nainoa Thompson	navigator	215
Keola Sequeira	wood carver, canoe maker	225
GLOSSARY		235

# INTRODUCTION

It is 1777. Hawai'i's people have evolved one of the most sophisticated societies in Polynesia. They've come from ancestors so skillful they explored the entire Pacific centuries before Europeans had ventured into the Atlantic. And they did so by navigating solely by their profound understanding of nature. On land, they were regarded as the best farmers in Oceania, developing more than 200 varieties of both sweet potato and *taro*. They watered their fields with a well-engineered system of irrigation. Their clothing came from the finest bark cloth made in ancient times. They knew no crippling diseases like diabetes, cancer, cholera or smallpox. They didn't even catch colds or flus.

One year later, Captain James Cook and his British sailors arrived. They met a people self-sufficient and enterprising, with a culture advanced and vibrant. Neither Cook nor the Hawaiians had any idea how quickly all of this would be undermined.

Only a century later, Samuel Kamakau, a famous Hawaiian scholar wrote:

The people of today are destitute; their clothing and provisions come from foreign lands, and they do not work as their ancestors did. . . . One cannot again find skilled persons who had a deep knowledge of the land; those who are called learned today are mere vagabonds. . . . Because of the foreign ways of the race, they have abandoned the works of the ancestors.

If Kamakau wrote this opinion in the late 1800s, what hope could there be 100 years after that? If the people of the 1800s were "destitute" and had "abandoned" their traditions, how could today's people have any native culture left?

They almost didn't.

Western ideas, Calvinist doctrine and introduced diseases nearly extinguished Hawaiian culture and its people. In the mere two centuries since Cook's arrival, Hawai'i has changed completely. A culture that had remained untouched and little changed since the twelfth century evolved rapidly in the direction of pop-top beer cans and cellophane *hula* skirts.

By the 1900s, there were few left who understood ancient traditions or were even interested in them. *Hula*, for instance, was seldom danced except in tourist hotels, and then it would be of the coconut-bra-Hollywood-Waikiki style. Ancient *hula* was rarely performed openly. The art of making *kapa*, the bark cloth that had clothed the ancients, was dead—not a single piece had been pounded in modern times; no one knew how any more. Navigation, the once all-important profession of these ocean people, was a lost art. There was not a single navigator left in Hawai'i.

Everything Hawaiian seemed of no value, and this once proud nation of people who traced their lineage back to the beginning of time was now at the bottom of the social structure. Many of the elders interviewed in this book speak of growing up inferior. Such low self-esteem took its toll. Hawaiians today have a long list of dreadful statistics: the shortest life expectancy of all ethnic groups in Hawai'i, the highest rates of heart disease, stroke, cancer and diabetes, the highest infant mortality rate, the lowest median family income, the highest incarceration rate, the highest school drop-out rate, among others.

Two hundred years of this, and change was desperately needed. It came in the 1970s, paralleling the national movement for civil rights. Then, the Hawaiians began a renaissance of Hawaiian culture that even surprised themselves—it came so quickly and with such a force of emotion. People began taking *hula* lessons, learning to chant, insisting that Hawaiian history be taught in school, speaking the language again, reviving the ancient crafts.

The people in this book were leaders of the renaissance, some quietly, some publicly. Through them, Hawai'i restored and rejuvenated its culture. Today they are elders, highly regarded as *kūpuna* have always been since ancient times.

Kupuna means elder. In old Hawai'i, *kūpuna* were respected as keepers of Hawai'i's wisdom and knowledge. Still, today, younger Hawaiians are told: *Nānā i ke kumu,* "look to the source."

Kāhuna was the term used for elders who were preeminent in their fields. They were the best at what they did—be it canoe building or healing or chanting. All 24 men and women described in this book would have been *kāhuna* in Hawai'i's ancient days. Each is an expert in some facet of Hawaiiana. Twenty-two of those interviewed are elders; the other two represent the next generation—two younger men who, nonetheless, are definitely *kāhuna,* one an expert wood carver and canoe builder, the other the most famous navigator in Polynesia.

It is not just the stories and personalities of these 24 that are featured here; through each individual we learn about a discipline, talent or skill valued in Hawaiian culture: through Mary Kaauamo, why *taro* was the most important agricultural crop; through George Nā'ope, the significance of *hula* in the culture; through Edith McKinzie, how genealogy structured society in ancient days.

These are 24 people who have led lives that matter; and what matters most to them is to keep lit the flame of a culture that nearly died. It is through their efforts that Hawaiian traditions will live into the twenty-first century. They prompted more than a cultural rebirth, they inspired a revival of spirit.

NATURE

Nature is where it all begins for the Hawaiians. In fact, they call themselves *keiki o ka 'aina*—"children of the land."

The *'āina* is not just soil, sand or dirt. The *'āina* is a heart issue for Hawaiians. The very word *'āina* brings forth deep emotion evolved from ancestral times when people lived in nature as an integral part of it. Mankind and nature were considered siblings born to the same parents at the beginning of time.

The word *'āina* literally means "that which feeds," and *maka'āinana,* a term for the common class of people, means "eyes of the land." Thus, nature feeds man and man watches over nature in return. The land gave the ancients everything they needed—not just food, but clothing, housing, weapons, tools, musical instruments, canoes—everything they crafted, wore and ate came from plants, animals or fish. Dependent on nature, they revered and respected it.

"My people have been cultivators from very ancient times; it was by agriculture that they made a living for themselves," wrote Hawaiian scholar Kamakau.

His people were considered the best farmers in the Pacific. They developed hundreds of varieties of sweet potato and *taro,* their two most important crops. They classified and named their plants before Linnaeus was born, and they knew how to use all parts of plants—wood, bark, roots, leaves, fruits and flowers. Their herbal doctors had a highly developed science of healing.

Their sense of place was so keen that every valley had a name, as did every waterfall, stream, mountain, gulch and beach. The rains also had a multitude of names, and the winds were named by the hundreds. Mists and light rains were blessings from the gods, and in poetry rain and water symbolized abundance and life. Water is the most fundamental element in island cultures. In fact, though there was no concept of monetary wealth in ancient times, the word for prosperity was *waiwai* (double water). In nature they found all the *waiwai* they needed.

MARY KAAUAMO
TARO FARMER

It is said that *taro*, Hawai'i's staple food, was birthed before mankind. A many-layered legend reveals that *taro* is actually the elder brother of man, both born at the beginning of time. In the legend, *taro* symbolically represents nature, and, as the elder brother, nature feeds and sustains man. Mankind, in turn, cultivates and cares for nature. They are two siblings in harmony.

It is a beautiful and symbolic message, one that Mary Kaauamo (pronounced Ka-wah-mo) has lived all her life. Yet, ironically, she has never read the legend and has never even heard it told. As a *taro* farmer for five decades, Auntie Mary knows all a farmer needs to know about *taro*, but she didn't get a bit of it from books. She learned *taro* by standing knee-deep in muddy water weeding, harvesting and replanting.

"I don't read those kine legend kine stories. I don't have the books," Auntie Mary

"My husband worked with nature. He always plant with the moon when he plants his *taro*. Then when you harvest the *taro*, underneath is good. Full moon. *Māhea-lani Hoku*—that's the good moon to raise *taro*. That's how in the olden times. Hawaiian moon calendar. They tell you what moon for plant *taro*, what moon to plant for potatoes. They have fruit moon, they have vegetable moon, they have *taro* moon. The ocean they have their own moon. The farmers have their own."

says in her simple, direct way. "It's interesting to read all those things to see what had come before. But I only know after—my time of living."

My time of living. It is a time and a way of living that's becoming as legendary as the myths of old. Few make a living with *taro* as Auntie Mary still does in her eighties. And few Hawaiians live in such a Hawaiian village as Wailua.

Wailua sits on Maui's famous Keʻanae Peninsula which was formed when a lava flow extended into the ocean. From a cliff-side overlook, hundreds of tourists peer down onto Keʻanae every day and marvel at the ancient feel of the scene. It is one of those postcard-perfect landscapes with crashing seas and swaying palms, but it's the rows and rows of rectangular *taro* patches that make the peninsula look so very Hawaiian. In fact, a population survey taken in the 1950s called Keʻanae the most Hawaiian place in all of Hawaiʻi.

Though she has lived here for six decades, Auntie Mary did not grow up in Keʻanae. She was raised on the desert side of East Maui, an area called Kaupō.

"My parents, they raised sweet potatoes, not *taro*. Too dry Kaupō. They don't have water. We eat *taro*, but had to buy from Keʻanae," she explains.

When Kamuela Kaauamo came courting in 1935, a young Mary soon found herself in rainy Keʻanae where her husband's family had grown *taro* for generations.

"He born and raised here with his parents. He taught me. The first time I didn't want to go in the mud. Just had to go little by little till you get used to it. So I get plenty used to it [now]," she admits with a laugh.

Actually, as she got older and developed varicose veins and poor circulation, her doctor told her that slogging through the mud of the *taro* fields was good medicine for her legs.

Taro is a root crop that grows an underground corm about the size and shape of a small pineapple. The corm is cooked like a potato; it cannot be eaten raw. The cooked corm is also pounded into a gooey paste called *poi*—the most Hawaiian of all foods. Tourists liken *poi* to wallpaper paste, but those who grow up with freshly made *poi* cannot live without it. As Asians eat rice at every meal and Europeans eat bread, Hawaiians eat *poi* as their staple food. Auntie Mary says her family eats it "every meal, every day."

The *taro* corm is a very nutritional complex carbohydrate. The plant's big green leaves are eaten like cooked spinach and have just as many vitamins.

The Hawaiians, who were extolled as the best farmers in the Pacific, reputedly had 300-some varieties of *taro*. Now there are only about 100 known varieties.

NATURE: **Mary Kaaumao**

To Auntie Mary, though, *"Taro* is *taro."* She doesn't worry about varieties. "Some they're so particular what kine *taro* they want, you know da kine. To me it's no difference. *Taro* is *taro*. The taste the same. I don't know why they want more of the red *taro* than the white *taro*. I don't know why. Same t'ing, no difference."

Taro is generally grown in paddies of water. In Keʻanae, stream water is channeled into neatly arranged ditches that feed into all the patches, called *loʻi* in Hawaiian. These precisely laid out *loʻi* that Auntie Mary and her neighbors work are the same patches the ancients worked. From above, the geometry of the *loʻi* is as symmetrical as Midwestern cornfields.

It is known that chiefs as far back as the sixteenth century did not wage battles in Keʻanae. The area was too important for both sides of any war—it was the breadbasket that fed the people.

Most *taro* farmers depend financially on outside jobs like construction or county road work. Even in Keʻanae, where *taro* grows in everyone's backyard, the Kaaumaos are a rarity. Mary and her husband never took on outside work. They spent 61 years together raising seven children and tons of *taro*.

> *Mary and her husband never took on outside work. They spent 61 years together raising seven children and tons of* taro.

"My husband never worked for nobody till he died [in 1995]," she says. "This [farming] is good job. You boss yourself. When it rains, you don't go, you stay home."

You must, however, be willing to live on what many would describe as poverty level. But, Auntie Mary says her life style is not about money.

"Over here is good for poor people," she says of Keʻanae. "If you're not lazy to go work *taro* patch and you live on your *taro* land, it's good fun to work. We all like. You cannot help. You gotta be patient, the main t'ing.

"The beginning we have our children. They were small. We raised them with the *taro*. Those days, in the beginning, we didn't sell any *taro,* but we used for eat."

During those early days of the 1930s and 1940s, there was no money in the Kaauamo household. At that time nobody was buying or selling *taro*.

How then did the Kaauamos buy things for the family?

They didn't.

"No money. No more nuttin. Just *taro*," Auntie Mary explains with a shrug, as if no big deal. "We had to live on *taro*. That's only what we live on. *Taro*. You worked for your family."

Things changed slightly after World War II. Then, *taro* became a fledging commodity.

"In 1948 people wanted *taro* from other places—Honolulu. That's when we started to harvest *taro*. But those days, we had only $3 a bag. One hundred pounds for a bag. That's true. In the beginning it's only eight bags a week. Now, we try to make 1,000 bags a year. It's $40 for 80 pounds now. From $3 to $40.

"Those days the food not too expensive like how now. We don't do much in buying; we go much more on ocean, mountain, fishing.

"Everybody go help each other. They go boat fishing and when they come back they share the fish with everybody. What we had, we all had together.

"Since my husband and I raise *taro,* and we have to make our living with *taro*. He don't go hunting. He don't go fishing. It's me I go fishing. He has to stay home and watch the *taro* patch. You have to work every day.

"We have fish, we have *lū'au* [taro top]. What little money we have from the *taro* we sell we buy cuttlefish and salt salmon from the store. That's the cheapest food they have in the store. That's what we eat. Salt salmon with *poi*. We don't need other things like how now we have."

The two acres of land that Auntie Mary still lives on today the Kaauamos got by homesteading in their early days. After ten years on the land, they were able to buy it for $2,700. There are four *lo'i* on her two acres, but she leases 28 more. "I lease," she explains. "You cannot get only four *lo'i* to make a living."

Mālama ka 'āina

–care for the land–

is the Hawaiian credo

the Kaauamos live by.

NATURE: Mary Kaaumao

Since her husband's passing, her son, Wilkins Penimana Kaauamo, comes daily to tend the *taro*—at least six days a week, often seven.

"Even if you do [seven days], you still can't catch up. Too much job," Wilkins says good-naturedly. "It's hard living. It's a broken-back job. But I just love it."

All the Kaauamo children learned farming from the time they were young. "It was our life; we just worked from childhood—six, seven, eight years old. During that time everybody has to work," he says with no regrets.

While his father was alive, Wilkins would help him on weekends, and, when laid off from his construction work, he'd work the *lo'i* almost every day. Then, his father died of a sudden heart attack after working all morning weeding the *taro*.

"He was 80 years old when he passed away," Auntie Mary says. "He was sick, but when you get *taro* business you have to do it. I went to senior citizen lunch and when I came home he was lying down dead already. Just one hour ahead before I came back."

"I didn't expect my dad to die so fast," Wilkins says. "But I just continue. It was my mother's say. I didn't ask her. She said I do the job. My mom decided to let me run the business, the *taro* farm.

"The construction job I made more money and I get good benefits. I leave one job for $26 an hour for small pay. But I just love the land."

He's following in the muddy footprints of a man devoted to this very land. "He was a good and strong and hard-working man," Wilkins says of his father. And like father, like son. "I like to be my own boss. I just love the life," he says.

Mālama ka 'āina—care for the land—is the Hawaiian credo the Kaaumaos live by.

"You have to take care of your land," Auntie Mary says. "My husband worked with nature. He always plant with the moon when he plants his *taro*. Then when you harvest the *taro*, underneath is good. Full moon. *Māhea-lani Hoku*—that's the good moon to raise *taro*. That's how in the olden times. Hawaiian moon calendar. They tell you what moon for plant *taro*, what moon to plant for potatoes. They have fruit moon, they have vegetable moon, they have *taro* moon. The ocean they have their own moon. The farmers have their own."

The Hawaiian moon calendar her husband followed is the calendar of his ancestors. The ancients observed the cycles of the moon, planting when the moon was full, ocean fishing when the moon was dark. Much of the calendar was based on practical sense. For instance, plankton come out during dark nights and they attract the deep sea fish; thus, ocean fishing is good during dark moon cycles.

The moon calendar was also based on spiritual beliefs. Several days of every 28-day moon cycle were devoted to certain gods, and these days were considered times for rest and renewal—no planting, no fishing, only play, celebration and religious ritual.

Like most farmers, the Kaauamos are practical folks, conscientious without making a big deal out of it. They don't, for instance, spray pesticides or insecticides.

"We don't spray poison. You damage the ground," Auntie Mary explains. "When *taro* get diseased you cannot do anything. Disease always comes to the bottom [of the *taro*]. Some have little insects on it. We don't know why come, but we don't spray. We just clean the patch and the thing dry up and let nature take over its business. You cannot do anything. You cannot poison them. Let nature take its own course. So if it comes good, it comes good, if it comes bad, what you gonna do? You can't do anything.

"Just like human being, eh? Sometimes you healthy, sometimes you come sick. And you get certain kine disease or whatever, same like the plant.

"We're having trouble with that yellow snail [a large water snail that eats the *taro*]. They tell us to spray them all. You do that, you gonna damage the *taro*. While you working you pick 'em up [pick the snails off]. We use our hands. God made our hands to do everything what you're supposed to do. Make use of it. My husband, his fingernails were thick. Almost like a hoof. Cause he use his fingers most on the ground, weeding out."

The Kaauamos live according to *lōkāhi*—unity, harmony—a particularly important credo when growing *taro* because the same stream water is used by the whole community. Fresh water has to circulate continually in the fields because standing water heats up and spoils the *taro* corm.

"You have to cooperate no matter what," Auntie Mary says. "*Lōkāhi*—get together. Everybody has to get together. See like me, I clean my own *lo'i*. The next neighbor clean and everyone clean their own. So, if the main ditch up the mountain hasn't got much water, all the growers who own *taro* patches, everyone cooperate and go up and clean. That's what they do. So everybody takes cane knife or sickle, the ladies go with the *'ōpae* net—that's fun, you know. The mens all in the front, they shaking the water, the water going down, the *'ōpae* [shrimp] and *'o'opu* [small fish] go in the net. That's what they do. Everybody cooperate."

Recently, a family from outside Keʻanae bought some *loʻi* land and decided to build a house on it. This united the community with *lōkāhi*.

"They bought from somebody here and then they don't want make *loʻi*, they want make house. We told them you cannot make house in the farm place. How you can go through the *taro* patches? You cannot take any truck or tractor to go over somebody's property. I wouldn't let them. The community have a meeting. It's not zoning house, it's zoning farm. We have to stop them."

They did.

Any development in Keʻanae would send shudders throughout the state. There are few places left that are still so Hawaiian. The academics call it a cultural *kīpuka*—an area of hope where old Hawaiʻi still exists as a living example for modern Hawaiians. In science, a *kīpuka* is an area that a new lava flow leaves untouched, often because it's on higher ground. A *kīpuka* is an oasis of greenery in the midst of desolate, raw lava. Seeds from the plants in a *kīpuka* germinate life in the barren rock all around. Culturally, Keʻanae is a *kīpuka* for the entire state. Here people live more traditionally and they live more in touch with nature.

Auntie Mary is not romantic about her life style; she doesn't consider it a symbolic *kīpuka*. She does not question it or extol it. She simply lives it. She does not "wax poetic," but she certainly agrees with those who do.

"Sixty-one years I married my husband and I live here and I raised *taro* from that time until today. We feel Keʻanae the best. The living with people is nice. You have more things to do. You have *taro* land to live on. Keʻanae is the *taro* land. That's how I feel. Nuttin else."

ISABELLA AIONA ABBOTT, PH.D.
PHYCOLOGIST AND ETHNOBOTONIST

Searching her memory for the name of an acquaintance, Isabella Aiona Abbott looks bemused, then says wryly: "As long as I don't forget the names of plants. I can forget the names of people, but not the plants."

It's doubtful that Dr. Abbott would ever forget her beloved plants. "Izzy," as friends call her, is a leading Hawaiian botanist and ethnobotanist who has taught at the University of Hawai'i in Honolulu since 1977. She has published 140-some scholarly papers and written eight books, including the current UH textbook for Hawaiian ethnobotany (the study of how ancient peoples used plants). But her real passion, her real love in life, is *limu* (seaweed). In fact, she is world renowned as a seaweed expert, a phycologist.

She doesn't know how many new seaweed species she has identified and named during her long career. "Lots of new species

"I'm trying to instill pride in the students, whether they're Hawaiians or not. I desperately want the non-Hawaiians to know these Hawaiians really accomplished a lot; no more should they be called a primitive society. If you're not Hawaiian, being able to say at the gut level: 'Boy, these Hawaiians were not just sitting under coconut trees, they were accomplished people.' . . . If students go away having pride in the accomplishments of the Hawaiians, that's my goal."

in California," she says. "And I have more here [in Hawaiʻi] than California. I've named several new genera here, too."

Dr. Abbott taught fall semesters at UH from 1977 to 1981 while spending spring semesters doing research and teaching at Stanford University in California. She had been at Stanford since 1950, but, by 1982, she and her husband, Donald (a renowned invertebrate zoologist at Stanford), decided to take early retirement to live full-time in Hawaiʻi. Stanford was her "other life," as she puts it, before she returned to the islands of her birth. However, in Hawaiʻi, the seaweed research of her California days takes a backseat to ethnobotany.

"I've had two very full lives already. In two fields. Because I teach ethnobotany, that's what they associate me with in Hawaiʻi. But I'm more famous as a seaweed person than I am as an ethnobotanist," she explains matter-of-factly. "There may be ten students in the botany department [at UH] who know what Dr. Abbott really does for research. It just stuns them when they find out that in their midst is someone who's internationally famous in seaweed studies."

What is it about seaweed that captured a young Hawaiian girl decades ago and led her into such an unconventional vocation?

As she tells it, she was encouraged by knowledgeable guides during her youth, beginning with her very Hawaiian mother.

"I used to go collecting seaweed with my mother when I was small. She and her Hawaiian friends. On nice sunny days they'd go to gossip and let the kids play. It was an outing. My mother knew all the Hawaiian names of the common seaweeds. When I wrote the first *limu* booklet I asked people if their mothers ever taught them names of seaweeds or plants and they said no. I have never met anybody my vintage whose mother or father knew Hawaiian plant names and taught them. So I was lucky that way.

"My mother loved plants. She learned like a farmer would: what time of year you do this to a plant, what kind of soil it likes, how much water it likes. The things you read in *Lāʻau Hawaiʻi* [her ethnobotany book] are mostly things my mother taught me.

"My formal introduction as an ethnobotanist is my first *limu* book; it records all the Hawaiian names of the common algae that are eaten. What I was doing was recording what I learned from my mother. There isn't anything in there, except the scientific names, that I didn't learn from my mother."

Her mother was her first, but not her only influence. "My mother had an uncle, therefore he was my great uncle, and when I was small I hung around him and he taught me a lot of things: fishing, growing things, pounding *poi*, cooking *taro,* making rope, how to catch octopuses. I remember him as a kind old man who was obviously very fond of me and who liked to teach me. He was my connection to the *kūpuna.*

"Then, when I was at Kamehameha [a school for native Hawaiian children], the principal of the girls school noticed that I was interested in plants, as she herself had been, so she encouraged me. I think she was the one who told me that I really should go into botany. So when I went to the university, I registered as a botany major."

Though her life's mission as a botanist seemed clear to her, it was a bit befuddling to her family. "My older brothers don't understand this sister," she says with an impish smile. "[They say:] 'Why don't you do something that we can understand and talk about?' They're proud, but not proud because they know what I'm doing."

Dr. Abbott was born in the remote Maui town of Hāna to a Chinese father and a Hawaiian mother. Her father had come to Hawai'i from southern China to work for the sugar plantations, but, after his five-year contract was up, he left plantation work and opened a country grocery store in Hāna. His Chinese picture bride died young, leaving him with six sons to raise, so he was seeking a partner to help him when friends suggested a Hawaiian woman who taught weaving at a girl's school on the Big Island.

"I've had two very full lives already. In two fields."

"I don't think it was very romantic," Dr. Abbott says of this match making. "But anyway, they got married. Then I was born and I have a younger brother."

With all these older boys to educate and no high school in small Hāna town, Dr. Abbott's father uprooted the family and moved to Honolulu when little Izzy was two years old.

"My father invested all the money he had in a variety of businesses in Honolulu, practically every bank or store. And he was a founder in many of them. He was very smart—he was Chinese with a computer in his head," Dr. Abbott says.

"I had a wonderful father. Every good thing you can think about Chinese people being kind and thoughtful and helpful—my father was one of those people."

However, living in Hawai'i, her father's daughter can't help but wish she looked more Hawaiian than Chinese.

"Some days when I look in the mirror I think: 'Who's that Chinese lady?' It's one of the crosses that I bear that I don't look more Hawaiian. With a name like Abbott [her husband's name], how would you know? But I am 100 percent Hawaiian in outlook and heart."

Why is it important to look Hawaiian?

"Because I'm so Hawaiian," she answers simply. "I think Hawaiian."

Then, the scientist in her corrects herself. "I should back up and say, in my professional life I think as a scientist first. The first thing that hits me when anybody says anything to me is: 'Where is your evidence? How can you say that? Do you have any evidence for saying that?' That's how I am as a scientist and that governs the rest of my life actually. I heave great sighs when my students come out with some of their statements. I've been teaching them all semester that you have to be able to back up what you say and here they are saying these wild things as if they have never been exposed to scientific discourse. It drives me nuts.

She wants her students to gain from her courses "an honest interpretation of the way the Hawaiians lived. Nothing romanticized, nothing half–baked, nothing excusing."

"One year in my advanced class, out of 21 students I had four who kept telling me: 'I wish I had taken your course earlier because you have done so much for me to awaken the Hawaiian spirit, and to make me feel responsible for what I say.'"

This combination of scientist and Hawaiian makes Dr. Abbott a role model for her students and gives her a sensitivity to their needs.

"Being Hawaiian, to me, is a softer approach." she explains. "It isn't that you don't see things the way a scientifically trained person would, but you don't hit it head on. When you're talking to Hawaiians it's the same thing—you don't hit a person head on. You never in your life would say: 'You've got it all wrong. I don't believe you.' You might think that, but you go around the back door, talk story. Fifteen minutes later you've diffused what they have said, but you have never told them to their face: 'You're wrong.' The language seems to lend itself to behaving that way. Straight out telling you the way it is—that's not the way Hawaiians speak in Hawaiian and therefore they don't think that way either.

"They're emotional people, and their language is kind of emotional too. It has a lot of nuances. The English I know as a scientist has no nuances at all. You tell something straight and that's it. I think that's why my students lapse into Hawaiian. They have to communicate in a different way than scientific English.

"So you can see it's kind of a sharp knife that separates one part of me when I'm dealing with Hawaiians and another part when I'm being myself [as a scientist]."

But there's no separation when she teaches ethnobotany. Both the scientist and the Hawaiian in her work hand-in-hand combining plants and culture. In her textbook, *Lāʻau Hawaiʻi,* she writes about the "vital link between Hawaiian flora and Hawaiian culture." Almost everything the ancients needed was supplied by plants: clothing, food, medicine, weaponry, housing, canoes, ropes and nets, musical instruments.

Agriculture was actually more important to them than fishing. "For every Hawaiian fisherman, there were hundreds who worked the land. Virtually all members of society spent some time gathering plants or gardening," she writes in her book.

"If you were as dependent on plants as the Hawaiians were for food you would have to respect them and treat them well," Dr. Abbott explains. "My mother, for example, always said that if you like pretty flowers, you have to pay attention to the plant when it's not in flower so it will flower for you. I think the Hawaiians were endlessly grateful to plants for what they furnished them for everyday living. I'm sure they were eternally grateful to the *koa* trees for being the source of their canoes."

Plants were involved in everything the ancients did. For instance, Dr. Abbott loves to tell her students about a seaweed called *kala,* which means "to forgive." It's used as a poultice on open coral cuts. It's also used in a mediation ceremony called *hoʻoponopono* to heal psychological wounds created within a family.

"When there's dissension in the family," she explains, "the mother usually gets some *kala* and gives it to each person in the family to eat. They sit around in a circle and pray and the gist of the prayers is forgive all of us for the dissension. You get the idea? Not forgive me, forgive ALL of us. Now, the psychological advantage of this is everyone is accepting blame for what happened in the family. So the ones who are mad at each other realize that the blame is being shared. You don't go away feeling that you're wrong, that you're always doing things wrong.

Sometimes it takes a week to ten days—every single evening until each person in that circle feels they can clearly forgive everybody else. This is a cleansing thing.

"You can pay $450 a night at Esalen in Big Sur for the very same thing. Psychologists are usually amazed when I tell them about this because they don't see how a primitive people could have figured this out. I tell them: 'That's where you're wrong, they were not primitive.'"

The role plants played in the lives of the ancients is "all tied to religion," Dr. Abbott says. In her text, *Lā'au Hawai'i,* she writes: "Hawaiian use and understanding of plants was thoroughly and profoundly religious." This was due to their "belief that maintaining a right relationship with the gods and the earth is humanity's basic spiritual challenge."

This may sound as if she is romanticizing the past, turning the ancients into perfect beings, but that is anathema to Dr. Abbott. She wants her students to gain from her courses "an honest interpretation of the way the Hawaiians lived. Nothing romanticized, nothing half-baked, nothing excusing.

"I'm trying to instill pride in the students, whether they're Hawaiians or not," she says. "I desperately want the non-Hawaiians to know these Hawaiians really accomplished a lot; no more should they be called a primitive society. If you're not Hawaiian, being able to say at the gut level: 'Boy, these Hawaiians were not just sitting under coconut trees, they were accomplished people.' For the Hawaiians, I want them to see that their people came [to Hawai'i from Tahiti and the Marquesas Islands] with a clothing fiber *[kapa]* which was adequate, more than adequate, and what happened? They weren't satisfied with that, they went up into the hills and found some other fibers that they made *kapa* with. They came with coconut cordage, perfectly good, nothing wrong with that. What did they do? They went and found *olonā* [a shrub that yields the strongest vegetable fiber in the world]. That takes experimentation. One species after another after another to find out how it works, what can be done with it. If students go away having pride in the accomplishments of the Hawaiians, that's my goal."

Another goal is to educate people about Hawai'i's endemic plants, species found nowhere else on the planet. Hawai'i has the highest rate of plant endemism in the world, yet many of these plants are now extinct or endangered.

"I call the endemic plants the first Hawaiians, so if they are the first, we ought to be interested in how they maintained themselves as the first Hawaiians," she says.

"The gingers and heliconias will grow elsewhere. The endemic plants will not. With some species you can count the individuals that are left on one hand.

You can be looking at a plant and it may be the last one, and you know this; it cannot help but affect you."

When asked: why bother saving threatened endemic species, she looks perplexed, as if the answer is obvious. "This is their home. It's like the Hawaiian people—they belong here."

As Dr. Abbott does herself. She has plans for a second retirement, but has no plans to live in California again. Hawai'i is home. She'll go back and forth between Maui and Honolulu.

"Time to do something else," she says of her retirement. "Or maybe nothing. Do nothing."

Doubtful. The Bishop Museum in Honolulu has "hundreds of specimens of seaweeds waiting for me to look at," she admits.

She hasn't seen enough *limu* in her life?

"Oh no," she says enthusiastically. "It's just like knowledge of any kind. You think you know it all and then you get another plant and you don't know it all. The old things that you think you know well, like an old friend, how come I didn't see that before? In a way it's testing your powers of observation.

"I think the Hawaiians were endlessly grateful to plants for what they furnished them for everyday living."

"Science is hypothetical, you know. It's always testing. You have a hypothesis, you name a species, you name a genus, you name a new family. These are hypothetical things, so the next seaweed you pick up may destroy this classification that you've been so carefully building. You'd never know that if you quit looking at things."

Dr. Abbott can't quit looking even on her time off. She has a condo on Maui where one might think she'd like to get away from it all, but, instead, she has a scientific experiment ongoing right outside her door—an underwater line stretching 180 meters from a coconut tree in front of her condo straight out into the ocean. She and her husband, Donald, began monitoring life along the line in 1979. It's a research study that involves both of their specialties—seaweeds and invertebrates.

Donald died in 1986, after a 43-year-marriage that always entwined their genuine love of scientific inquiry. Their two specialties "dovetailed very nicely," Dr. Abbott says. "My husband was supportive of me in every way, especially my scientific career. He was more famous than I—in invertebrate zoology: snails and crabs and other creatures like that."

Whenever he went on research expeditions, the gifts he'd return with were seaweed specimens—the perfect souvenir for a wife like Dr. Abbott.

"My husband was such a dear to me, so helpful and caring. People would think it was 'sweet' of him to bring me seaweeds, but it enlarged my data base greatly, and, as a scientist, I appreciated specimens."

She is continuing with the baseline study they both began on Maui, monitoring it now with the help of friends.

"It's one of the only baseline studies in the Hawaiian Islands," Dr. Abbott says. "Every meter we collect things. Our emphasis is on sea urchins and what they eat because most sea urchins are algae eaters. We want to know what species they eat. Sea urchins are sedentary. They travel around within 20 feet of where they live but they come back to the rock they were sitting under. And algae are attached. So, if you found out 20 years ago that they ate sea lettuce and the same species of sea urchin is still there, but there's no sea lettuce there, then what are they eating? It's those kind of changes you can monitor. Some species come, some go, maybe they never come back.

"Unless you have that kind of information, you're just talking off the top of your head. You hear people talking about terrible pollution, or there's no pollution, and the evidence is right there that can tell you what was happening over a period of years.

"In the marine environment, there are very few baselines of this kind anywhere in the world. So, I'm very happy that we have one right outside my front door."

Watching her join a group of Maui students scouring the beach for seaweed, it's evident the scientist and teacher in her will never retire.

"We're so lucky to be getting her on Maui," says their teacher. "Honolulu's had her for years. We could really use her knowledge here."

Meanwhile, the students crowd around Dr. Abbott on the beach, deferential and respectful, all clearly eager to learn from the legend.

"How do you tell parasite bumps from other bumps?" one of them asks as the group stands knee-deep in the ocean.

"How do you classify this?" another interrupts, holding up a slimy morsel.

"Do you have to cook *ogo* before you eat it?"

"Do most seaweeds have air in them to keep them buoyant?"

"Can you eat this one?"

"Is that calcium carbonate?"

Dr. Abbott is as eager as they are, answering their questions as if she hasn't answered similar ones for decades of students. Her interest and patience never wane.

"The quest for knowledge," she calls it. "Science is a game that never ends."

EDDIE PU
NATIONAL PARK RANGER

To Eddie Pu, the *'āina* is everything. He has worked outside, on the land, every working day of his life, first as a lifeguard at a beach in Hāna, Maui, then, since 1972, as a national park ranger in Kīpahulu, Maui. As a result, he has a profound sense of the importance of Mother Earth.

"I love the *'āina* so much," he says. "The *'āina* is my whole life. Without her, I can't enjoy. I sense that the land provides energy.

"Maui is my island. She brought and raised me here. I call her my mother. Every morning I say, 'Mother Maui, I love you.' When the sun rises in the morning, I say, 'Thank you, Lord, for this beautiful morning; thank you for giving us this sun. Let me receive your sun rays into my body so I can share with all I come in contact with.

"When I come to the park, I say, *'Āina*, accept me for this morning and receive me as

"I'm greeting about 2,000 people a day, and 90 percent of them are perfect energies, but 10 percent are wobbly. So, five days a week my body is wobbly, out of balance from their energies. I use this [spiritual] walk to bring it back.

I go out and gather all the energy from various parts [of Maui]. I pick a spot to meditate. I collect all the energy and when I go back I release all the energy to the people."

I come through. I may not be humble today, but let me receive your energy into my body. I know you will guide me through the day.'"

Before starting his work day, Pu centers himself by rising at five a.m. to sit and meditate while waiting for the first hint of the sun. He has been meditating for 30 years, introduced to it when he became involved in the Japanese martial art of aikido.

"I keep that orange clear in my mind, that first glow of the sunrise. I just circle right on the energy of the *lā,* the sun, because she's the strongest energy that we receive here today. I'm waiting for her to come up in the darkness, up into brightness.

He calls it his spiritual walk and he's been doing it every year since 1976, because, as he says, "I can't stop."

"That's where my energy comes from—the sun, the land."

Pu needs that energy five days a week because he greets up to 2,000 people a day in his job as a park ranger. He works surrounded by beauty at the waterfall wonderland of ʻOheʻo Gulch, one of the most popular areas of the 28,665-acre Haleakalā National Park. When he was hired as a ranger in 1972, park visitors were few, but today, the parking lot is always full during peak hours. An endless stream of people flows alongside ʻOheʻo's famous stream, asking the same questions over and over, many of them still on hurried Mainland time. It takes a man filled with patience and *aloha* (love, compassion) to handle the job with grace. Pu does it so well, he is often called "Smiling Eddie."

"People ask why am I always smiling? I don't know that I am," he says when questioned about his radiant face. "When the wind blows, the leaves are waving—they're smiling. When you throw a rock into a pool and the ripples go out—the water is smiling. That's the energy. That's what I call my energy."

Every person encountering him at the park is addressed by his welcoming *aloha,* and he is adamant that every ranger at ʻOheʻo use this Hawaiian greeting with the tourists.

"*Aloha* means welcome," he explains. "In our ranger station, when people come in, first thing you hear is 'howzit!' [local lingo for 'How is it?' or 'How are you?']

NATURE: Eddie Pu

This is impolite. We sit down and say, 'Okay, let's take a minute break. Do we respect these people who've traveled so far to come here and say 'howzit?' Then what can you say?—*aloha*.

"We have a new ranger from San Francisco. She says, 'Why can't I say welcome?' I said, 'This is Hawai'i, the *aloha* state, we like to say *aloha*."

Does he mind the hoards of people who come daily to the park?

"Not really," he says. "Nothing I can do about it—just receive them. I love them all. I know every day I'm going to have more and more. Every year.

"That's my purpose for being here. This is my roots. I ran around here as a kid, not knowing how valuable the park would be today."

Walking with Pu is an exercise in observation. He knows the plants, endemic and foreign, and greets them as an old friend, believing they all have their own feelings.

"Excuse me," he says to a weedy-looking plant as he picks a leaf. "*Mahalo* [thank you]." Then he demonstrates how he'd crumple the leaf to use the iodine in it if he had a cut.

He picks a large *tī* leaf, a plant sacred to the Hawaiian god Lono, and puts it on his forehead as a headband.

"This helps me release my inner feelings," he explains. "It helps me to be humble.

"See this *hau* plant? You make a *hula* skirt from its bark."

"This one [blue vervain], you get the leaves and mash them and put them on any laceration and it burns like hell. Stops the bleeding. Put it on three or four times, wrap it in *tī* leaves and it leaves no scar. It makes a wonderful tea for blood circulation. But people are afraid to use it because it's not bought in the store.

"See all the bamboo? Terrible. Fastest growing plant in the world. It's out of control here and there's nothing we can do about it; it's way up in the hills. But it was here before I was around.

"On a walk once I told a Los Angeles police officer that the bamboo [in the far distance] was cannabis. He wrote that down in his book. 'What do you do with it?' one lady asked. 'Smoke it!' I said. Then, when we got up to the bamboo and saw what it was, they were surprised."

Pu takes off his ranger hat once a year and leaves the crowds far behind. Two days after his November birthday, he puts on his hiking boots, packs a small bag and heads out to walk all around the island of Maui at the coast level, a walk he estimates to be about 150 miles.

He calls it his spiritual walk and he's been doing it every year since 1976, because, as he says, "I can't stop." He has tried to do it quietly, but his fame keeps preceding him, and every year people call, trying to accompany him.

"Finally I had to get an unlisted number. A phone call breaks my spell," he says. "Doctors, professors, police, firemen all want to walk with me. But no one walks with me. I talk to the trees. I talk to the plants. I talk to the water. I yell out. And people might say I'm crazy. They would stop my thing like I like to do it."

One year two young people, who had heard of Pu's walk, met him and immediately asked if they could accompany him the next year. Not wanting to be rude, Pu tried to let them down easily by saying he might instead kayak around the island next time. Great, the enthusiastic young woman answered, they had kayaks themselves and would love to do it that way.

Within no time, Pu was receiving calls from professional kayakers, people who owned kayak tour companies, who said they'd like to go along too. Feeling he'd really stuck his foot in his mouth, he finally had to beg off by saying his wife, Beverly, thought it was a bad idea—that he might just end up in Japan. Having never been on a kayak, he had no intention of getting off his famous feet.

On his first walk back in 1976, Pu felt he was being led and instructed by his deceased grandfather. He admits that on this walk: "I didn't know what to do. I gathered my things together and started walking. And I could feel someone is ahead of me leading me, not realizing it's my grandfather.

"My first night camp-out in Kaupō there he was again in my sleep, smiling. He said, 'You going to walk the coastline from Mokulau to Nuʻu.' It took me two days to walk that coastline. From there he says the *alanui* [the road] continues on. So it's like he's telling me to go right around Maui.

"My second year I didn't do it; I figured it was just the first year, but he came back to me again and said there are more things to see than staying around the house. I bought a camera, rolls of film and I took pictures, but when I came back and developed them, nothing showed, everything's black. I buy a new camera, go out my next year, take a picture of all the sites I see, and nothing shows again. It happened three times.

"My grandfather says: 'This is your camera,'" as Pu points to his head.

"It's like there is a spirit that's pulling me off to the left, then sit there, then lift up and off to the right, then sit there, off to the mountain and down the coastline. I see things that when I drive a car I won't see—plants, archaeological sites, burial sites, artifacts."

The walk usually takes a couple of weeks, yet he only carries a gallon of water with him, some trail mix, a 10-by-10-foot piece of plastic, a thin metallic space blanket and extra clothes. He does pick up more food and water along the way when it's available.

He rarely has any problems on his walk, but, one year he did, when two young men, one *haole* (white) and one Hawaiian, approached him in a remote area where he had bedded down for the night. It appeared they were up to no good, so Eddie stood up, holding onto his walking stick, and said: "I don't have anything if you want to rob me. Just my dirty socks and some trail mix and water."

The Hawaiian called out in the dark: "Where are you from?"

"The *'āina,*" Pu responded characteristically. He then told them not to come within his "circle"—the space he was claiming for the night.

"I was accepted there and it became my place for the night," he explained later. "This circle was given to me to bed down."

> *"The 'āina is my whole life. Without her, I can't enjoy. I sense that the land provides energy. . . . That's where my energy comes from— the sun, the land."*

He quietly indicated to these boys decades younger than he that he would flip them over the cliff if they stepped within his circle.

The Hawaiian asked again: "Where are you from?"

"Maui," Pu said simply.

Did he really think he could take on two guys with his walking stick and his aikido training?

"Yes," he insists. "I knew she would help me, my Mother Earth. They tramped into my premises and that was wrong. I was accepted there."

"Where are you from?" the Hawaiian asked a third time.

"Hāna."

"I have relatives in Hāna," the kid said, warming up. "Maybe you know them. My uncle is Eddie Pu. Do you know him?"

"Yes, I do," Pu answered.

"Well, the next time you see him," the kid said with bravado, "tell him I said hello." He then gave his name.

"I'll do that," he agreed. Pu had never heard of the kid.

After they left him, Pu bedded down. Then the next morning, he stopped in the nearby village to visit old friends. A woman answered the door, very happy to see him.

"Kids, come meet Eddie Pu!" she said excitedly to her children. The young Hawaiian man from the previous evening's encounter came when his mother called, only to discover who Eddie Pu really was. In shock, he went down on both knees, admitted to Pu that he and his buddy were planning to "rough him up" and rob him, and asked Pu to forgive him.

That same year, not from fear, but from some new inner drive, Pu started walking more at night.

"It's beautiful to walk in the moonlight," he explains. "Beautiful. I put in miles at night. I see things that people normally don't see. And I just sing away. I dance and say 'thank you, *mahalo*' and sing. Then about four o'clock [in the morning] I find a space, settle down to meditate; then, when the sun rises, I go to sleep for a few hours; then I'm up again. I walk up the hills, just follow the stream. Nobody around. Take my clothes off, swim, all alone, singing away. The birds all singing with me. The waterfalls, the water rippling. I just love it."

Everyone, naturally, asks Pu what spurs him to keep doing such a strenuous walk year after year, well beyond a normal retirement age. Besides the fact that it's part of his spiritual quest, he says it keeps him sane on the job during the rest of the year.

"I'm greeting about 2,000 people a day, and 90 percent of them are perfect energies, but 10 percent are wobbly. So, five days a week my body is wobbly, out of balance from their energies. I use this walk to bring it back.

> *"When the wind blows, the leaves are waving—they're smiling. When you throw a rock into a pool and the ripples go out—the water is smiling. That's the energy. That's what I call my energy."*

"I go out and gather all the energy from various parts [of Maui]. I pick a spot to meditate. I collect all the energy and when I go back I release all the energy to the people.

"I'm just a simple Hawaiian," he says with a broad grin and a shrug. "I like to do for the people."

SPIRITUALITY AND HEALING

A canoe maker prays to the goddess Lea before he fells a tree. If she arrives in the form of the *'elepaio* bird and pecks on the tree, he knows it's a sign the tree is not perfect for a canoe.

A nursing mother prays for enough milk to Nuʻakea, goddess of lactation.

A family prays to their ancestral *ʻaumākua* (family guardian gods) at the dawn of day.

A fisherman acknowledges his family animal *ʻaumakua,* the shark, before casting his net.

A *hula* dancer gathering ferns in the forest asks permission of the goddess Laka.

Nothing was done in ancient Hawaiʻi without acknowledging the presence and power of the gods and goddesses. There was no word for religion in the ancient days; the entirety of life was religious.

Mary Kawena Pukui, this century's most famous Hawaiian scholar, wrote: "Everything they did, they did with prayer."

Though there were four major gods (Lono, Kū, Kāne, Kanaloa), there was such a pantheon of related and minor gods and goddesses that no one really knows how many there were. It appears they kept multiplying as needs arose. Like the ancient Greek and Roman gods, Hawaiian gods had human qualities—anger, jealousy, passion, lust, compassion, kindness. And, as in Greece and Rome, the tales of their gods became an intricate, compelling mythology.

Healing and medicine were also based on spirituality. If one was sick, one did not search for a microbe or virus to blame, one searched one's very soul. What had gone wrong in the person's life to upset the balance? How had mental or emotional problems caused bodily harm? Was it a problem inherited from the ancestors? Was a god displeased?

Families would try to resolve sickness, conflicts or *pilikia* (troubles) with a mediation ceremony called *ho'oponopono*. With an elder leading the group, each family member would contribute until the problem was settled.

If the family could not resolve a sickness, a *kahuna* would be called in, and, just like today, their doctors were specialists—bone setting, birthing, baby ailments, massage, diagnosing, healers of the spirit, herbalists—there were numerous *kāhuna*. However, their illnesses were mild compared with today's.

As Kamakau writes: "Foreigners had not yet come from other lands; there were no fatal disease, no epidemics, no contagious diseases, no diseases that eat away the body, no venereal diseases."

In 1820 when the missionaries first arrived, the Hawaiians had, ironically, just done away with their *kapu* system (their society's laws), and, since these laws were interwoven with their religious beliefs, they also destroyed many of their temples. It was a time of great change in Hawai'i—foreigners had been influencing them for forty years (since the arrival in 1778 of Captain James Cook); and, since foreigners broke the *kapu* regularly with no repercussions, the Hawaiians began to question their own system's validity. Thus, when the first Calvinists stepped on shore, they met a deeply spiritual people who no longer had religious rules or rituals. The new Western god and the new book (The Bible) were fascinating to them.

The change was not easy, however. This new god did not allow room for the ancient gods; old Hawaiian names that were imbued with poetic meaning had to be replaced by Christian names; sex outside marriage was sinful; nakedness was sinful; mankind itself was deemed unworthy and sinful by nature.

Though sinfulness is foreign to Hawaiian thought and philosophy, Calvinist doctrines prevailed, and most Hawaiians are Christian today. Reverend Kawika Ka'alakea (in this chapter) was raised very Hawaiian, for instance, but he believes in and preaches the new ways, not the old. Still, though a Christian minister, Ka'alakea has revelations from God, casts out spirits and heals with prayer and herbs, much as his ancestors would have done.

The ancients did not separate mankind from either the supernatural or the natural worlds. Gods, spirits, nature and humans were all part of the life force. They were a people who believed in symbolism, in *mana* (spiritual life force), in dreams, in visions, in sorcery, in magic, in prophets, in spiritual healing, just as readily as they believed in the humdrum of their daily lives. As Mary Pukui writes: "There are many references to supernatural or mystic occurrences. . . . Hawaiian life and thought cannot be understood without knowing about them."

MARGARET MACHADO
LOMILOMI MASSAGE MASTER

"The spirit of aloha *is what she embodies. She is the spirit of* aloha.*"*
　　　　　　　Glenna Wilde, naturopath
　　　　　　　Juneau, Alaska

"I've seen things that she's done that would be considered miracles."
　　　　　　　Makaʻala Yates, *lomilomi* instructor
　　　　　　　Oregon

"She hardly asks a person any questions, but she can tell when a person is troubled. She just loves them, and they eventually learn to love themselves, and their bodies heal, and they're able to handle some of these long, painful, traumatic childhood experiences."
　　　　　　　Daughter Nerita Machado, nurse
　　　　　　　Hawaiʻi

"This was the first time in my life that I experienced unconditional love—from Auntie, from the place, from the healing."
　　　　　　　Pamela Haggerty, student
　　　　　　　Hawaiʻi

"I can go right through you and tell you just exactly where it is. When I look at you I know all about you. You don't have to tell me about yourself. It's written on your countenance. All your muscles and your bones reflect your countenance, how you work with your body."

Auntie Margaret Machado never says these things herself. She merely looks in your eyes, holding your gaze without breaking it, seemingly without blinking, and reads your face.

"You've got tension in your left jaw," she'll tell you, never breaking her smile or the impish, loving look in her eyes, as if she's telling you something absolutely delightful.

Of her fame for healing, her husband Daniel says: "She never claims to take credit. Never. She says the Lord's virtue passes through her. She's a very humble woman and a very godly woman. The Lord is her master."

Still, as her husband speaks, she looks you steadily in the eyes, unblinking, unfazed, not saying a thing, just smiling.

Auntie Margaret is renowned as a master of *lomilomi,* traditional Hawaiian massage. She is the only person state certified to teach *lomilomi* in Hawai'i. People come to her from all over the world and attribute miraculous cures to her work, but she doesn't make those claims herself.

"She does not heal. And she'll be the first one to tell you that," naturopathic doctor Glenna Wilde says. "She heals with her love of God. It's never about herself, or 'I did this;' it's about how she was privileged to experience and witness God doing this. I have seen her be a conduit for God on many occasions. She absolutely with every ounce of her being loves God. Her whole message in massage is to love the body. I can still hear her voice in *lomilomi* class: 'Love the body, Glenna, love the body.' She touches people as though she were touching their souls."

Lomilomi is handed down within families for generations. Her family's knowledge was transmitted to her by her grandfather, a man she didn't know well. Auntie Margaret was not raised by her Big Island family; instead, before her mother died, she sent young Margaret to a missionary home in Honolulu for a Christian upbringing.

When Margaret was ten, her grandfather flew over to give her his blessing and to impart his wisdom and lineage. Before her birth, he had named her *Kalehuamakanoelulu'uonapali,* a name that indicated he had chosen her to carry on the family secrets. Within the name are several meanings: the *lehua* flower, eyes, mist, scattered pollen, precipice.

"I was the chosen one of the family to receive the blessing," she explains. "Because my grandfather named me *Kalehuamakanoelulu'uonapali,* he had to see this little girl. He wanted to give me the blessing because he named me before birth. Hawaiian children are named before birth. The parents or the grandparents are given a dream of what to name the coming baby.

"So he blessed me and he chanted over me. It was a long, long chant. And his tears ran down his cheeks. After that he kissed both cheeks, my forehead and the top of my head and he left. He didn't live too long after that and he passed away. Then when I was sixteen I came home.

"When I grew up it was natural for me to love anybody, no matter what. Then when I went into my work and graduated from high school, it was natural for me to massage. I was just gifted that way."

Typically, the knowledge of her lineage was kept within the family. As Auntie Margaret says: "My family didn't want me to teach. They thought maybe it belonged only in the family. But because I was raised up in a missionary home, I want to share it. The Lord wants me to share it. Even now my relatives say, 'Don't teach, Auntie. Don't teach.' I say because it's love work, and because I love the Lord, I'm going to teach."

And thus she has done so since the 1940s. She has no idea how many people she has taught in her one-month classes, and has no idea how many people she has massaged over the years. What she does know is that from her own name comes her inspiration.

People come to her from all over the world and attribute miraculous cures to her work, but she doesn't make those claims herself.

"My name means my work. *Ka lehua* means flower—I'm a flower. *Maka* is the eyes—I'm looking at you. I can go right through you and tell you just exactly where it is. When I look at you I know all about you. You don't have to tell me about yourself. It's written on your countenance. All your muscles and your bones reflect your countenance, how you work with your body. When I look at you, I know that all this is coming up from your hands and feet to your countenance. It shows on your face. I look at your face, one side is tight. I look at your brain, one side lacking oxygen.

"They ask me, 'How do you know?' I say, 'It's there. I didn't do it. You did it. That's your face, that's your body.'

"Your body is a temple of the Holy Spirit. That's why *pali* [is in her name]—

this is your *pali,* this is my *pali,* my mountain, my temple. So I'm going to open it up so you have better circulation so you feel better. I want you to feel better."

Lomilomi is the only massage Auntie Margaret uses. She knows of the other massage styles, but finds them too rough. "They dig in," she says. *Lomilomi* she calls "very thorough," and says it's "just working with the heart."

There's a one-two-three rhythm to *lomilomi;* the body is always rhythmically massaged in the direction of the heart, thus creating better circulation.

"Lomilomi is to and from the heart, taking the blood faster to the heart," she explains. "I massage to and from the arms and the legs, pushing the blood to the heart faster, to and from. Pushing to and from, to and from. The one-two-three is the same as they dance the *hula. Lomilomi*—one two three. One two three pinch off.

"Lomilomi is a loving touch, letting them feel you. When they feel loving hands on their body, they'll respond: 'She loves me, she'll take good care of me, and I'm going to get well.' It's your talk and your approach. They know that you love them. Getting them to relax their body so there'll be no stress. It's love!

"If your hands are gentle and loving, your patient will feel the sincerity of your heart. His soul will reach out to yours. She'll know you love her and she'll just let go of herself.

"The Lord does the healing. I don't heal," she reminds you. "That's why I say prayer. I ask the Lord to intervene. It's said that Hawaiian massage is praying work."

Prayer and the Hawaiian art of family mediation *(ho'oponopono)* are what Auntie Margaret considers her special ingredients for healing.

"We pray and sing every morning," she says of her massage students, "because I want them to empty everything in their hearts to be ready to help somebody. If you have problem, empty the problem out.

"I tell my students, when you go out to pick herbs, pray; when you prepare

> *"Don't worry.*
>
> *I never worry.*
>
> *The Lord going*
>
> *to open the way."*

them, pray; when you give them, pray. Your patient going to get well.

"And the secret part of it is that before the sun goes down you *hoʻoponopono*, you search your heart. *Hoʻoponopono* meaning we empty all ourselves and ask for forgiveness before the sun goes down. You can't go to sleep with a troubled mind or troubled heart. You feel good because you're open minded.

"Do it as a family. Always gather together and sit down on a *lau hala* mat [mat made from leaves of the native *hala* tree] and pray. It was in our family every day. It was beautiful. My aunt would pray, my uncle would pray and everything was over. Every day with my family, every day you ask forgiveness. So your blood vessels open, your nerves open, your muscles open, you relax. Don't worry. I never worry. The Lord going to open the way."

Naturopath Mark LaMore, who helps Auntie Margaret teach her classes, has seen many people come and go up the wooden steps to her beach house, and prayer is always their introduction to healing. "When someone comes here, the first thing she does is pray," he says. "That's where she gets more inspiration. If you don't know right off the bat what to do, you pray; it'll come to you."

All her teaching and healing work is done in a setting straight from old Hawaiʻi. She has an old, plantation-style wooden beach house just a few steps from the ocean's edge on "The Big Island" of Hawaiʻi. Students and patients must drive far off the main highway down a rutted dirt road to Auntie's house to sleep on futons under the stars. Many patients come specifically for her famous ten-day cleanses consisting of fasting, herbs, enemas and sea water drinks.

One patient from New Mexico, who prefers to be unnamed, came to Auntie as a last resort after nearly dying of a rare skin disease. In her own words:

"Auntie Margaret has had such a powerful impact on my life. I had been on a healing path for two years working with naturopaths, but I was tired. It was two years of work, and I was still not getting anywhere. I was still manifesting the same symptoms—my skin was falling off and I had tremendous daily pain. I was scrawny, 88 pounds, and I had very little hair left. I looked like a chicken with no feathers.

"A friend of mine sent me to Auntie Margaret. I thought it was really funky— on the beach, sleeping on these futons. And here's this simple Hawaiian lady.

"They wake you at four a.m. and the first thing you do is pray. And to me, that was the simplest thing I was missing—prayer. That was the missing key that she gave me, besides really cleaning my colon by drinking the salt water. The Hawaiian herbs pull the toxins out and the sea water pushes them out.

"When I saw what came out of me, I said, 'Praise the Lord,' as she said it. I couldn't believe what was coming out of my body. Basically, it blasts out of your

body.

"My eyes were jaundiced, and on the eighth day I released all this yellow stuff. A gush of all this yellow and my eyes cleared up. The last day, the tenth, something like tar was coming out of me.

"She said now that I'd released on a physical level, I'd release on an emotional level. She said my eyes would start twitching and I'd start drooling at night and I did. It was unbelievable.

"It was one of the most powerful healing experiences. You saw what came out of you and you couldn't deny it."

These results didn't surprise Auntie Margaret, of course. She's been getting them for years from everyone who tries her cleansing regimen.

"I give plain warm water enema," she says frankly. "Some of them don't move their bowels three days, five days. Wow. A lot of the students here never saw an enema.

"We give a colon program to clean out the colon. I fix sea water in a formula in a two-quart jar. We go to the laboratory and buy sea water; they go down 2,000 feet to get it. Too many boats out there." She points toward the ocean in front of her house, explaining why she doesn't scoop sea water straight from the source. "They drink a quart in the morning, first thing they get up. One-third sea water, two-thirds fresh water."

Sea water was called "the universal remedy" by Hawaiian scholar, Samuel Kamakau. In a newspaper column he wrote in the 1860's, Kamakau described what he knew of this ancient cure: "For *ka po'e kahiko* [the people of old] the sea was the remedy upon which all relied . . . when people took sick . . . a drink of sea water was the universal remedy employed . . . the sea water loosened the bowels, and it kept on working until the yellowish and greenish discharges came forth."

Auntie Margaret adds her own modern touches to the salt water cleanse: "We give them sea water at six o'clock in the morning. At nine o'clock they have psyllium and bentonite for roughage in grape juice. Grape juice has a natural sugar, it gives you enough energy so you won't faint. Twelve o'clock, three o'clock and six o'clock they take psyllium, bentonite and grape juice. Oh boy you smell. But, after you clean out your colon you feel ten years younger.

"No food till the fourth day. Fourth, fifth, six, seventh days fruit in the morning, vegetables in the afternoon. No meat, no fish, no crab, no flesh food. For the soups, all sea water. Sea water is same as human blood—97 elements in ocean water, same as in human blood.

"You feel good. Exercise is very important because it opens up the blood vessels and the nerves and muscles so you have better circulation. They go walking, they go swimming and they take steam baths every day and sweat out the pores. From there they go on a slant board to put the diaphragm back in position. They're inhaling and exhaling. You feel good.

"After you learn the lesson, you take care of yourself. You don't do the same thing you do before. You change. If you don't change, then you don't want to take care of yourself.

"I have people come from all over—Germany, Switzerland, Norway, from Japan, from Alaska, from Canada. From all over. I feel sorry for them—they have a lot of stress."

Naturopath Glenna Wilde has helped Auntie Margaret give these cleanses and finds them remarkably effective. "Auntie never advertises her cleanses," Wilde says. "Never did, never had to. It's all word of mouth. People would come from all over the world and they would be so sick. I guess the most graphic ones are the people who have skin afflictions that clear up. People with horrible oozing, weeping psoriasis would come and spend ten days and they'd leave and their skin would be as pink as a baby's butt."

Over the two decades that Makaʻala Yates has known and worked with Auntie Margaret, he has seen many a cure that could not be explained medically. "I would ask Auntie Margaret: 'I saw, I was here, but what the heck happened?'" Yates says, still amazed. "She would say, 'I don't know, Makaʻala. But it's the power of prayer.' That's how she'd typically respond to my questions—very simple with faith and belief."

"It's just love," she explains over and over.

LANAKILA BRANDT
PRIEST OF LONO

"*Mana* is life force, the power that enables us to live. . . . The gift of *mana* is all of ours, and we can command this *mana*. You generate *mana* through prayer, through deep breathing and through meditation."

"Aloha e ka lā, e ka lā!
E ola mai e ka lā, i ka honua nei."
"Greetings to the sun, life, the earth."

Lanakila Brandt chants this greeting to the dawn arrival of the sun as it lights the sky behind the Big Island's massive volcano Mauna Loa. Brandt is *kahuna pule* (temple priest) of one of the most impressive temple sites left in Hawai'i—*Pu'uhonua o Hōnaunau,* called Place of Refuge in English.

In his yellow robe and his *tī* leaf headband, Brandt prays in front of a stone and thatched structure that once housed the bones of 33 generations of the ruling Keawe line of sacred chiefs and priests of *Hōnaunau*. The bones are long gone, but the sacred feeling remains as giant wooden *ki'i* (images) stare down from their temple perches guarding what once was.

"To greet the sun as it rises—this was the tradition of the ancestors," Brandt later explains. "Everyone would turn to the sun with prayers of love and gratitude because native practitioners believe that with the coming of the sun the *mana* [life force] returns to Earth each day. With *mana* comes healing, growth, life itself, for all creatures and the Earth."

Brandt is a consecrated *kahuna* of the *Moʻo Lono,* or Order of Lord Lono. As a boy he was trained by his great-grandfather who descended from a long line of Lono practitioners. Lono is the Hawaiian deity dedicated to agriculture and peaceful activities. In Brandt's lineage, the Lono people were also considered healers.

"My education in the ancient traditions started when I was very young. Despite my inherited Austrian father's blue eyes and fair skin, I am my Hawaiian/Portuguese mother's child. I had four brothers and I was the last one. The next youngest brother was 13 years older than me," Brandt says as he begins his personal story.

"My father was a very successful Austrian businessman, imports, exports out of Hamburg, Germany. He was constantly on the go between the islands on the old steamers; consequently, I did not see a whole lot of him. His English wasn't too great, but he spoke Hawaiian beautifully.

"Usually in Hawaiian families, the grandparents had the option to ask for the first-born child. And it was proper for the young couple to give the grandchild away. In my family, my father did not agree with this because the first four boys he refused to give to Tūtū Man [Lanakila's maternal great-grandfather, Kehauleo Waiwaiʻole]. But my father wasn't around to raise me, and my mother, by the time she got through raising four boys, didn't figure she wanted to raise another one.

"So when I came along, my great-grandfather was waiting, and he said: 'You're the one.' He repeated it many, many times: 'You're the one I've been waiting for.'

As a result, little Lanakila was taken into the ways of the ancients by Tūtū Man and his friends, all Hawaiians born in the 1800s.

"Tūtū Kehau was over 100 when he died," Brandt says. "He was active all the way. Wherever he went, I walked along with him. With *kūpuna,* children talked little, but we listened and learned. And so, that's what I did. I loved being with the old people.

"I had the advantage of growing up in another age when my teachers were of the last century. They grew up in the Hawaiian culture and most of them were pretty unacquainted with Western language and traditions. They were always into healing or the religion or things connected with spiritual life. That's how Hawaiians were—their whole life was spiritual.

SPIRITUALITY AND HEALING: Lanakila Brandt

"When I was eighteen I was consecrated by two very old priests of the Lono rite at the head of Kalihi Valley on Oʻahu, which was at that time my great-grandfather's *taro* land."

But it was a different world that Brandt inherited. There was no way one could make a living as a Lono priest, so Brandt, who had also been trained in *hula* and chant, developed a successful career entertaining at the big hotels with his *hula* troupe.

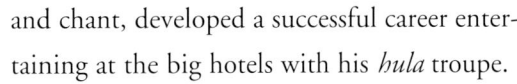

Still, he continued to study healing and Hawaiian spirituality. One of his first medicinal healing teachers was Auntie Ida (whose last name he prefers not to reveal).

"I met her when I took a friend with a broken arm to her house for healing. Auntie spoke mostly Hawaiian, so she asked me to help," Brandt says of their first encounter. "She used salt water from the sea, added to it *ʻōlena* [tumeric]. She was praying all the time to her *ʻaumākua* and to the healing gods. At the same time she was reading the water, reading the pictures in the water. She said everything looked favorable, so she would go ahead with the healing.

"When she was through, she told him to pick up the kitchen chair. He tentatively raised the chair, his worried expression telling us he was expecting his two bone-ends to pop out any second. They didn't. He gave a loud sigh of relief, then hoisted the chair four or five more times and stood grinning at Auntie Ida.

"Auntie told him to come back again two more times. Everything in our healing is always done in threes or fives. All people that practice traditional natural healing work in sacred numerical combinations, usually threes, fives or sevens.

"When he came back, the skin was healed entirely. He went back to the hospital and asked for X-rays and there was no sign of his arm ever being broken. The doctor immediately realized that he had been to a *kahuna*. In those days the laws said that a practicing *kahuna* could be imprisoned and fined $1000, so this doctor was going to have her imprisoned and pay a fine for healing this man. But the word spread very quickly in the community and he got off her case.

"Auntie Ida had five children who were grown and none of them wanted to learn anything of this wonderful gift that she had. She was an instant healer, which is something that I don't think is found in Hawaiʻi anymore. Most of the healers now are very limited in what they can do.

"She offered to teach me because she did not want to die without passing on her skills. So I took that offer and I spent about a year and a half with Auntie Ida. She was very famous. People came from different parts of the world to see her.

"Auntie was descended from the shark line of *'aumakua*. Hawaiians believe that we are descended in certain lines—the shark, the Hawaiian owl, the turtle. Everybody is descended from some line.

"At least once a week, we would get up early before sunrise to feed the shark. We put together *'awa* [a traditional drink], fish, bananas. Auntie Ida always wore her *mu'umu'u*, the original pup tent. We would pray to the *'aumākua* on the beach. When the sun came up she would start calling and chanting: 'Shark, come.' I never saw a time when she would not get a response. The sharks would come and one would swim back and forth the way sharks do, working his way in. The beach we were on was shallow quite far out, so she would go out there and hold out her hands, holding the offering and chanting to the shark to come. It would come right up in front of her and stop. She always had in her hand a piece of coral and she would be talking to him and rubbing his back with the coral. And she would give him the offering. It was pretty incredible."

The shark is also Brandt's Waiwai'ole family *'aumakua*. The *'aumakua* is a personal guiding spirit, either a creature guide or a family ancestor. A person may have several *'aumākua* to call upon for aid.

"It is our *kahu* or caretaker since the moment of conception. Its role is that of primal guide. The *'aumakua* is always at your side. It is yours to call on at any time of life. Any time I'm in a difficult situation, I pause a moment and I ask for help," Brandt explains.

"Every person has a family *'aumakua*. This is your guardian spirit, guardian angel, whatever you want to call it. We all have it. But few people know how to work with the *'aumakua*. The *'aumakua* is there to help protect you and your family, to give you wisdom, vision to move ahead safely through life, to succeed.

Brandt's chief ancestral *'aumakua* is his beloved great-grandfather, Tūtū Man Kehauleo. "He has appeared to me on many occasions, and always in a case of warning," Brandt says. "In the early '80s my heart was giving me a bad time. The doctor was very frank that he was iffy whether I was going to make it. I was taking all kinds of tests, and I was going to specialists, and everybody gave me medicines. At one time I had 18 kinds of medicine and I was getting sicker and sicker and sicker.

"One night I was sleeping, and all of a sudden I was wide awake and the room was brilliantly lit and my great-grandfather was right there. He told me frankly: '*Keiki* [child], you are close to death.' He told me that everything I was doing was wrong—the doctors, the medicine, wrong. If I wanted to save my life and raise my kids, I was going to have to change my life completely.

"He said: 'In order to live, you need to throw away all that *lā'au haole* [Western medicine]. You have to get back on the *lā'au maoli*,' meaning that I had to go back to one of the herbal healers who could give me Hawaiian medicine. 'You have to go back to the temple—now.' He meant now! I had been so sick I had not been to the temple.

"All of a sudden I was out of body and I was watching my body lying stiff on the bed as if dead. Then all of this faded out, and he came back again and gave me a blessing and then he left. That was four o'clock in the morning.

"I called my kids and told them we were going to the temple. They never questioned me. I put on my robes. My son picked a bunch of *tī* leaves for the temple. My daughter made *'awa*, the offering. They had to

"When I came along, my great-grandfather said: 'You're the one.'"

help me, I could not walk. I tried to chant from my prone position. Then, as the sun rose, they started praying. I fell asleep or went into a trance. I awoke feeling very strong, very well, feeling that I needed to get up and get on with my life. So I got up on my feet without any help. We came home and I put on my sweats and went for a run."

Since such magic doesn't happen for everyone, Brandt suggests meditation as the best way to call upon personal *'aumākua*. He stresses that meditation is the foundation for any spiritual life "because it is through meditation that we are spiritually guided." Meditation, he says, is "the time when you are directly in touch with the *'aumākua,* directly in touch with the gods."

He follows an eight-step technique through which, he insists, "you will reach the light and generate *mana.*" His technique is not an ancient practice, but something he has evolved on his own over the years.

"We teach that practice is the thing. I don't think 30 minutes of practice a day is the answer. I don't think it's possible to obtain the illumination you want on a 30-minute casual practice. I believe you need to practice in the morning and practice at night. The Buddhists do this—at least two full meditations a day.

"If you follow this technique, it will happen. All I can say is that it will happen. Because this technique has been used by thousands of people."

His eight-step technique is:

1) **Schedule**

"Develop an established place and time. If you get into a familiar situation, after you've done it a few times, you'll notice that the moment you sit down that everything seems to feel right, that everything's flowing. We need that familiarity."

2) **Atmosphere**

The place must be: "familiar, comfortable, secure. Sit cross-legged or upright in a chair. No interruptions by telephone, traffic, kids or anything else disruptive. It will destroy your meditations."

3) **Opening prayer**

"This is a ritual prayer to the power you worship to open the way. You call on your deities or your ʻaumākua to empower you. Whether you want to pray or whether you simply want to state your purpose, it's up to you."

"Meditation is when you're directly in touch with the ʻaumākua, directly in touch with the gods."

4) **Goal**

"This is the big one: your statement of goals. State and fix your mind on a goal or need. I do stress singular—one object you want to accomplish in this meditation. If you just want the peace of meditation, you simply ask that you be guided into the light and then you enjoy your peace and quiet and your empowerment."

5) **Breathing**

"Deep breathing: this is a critical part of the entire process because if you don't do this well, it is very likely that nothing is going to manifest. Through your breathing eliminate all the junk thoughts in your head. Get yourself right on focus where you don't hear anything, not even your own voice. I just breathe until I see this little diamond light. As I breathe I feel myself growing lighter, and the light and I are moving together until at some point I'm really enveloped in the light and completely in trance."

6) Light

"You may perceive, if you focus upon it, a tiny bright light in the distant ether which expands until you are enveloped in its brilliance. Occasionally, your conjunction with the light is instantaneous—zip, you're there. When you reach it, you are empowered, and you will stay that way for a considerable period of time."

7) Focus

"All this time when you're traveling in time and space, keep yourself focused. Keep your mind on your goal until the light wanes and power mellows."

8) Ending

"Stay as meditative and alert to counsel or guidance as possible. Hold yourself open and free until your senses confirm that the work is completed."

Brandt says he approaches meditation with "absolute confidence that, if I do this right, everything is going to happen, and it does. If you approach this work with a lot of doubt about yourself, then it won't work. If you have studied it well, and you have confidence in yourself, it will work—you will receive the *mana*, you'll receive the guidance."

Mana is one of Brandt's major reasons for meditating. He teaches people how to "target their *mana*"—how to empower themselves.

"*Mana* is life force, the power that enables us to live," he explains. "So many people go throughout life without even using *mana*; they walk through life like they are in a fog. With *mana* you perceive what life really means and what it's saying to you.

"The gift of *mana* is all of ours, and we can command this *mana*. You generate *mana* through prayer, through deep breathing and through meditation. Do you have a great need to manifest something in your life? More wealth, better health, how to be a better person? Fine, then you focus on that.

"What blocks *mana*? Being unable to focus. We need to bring ourselves to a sharp focal point   block out all the extraneous junk in our heads. We can do this through proper deep breathing. Breathing is the key."

Healers, obviously, have powerfully developed *mana*. Brandt, who has done spiritual healings throughout his life, insists that anyone can be a healer if sufficiently focused. "You call upon the ʻaumākua, the gods, to release the *mana* and empower you," he says.

However, certain illnesses, he stresses, should only be handled by an experienced *kahuna*—illnesses imposed by sorcerers. This black magic is called *'anā'anā* and the only cure is to send the curse back to the sorcerer.

"I send it back and punish that individual. I do counter sorcery. I've done it many times successfully," Brandt says.

"One was a woman from France. Seeking to escape a curse, she and her husband fled to England, then to Australia. But, you can't run away from the curse, it travels with you. After they'd been around the world trying to obtain healing for her, he called me from Australia. They soon arrived on the Big Island and we spent five evenings together engaged in a really heavy trip. I was being picked up and bounced on the floor, but I was strong enough and I knew enough to hang in there with it. And in the end I completed a successful counter sorcery. If I had failed, I could have been destroyed."

Apparently, the man's first wife had spent time in Africa and had asked an African witch doctor to place the spell—unbeknownst to the couple. After Brandt's spiritual healing, they flew back to Australia, then called to tell him about the witch doctor—apparently she died while Brandt was doing his healing.

"And so with her death, this French woman was released," Brandt says. "It is really this serious. This is no joke. There are countless cases where this is recorded. It's a very real thing. Been done to me. Obviously it didn't work."

When Brandt was a young man, a girlfriend's ex-husband asked his aunt to send the death prayer to kill Brandt. "His grand-aunt was a *kahuna 'anā'anā*, which I did not know," Brandt says. "No trained *kahuna* will ever be killed like that or endangered if they're doing what they're taught to do, which is to protect ourselves. We do this twice a day through prayer, through commitment to the gods. It's just part of our spiritual offering. But, it never occurred to me that I was cursed. That was my stupidity. I knew enough to be aware, but I was madly in love and got lost, I suppose."

He found himself in the hospital, and after a week he overheard the doctors tell his sister there was nothing more they could do.

"I asked her to go call Auntie Luka, but admissions wouldn't let her in the hospital because they knew who and what she was. At that time practicing *kahuna* was still a crime, punishable by law. But she didn't have to come in. The plantation hospital had a *lānai* [porch] all around it. So she came by my room where she searched my astral body, then perceived what was wrong with me."

She took him from the hospital to her own home where he spent a week going in and out of consciousness. He finally awoke 35 pounds lighter and very weak.

"Auntie Luka told me in plain language she didn't know how I could be such a *lolo* 'stupid head' because I had almost been killed by *'anā'anā*. She even told me who it was, not by name, but by location, so there was no doubt about it. Auntie Luka said we had to send it back to her, so we did, very successfully."

In 1967 Brandt started a nonprofit foundation called Kahanahou (renewal) Hawaiian Foundation to teach Hawaiian youth about their culture. He retired from entertaining at resort hotels to devote himself to the foundation.

"We were still quite successful [in entertainment]," he says. "But my great-grandfather manifested himself during my sleep again. He told me that he thought it was the time in my life when I should give myself more deeply to our culture, our people. He said concentrate entirely on the *hula maoli,* our native dance, and chant.

Brandt, who has done spiritual healings all his life, insists that anyone can be a healer if sufficiently focused.

"We had about five of us working in what was the donkey barn, carving, and I was making drums. Then other Hawaiians came by. Pretty soon we had twelve of us working there. Then parents were stopping by, saying: 'Why you not teach then?' So I did. We built up a *hālau* [school] in no time. It was never a big deal. Just a bunch of Hawaiians working together. For the first 17 years we did not teach anyone but Hawaiians and nobody else practiced with us except Hawaiians.

"But, at that time the New Age was upon us, and I had been befriended by Peter and Eileen Caddy [of Findhorn Foundation in Scotland]. Other New Age teachers were drawn here for various reasons. So I really had a lot of exposure to New Age philosophies, and I did not dislike them. I liked it a whole lot better than the Christian, *haole* community. So we began to lend ourselves to these people and I had my own revelation about this.

"We opened to everyone. And I'm not sorry that we did that. We've been sharing it with whoever wants to learn. We have people from a great many countries coming here to study with us. Searching for Hawaiian cultural truth.

"It's a time of great change. And the change has just only really begun. It's going to be much more radical and totally different from anything my generation ever envisioned. Fortunately, I've been so exposed to the New Age that I'm really quite comfortable with the changes to come."

KAWIKA KAʻALAKEA
MINISTER AND HERBALIST

"I have spirits in my head." As he hesitantly speaks these soft words, the bearded, 40-ish Japanese-American man cries quietly, his body bowed under the strain of his secret.

His parents have brought him to meet Reverend *(Kahu)* Kawika Kaʻalakea, a Pentecostal minister who has dealt with spirits and miracles all his life. Kaʻalakea is a talkative, friendly, humble man who embraces all situations with *aloha*.

"Can you heal him, Reverend?" the man's mother asks. "He no sleep nights. He thinks spirit in his head. He used to live with us, but now he stay in dirty shack."

She stands with her husband, who never says a word, both of them frail and thin as bent coat hangers. She speaks in a lilting pidgin English familiar to the descendants of sugar plantation workers.

Kahu Kaʻalakea (pronounced Kah-a-la-ke-a) puts his big hand on her

"When God created Heaven and Earth, there was only water at that time. So drink water to keep you healthy. Water is life. There is something in the water that you no see and I no see. But according to the will of God, the spirit of God moves in the water."

son's head and commands Satan to leave him. "You don't belong to him," he tells the man. "You belong to God. You carry the image of God."

As Kaʻalakea quotes the Bible from memory, the man interrupts: "I am not a Christian. I'm a Zen Buddhist. I do not believe in a personal god. But I believe that Jesus existed."

That's fine with Kaʻalakea. "That's what I like," he responds. "You make your choice." But he does want to come by the man's shack to see if he can rid the place of the unseen and the unknown—spirits that might linger there. "You need to clean house," he admonishes, meaning spiritually, not literally.

"He's a good boy," his mother says of her troubled son. "He's honest. He tells the truth and he believes in the Hawaiian *kahuna.*"

Reverend Kaʻalakea does not liken himself to the powerful *kāhuna* of old. Many of them had such *mana,* their alleged powers seem magical today. Kaʻalakea considers himself merely a country minister. But, he is actually a blend of ancient and modern—a very Hawaiian man who practices *lāʻau lapaʻau,* herbal healing, but prefers hands-on healing while praying fervently to the Christian god.

He lived a Hawaiian childhood that no one gets to live anymore, growing up in a paradise called Kīpahulu, Maui, where the air is pregnant with the smells of flowers and ripening fruit, a place where plants develop gigantism from the lushness of rainfall, sun, volcanic soil and *aloha.* The jungle-green earth is lulled on one side by the blueness of unpolluted ocean waters; on the other side it's guarded by a 10,000-foot gentle mountain named after the sun, Haleakalā. It is a place Kaʻalakea speaks of in hushed, reverent tones as if he were referring to a great cathedral. It's a place he remembers with much nostalgia.

"I was born Dec. 8, 1919, in Kīpahulu," he begins. "I'm pure Hawaiian. Living in Kīpahulu it's a wonderful life. Everything—mountain, ocean and land—everything was there. Mountain was so important. I learned all the skills of the mountain. I go all myself. I never get lost one time. I know all the plants up there, what is medicine, what is not medicine, what to take, what not to take, how to cut.

"Up the mountain, down the ocean. I was taught many good things. I was lucky. I learned all the land. I learned how to plant *taro,* sweet potato. Fishing. All those things. That's how we survived. We had to do it; nobody gonna do that for us. That's why my grandmother said: 'Put your hand on the land. And what goes in the land it will take care of you.'

"In the land is many things. That's where our food comes. That is where our culture comes and our language comes from the land. Everything. That's *ʻāina.* We Hawaiians come from the *ʻāina.*"

As a young man, he never gave spiritual matters much heed. He left school after the fourth grade and began helping his father with his fishing business. By the time he was 14, he was working on the local ranch as a ranch hand. He was married in 1938, and six years later as the father of three small children, he had what he calls his first "conversion"—an intercession in his life by God.

"I received the Holy Spirit," he recalls. "I was pulled by my oldest brother to the pulpit to be prayed for. I felt something that I never felt in my life and I began to weep. After that, I didn't smoke. No more drinking."

Though he believes that was his first call, he still continued life as usual. Days he worked at the ranch as a cowboy and nights he played steel guitar in a popular band at the only hotel in the town of Hāna, ten miles from where he grew up. He didn't yet understand where life was going to lead him. It took nearly losing his life for the light to dawn.

"In 1948 I had an accident," he says as he begins to tell the story that changed his life. "My father [as deacon of the church] asked me to assist him, to prepare the Lord's Supper on Sunday. But my friend came, so I went with him. We took our nets. Go fishing.

"The sea was rough, rough. I always go that place, but this time I had something happen to me. I fell down about 20-40 feet. I fell down on this rock, fell down into the water. When I look up, oh, I'm in the water. My friend sees me in the water, so he runs. But I thank God—it was the love of God that saved my life. I could have died out there. The sea was rough. No man can stay in water like that. The wave picked me up and throw me up. My friend reached over there. Big wave. My friend hold my hand and pulled me up. No can walk. We crawl up. He put me on the horse and went home.

"My father went go get the medicine for my back. I thought my back broke. He dragged me outside into the afternoon sun and he asked God to forgive. So he put that medicine on my back five times. *'Ekāhi, 'elua, 'ekolu, 'ehā, lima. Hā.* [One, two, three, four, five. Breath.] Five times. He put the breath on me. He make the medicine on top my back for three days. *'Ekāhi, 'elua, 'ekolu*— one, two, three. *Pau* [finish]. I stand and walk. It's a miracle. I walk. I no feel nothing. I no feel sore. I go back work. My friend say: 'You come back work? Too early you come back work. Your condition no good. You broke your back!'

"From that experience I know what God wants me to do—to assist my father. I was the only boy left at home with my father and my father always looked to me. It was my duty to help my father in the church. So I get hurt. God make me that way. Good thing he not broke my back. He just warned me: according to the will of God, there was the wrath of God to fall upon the children of God."

But still . . . the wrath of God had some punch left. Kaʻalakea was not only going to be on his knees, but flat on his back before he truly understood how Hawaiian his ministry was to be.

"In 1948 I fell down. Not enough yet. God saved my life. And I lived well. 1953, not enough yet. God still loved me. He put me in the hospital.

"My wife tell me: 'You better go to the doctor, you're not well.' I said: 'No I'm all right.' She said: 'No, no, no.' My wife hard head. She throw me in the car and take me to the hospital. They took my X-ray and put me in the hospital. I had TB [tuberculosis].

"The doctor there talked to my father and my wife and said: 'You brought that man too late to me. I cannot do nothing for him. Too late. Look at his X-ray.'

"So they put me in a room with a Filipino man. I stayed about one week. Then my father came, he look up to heaven: 'Father, thank you today. If you think my boy go home with you, take him home. It's your will.' He speak Hawaiian. Then he called me: 'Kawika, you and I pray The Lord's Prayer in Hawaiian.'

"You know, I never prayed in Hawaiian in my life. I only prayed in English. It's my first time. I prayed The Lord's Prayer for the first time in my life with my father. [In chant-like rhythms he begins praying The Lord's Prayer: *E ko mākou Makua i luna o ka lani, e hoʻanoia kou inoa. . . .*]

"The Lord's Prayer has so much meaning, everything for us today—how to live, how to repent, how to make ourselves right, how to love, and all that is in one prayer. The most powerful prayer for today.

"My father stands up, picks up his hat, he walks straight for the door, he never says nothing to me, no goodbye, nothing. Two days after that, I see this revelation. I see this small light coming towards me and it's a beautiful land, wheat growing as far as your eyes could see, and this light in the center coming. There was somebody behind this light, coming towards me. Like lightning. Oh, wow. Lightning came three times. I don't know what is that lightning.

"I dreamed these two doctors reading my X-rays. The first X-ray, the second X-ray, they were putting back and forth these X-rays. They were shaking their heads. They no can believe.

"One week afterwards they take X-rays. The doctor came see me: 'You will be all right.' At that time, they didn't have the drug for TB.

"But the Filipino man died. He took my place instead of me going up. I was supposed to go, me. God has a plan for me. It was God's plan to save my life, take him [the Filipino] home.

"The funny thing, I stay in the hospital for two long years. I was well, but God put me there two years. There was a reason God put me in there; I began to work with the patients, I prayed for the patients. It was God's plan.

"I saw this light and it was Jesus Himself, He came to me; He was the light of the world. That's Him.

"How many times God warned me? Two times already. God's plan was to call me to the ministry. My brother is a minister, my other brother is a minister, my uncle is a minister, my older sister is an evangelist.

"When I first came home from the hospital, my first mission was to gather all my family. They look at me and cry. I was filled with the spirit of God. We get all together and I speak Hawaiian. From The Lord's Prayer, I began to speak in Hawaiian, preach in Hawaiian, read in Hawaiian, pray in Hawaiian. God wanted me to speak the language. I take the Hawaiian language all over the island. This one language, most powerful."

It is a place Kaʻalakea speaks of in hushed, reverent tones as if he were referring to a great cathedral.

After he arrived home in 1955, he discovered his brother had been paralyzed for a year, after a cow attacked him while he was branding her calf.

"Paralyzed. No can walk," Kaʻalakea says. "Doctor give up. No can. I come home from the hospital; I was filled with the presence of God. So I went to visit my brother. He was a minister, long time. He was on the bed. He seen me, he cried. I look up to heaven, say: 'Father, this is my brother. I love my brother. Can you make him walk?' This is the way I talk. I pick up my brother and hold him, and he began to walk. He walk. That's the first miracle God showed me. From that time I know God called me. There are many miracles after that.

"I see something happening when I started with my brother. From that time on, I believe maybe God want me in the ministry. This is what he tells me: 'Go, and save His children.' Every time I stand up behind the pulpit, I'm filled with the spirit of God."

Kahu Kaʻalakea is not just a caretaker of souls, he also knows how to heal physical ailments using the ancient Hawaiian tradition of herbal medicine. He comes from a family of *kāhuna lāʻau lapaʻau* (herbal doctors), but he only began practicing it himself in 1986. As a child he watched his father and his grandmother and grandfather practice their medicine, but, in typical Hawaiian fashion, they never taught him outright—he just watched and asked no questions.

His father's specialty was broken bones. In the olden days, it's said his type of *kahuna* could heal bones very quickly, almost magically. Kaʻalakea saw his father do just that, but today does not know how it's done himself.

"I cannot do what he do. It's a secret method between him and his God. He doesn't tell you. People gotta be humble and quiet for four days. Then on fourth day healed. How he do it, I don't know. Certain kinds of methods they don't teach."

He believes *kāhuna* were more powerful in the old days because: "Not so much people. Not too much activity. It was quiet. I know my father always go up to the mountain, spent four days up there. So they get the knowledge from God in a secret manner and they keep that to themselves."

However, it turns out he received his own knowledge in much the same way. Though he learned some from his family, he feels he received most of his medical knowledge directly through revelations from God.

"God called me to take the valuables to my people," he says. "The children of God. God taught the medicine to me. I began to speak according to what He told me. I never read the books. No. Revelation comes from God . . . this is for the asthma, this is how to go get the medicine, this is how to mix it. Castor bean apply the leaf to the arthritis. Wrap it three times. My father had arthritis, even I had arthritis. I'm fine.

"*Lāʻau lapaʻau* is for everything. It can be for your eye, for your hair, for your nose, for your ear, for your tongue, whatever. You have ulcer, you have hemorrhage, every disorder of the body we have medicine for that. *Lāʻau lapaʻau* is a powerful thing."

Still, he has nothing against Western medicine. "They're the same. It doesn't matter," he says. "It can be Western medicine, it can be Hawaiian medicine. It's all the same. From the herbs they make capsules. It's given to me to share Hawaiian medicine."

His true preference, though, is spiritual healing. "If I have to give herbs, I give. But mostly I don't give," he says. "I pray for them. Prayer healing. That's what

I'm doing—spiritual medicine. Prayer is stronger. Jesus used His hand, only hand, His medicine. He made the blind to see, He made the crippled to walk, He made the dead alive, only by His hand. I use my hand. I do believe in prayer."

When asked advice on how to stay well, Ka'alakea's answer is simple and surprising: "When God created Heaven and Earth, there was only water at that time. So drink water to keep you healthy. Water is life. There is something in the water that you no see and I no see. But according to the will of God, the spirit of God moves in the water.

"Two kinds of water: hot water and cold water. Hot water you take your time, you never rush. Cold water is too cold. The sun is life—makes the water hot. I put my medicine outside in the sun, the sun cooks the medicine.

"To clean inside the body, you get ocean water, salt water, with half and half pure water, you put lemon in there and you cleanse. The most important thing in life is to cleanse."

And the final answer, beyond medical and herbal healing, he believes, is: "The only thing is you yourself. You believe, you're well."

Reverend Ka'alakea receives all his directives from God, both on health and spirituality. He didn't train in a seminary to become a preacher, he didn't read books or study in school to become a healer, he simply began doing both on his own.

He considers his church Pentecostal and the building is on land that he owns. He bought the land in the early 1980s, then moved an old Mormon church onto it. After fixing it up and planting the land, he now has one of the sweetest properties in a very busy tourist area called Kihei. His tiny white church is an incongruously peaceful oasis in a neighborhood of concrete condos and shopping malls. With its quaint little steeple and simple wooden construction, Ka'alakea's antique building is a reminder of what this busy area used to be before Maui was "discovered."

He believes his is the only church where Hawaiian is used as liberally as English. His 10 o'clock Sunday service consists of Hawaiian hymns, Hawaiian prayers and a sermon, mostly in English. There is no ceremony, no ritual, and, there's no altar, just a small wooden pulpit. A sign proclaiming: "God is Love— *Aloha Ke Akua*" hangs behind the pulpit above a simple wooden cross. That message is Ka'alakea's standard: *Aloha Ke Akua*.

PRESERVATION AND HISTORY

Captain Cook estimated there were 300,000 people in Hawai'i when he arrived in 1778. Others theorized there were up to a million. Cook was well-intentioned and well-mannered, but his men didn't think past their own desires. As a result, they, and everyone after them, introduced diseases previously unknown in The Islands—venereal disease, smallpox, cholera, measles, colds, flus. A majority, perhaps as many as 80 to 90 percent, of Hawai'i's native people died within a few decades.

The ancients had no written language; they transmitted their traditions orally, one generation to the next; so, when the elders and the *kāhuna* began dying from disease, with them went their expertise. Much ancient ritual and knowledge was lost forever.

To complicate matters, when the missionaries came in 1820, they saw little about the Hawaiians and their culture that pleased them. Head missionary Hiram Bingham was appalled at his introduction to Hawai'i's king when Liholiho, attired in his customary *malo* (loincloth) met "the first company of white women he ever saw . . . destitute of hat, gloves, shoes, stockings and pants." Bingham later wrote of "the appearance of destitution, degradation, and barbarism, among the chattering and almost naked savages."

Yet the early missionaries were loved by the people and their powerful new god was of great interest to the deeply spiritual Hawaiians. To their credit, these dogged, hard-working New Englanders learned the Hawaiian language, printed school books in Hawaiian and taught the people in Hawaiian. Within four years of their arrival, there were 900-some schools throughout The Islands, most headed by Hawaiian scholars trained by the missionaries. Hawaiians knew little about the rapidly infiltrating West, so the chiefs pushed the missionaries to teach their people *palapala*, "the book learning." Within 20 years, Hawaiians had the highest literacy rate in the world. While slaves, pioneers and Indians had little opportunity for schooling in America, in Hawai'i every child went to school.

Yet, as strict Calvinist thought permeated society, and as Western technology overwhelmed native techniques, all things Hawaiian became second rate. Even the Hawaiian monarchy would not last long (less than a century) before it was overthrown by Westerners.

The landscape itself changed as people moved from traditional villages to Western cities, and as huge sugar and pineapple plantations cultivated the *'āina* into sameness. King Kamehameha III legislated land ownership for his people, but many of them never understood the concept, or failed to fill out the required paperwork, or sold their land for needed money. The upshot was that, over the years, the majority of Hawaiians became landless on their own soil.

Preservation of whatever remains from the past two difficult centuries has become an obsession for today's Hawaiians. Burial grounds, archaeological sites, water rights, fishing rights, gathering rights—all have become part of the battle cry for Hawaiian rights.

By the 1960s, tourism was becoming Hawai'i's major industry, and jobs were so needed that development started to grow like Topsy. Kā'anapali, Maui, the first large resort area built in Hawai'i, leveled numerous archaeological sites to make room for hotels, condos and shops—all necessary to draw income to the island. Mā'alaea, Maui, contained what Bishop Museum archaeologists in Honolulu considered one of the best fishing villages on Maui, and they planned to excavate and study it in the future. Instead, a temple, a fishing shrine, several petroglyphs and 45 house sites were destroyed to construct a harbor breakwater.

There was no future for this village, but, by the late 1980s, preservationists began to battle developers and win. When an expensive hotel chain broke ground for a luxury resort in Kapalua, Maui, the developers found they were building on an ancient burial site of more than 1,000 bodies. A Hawaiian group went to court to halt removal of the bones and they won—a major victory over "progress." Another Maui hotel in Mākena wanted to block the public from crossing hotel grounds to walk the ancient Pi'ilani Alanui, a roadway engineered in the 1500s to circumnavigate the island. Once again the Hawaiians won.

As tourists become more and more interested in the "real" Hawai'i, and as admiration for the native culture grows, preservationists and history buffs will be more readily heard above the clanging of hammer and nails.

Lydia Namahana Maiʻoho

KAHU OF ROYAL MAUSOLEUM

"We are descendants of the chiefs who took care of the bones of Kamehameha the Great..."

When Hawaiʻi's greatest king, Kamehameha I, died in 1819, his remains were taken secretly and hidden by two of his most trusted chiefs, two brothers named Hoapili and Hoʻoūlu. They kept their mission so clandestine, that, to this day, no one knows where the hiding place is.

That's the way it was done in ancient times—bones of the high *aliʻi* (chiefs/chiefesses) were so imbued with *mana* that they were hidden away so no one could misuse them or take power from them.

Kamehameha was Hawaiʻi's first king, and he still lived the ancient ways. However, all seven monarchs after him faced a more modern, Christian world. Thus, their *iwi* (bones) were not stripped of the flesh and secreted away. Their *iwi* are, in fact, in the middle of Honolulu, situated between a very busy business street and a roaring highway. Their *iwi* lie on the grounds of Mauna ʻAla, the Royal Mausoleum.

Still, the power of these *ali'i* remains. Though the big city thunders around Mauna 'Ala, there is a stately silence within its 3.7 acres. Oddly, not a car can be heard.

"Don't you find it peaceful? It's just a quiet, quiet place. It seems like we're far away in a remote place." Lydia Namahana Mai'oho mentions the silence several times as she sits on the front lawn of her cottage, weaving the history of Mauna 'Ala through her own life's history. Her presence as *kahu*, or caretaker, proves that tradition does not die easily in a land where the high chiefs were once revered as *ali'i akua* (chiefs of the gods). Mrs. Mai'oho (pronounced My-o-ho) is a descendant of the two chiefly brothers who were entrusted with Kamehameha's remains. Her family has continued the tradition through modern times. The kings and queens who are buried at Mauna 'Ala are under the constant care of a woman who takes her job seriously, a woman whose lineage gives her absolute right to be keeper of the bones. Though she comes from *ali'i* stock herself, to live alongside these great Hawaiians is an honor she feels deeply.

Slowed by acute arthritis that barely allows her to walk, Auntie Namahana has turned over all official *kahu* duties to her son Bill who lives with her in the small, green cottage built for her father in the 1940s when he was *kahu*.

"We are descendants of the chiefs who took care of the bones of Kamehameha the Great," she explains, adding a bit of family lore to the 200-year-old tale. "We were always told that even Kamehameha could not trust because he had so many chiefs. How was he going to know which ones would he pick? What he did was to call all of his chiefs to see who he would pick. But only two of them came in their *malo* [loincloths], and that was Ho'olulu and Hoapili. The rest came in their feather capes and helmets and stood before him. But he did not choose them. He took the two chiefs. And do you know why he chose them? Because they did not take the time to dress. When he called them, they immediately came, and he knew that these were the two that he could trust to hide his bones secretly.

"So many people want to know where he is buried. The only thing we know is that when the two chiefs came back from hiding the bones, Ho'olulu went to his wife and she had just given birth to a son. Hawaiians had an instinct to name a child after an event. So the child was named Kaihe'ekai, which meant the receding waters. So figure that one out: did the waters recede? They must have gone into an underwater cave.

"Kaihe'ekai was the first caretaker at the cemetery at 'Iolani Palace. And when he died, it was still in the family. His name was given to my dad, my dad to his son who died, and finally to my son, Bill, and now my grandson also carries the name Kaihe'ekai. Our direct line comes from Ho'olulu."

PRESERVATION AND HISTORY: Lydia Namahana Maiʻoho

Until 1862, Hawaiʻi's deceased royalty were kept in a mausoleum near ʻIolani Palace in Honolulu. During that year, King Kamehameha IV and Queen Emma lost their only child. There was no room in the mausoleum for little Prince Albert, a four-year-old named after the husband of his godmother, England's Queen Victoria, so his parents decided to move the royal cemetery to its current spot.

According to Auntie Namahana: "No one lived on this site when they chose it. It was barren ground. You don't choose a site that someone has lived on. It has to be clear of everything—that there was no desecration to it at all."

Her presence as kahu, *or caretaker, proves that tradition does not die easily in a land where the high chiefs were once revered as* aliʻi akua *(chiefs of the gods).*

The new Kamehameha mausoleum was not finished in time for the next tragedy—only 15 months after his son's death, the 29-year-old king died of an asthma attack. It's believed that guilt and sadness over little Albert's passing prompted his early death.

Faced with this crushing dual loss, Queen Emma actually pitched a tent on Mauna ʻAla's grounds and slept in an unfinished wing of the mausoleum's chapel alongside her husband and son.

Bill Maiʻoho, Auntie Namahana's son, has such an obvious love of history that he speaks of Hawaiʻi's past in the present tense while giving tours of the mausoleum's ground. "Queen Emma is so overcome with grief," he says, "that she camps on the grounds of Mauna ʻAla and sleeps inside a wing [of the chapel] for about a month to six weeks. They try to talk her out of it, but she won't hear of it."

A year's period of mourning was observed before construction was continued on the chapel, a structure built in the form of a Christian cross. When finished, the rest of the Kamehameha family were brought to the chapel from the ʻIolani Palace cemetery. These were such high *aliʻi* that the only people who could disturb their remains were their own descendants.

Bill describes the torch-lit procession of Hawaiʻi's greatest family of modern times: "On the evening of October 30th, 1865, King Kamehameha V and his father, Kekūanaōʻa, bring from the grounds of ʻIolani Palace 18 members of the

Kamehameha Dynasty. It is a night-time procession—*kāhili* [feather standards that indicate royalty], *kukui* nut torches, chanting the *mele* [chants]. They lay wreaths and *pili* grass alongside King Street and Nuʻuanu Avenue onto the grounds of Mauna ʻAla. The king and his father lead the procession. They bring the Kamehameha Dynasty here, and place them inside the building on biers or casket stands."

Mauna ʻAla, which means "Fragrant Mountain," is perhaps the most Hawaiian place in all the islands because, as Auntie Namahana says: "It is the only sovereign land in the state of Hawaiʻi. The state is in charge of taking care of it, but it belongs to these people buried here. It is sacred where they're buried."

Bill explains that "sovereign" means that "only the Hawaiian flag flies here. It is the only sovereign land recognized by an act of Congress [in 1900]."

Due to the power of the people buried here, Mauna ʻAla is considered spooky or eerie by many of those who believe in the magic of old Hawaiʻi.

"A lot of them say: 'I don't know how you can live here with these people,'" Auntie Namahana says with a wry lift of her eyebrows. "It's mostly Hawaiians who say that. They have this feeling that if you're here you get spooked out—that the dead are coming out, doing this or that. Not me. I'm not bothered—I'm happy to be here. It's so peaceful. Serene. Never had a problem. The caretaker is here to see that no desecration comes to the *aliʻi*—that nobody hurts the tombs or the chapel. That's our concern: to see that they're safe in here. Which they are."

(Her) lineage gives her absolute right to be keeper of the bones.

Old Hawaiʻi does rear up on occasion and surprise its modern citizens. When the chapel was restored in 1976, nineteen sets of bones wrapped in *kapa* cloth were found buried on the outer and inner perimeters of the building. Those outside were facing the chapel; those underneath the building had their heads turned to the outside. Anthropologists and archaeologists were called in to examine this phenomenon and many theories were proposed, but the new *kahu* of these *iwi*, Bill

Maiʻoho, believes the *iwi* were buried in keeping with the ancient ways.

"When the high chiefs passed away in ancient times, other high chiefs would willingly give up their lives to go with that high chief," Bill explains. "It was a tradition called *moepuʻu,* or, to sleep with the chief. Kamehameha the Great forbid it at his death. He said the men were sacred to his son and his son would need them more than he would need them. And so that practice was done away with.

"Everybody's got an opinion, but in reading about Kamehameha V and his strong adherence to the culture, I think he had these individuals placed that way in a spiritual connection to protect his family members inside the mausoleum."

Bill is not saying the nineteen were killed by Kamehameha V. Their remains were old, as was the *kapa* cloth wrapping them, so he thinks they were dug up from their original graves and reburied when the chapel was built. Bill believes they were all high chiefs because they wore *niho palaoa,* the whale's tooth necklace that symbolized *aliʻi.*

"Chicken skin" is the phrase Hawaiians would use.

Auntie Namahana has her own tales of mystery. One can barely get inside Mauna ʻAla's imposing iron gates before being faced with the first of these intrigues. A few feet beyond the gates stands a massive, stately tree with giant limbs and huge, exposed roots that bond the tree to the earth. The tree has a powerful, ponderous presence like a nature spirit from a Gothic children's tale. Not surprisingly, this Hawaiian *kamani* tree reputedly speaks. As it did once to Namahana.

"Hawaiians believe it talks and chants," she says. "And I've seen it does. When I came back at midnight one night and opened the gate, I heard this voice above me saying: 'Namahana, Namahana.' I was so scared, but I didn't answer back because my mother said don't answer the call.

"Another experience happened in 1956. A young Air Force man, a *haole* boy, came to the door and said he was going to write about *Menehunes* [legendary small people], so he came to take pictures. My mother explained to him that only the *aliʻi* are buried here, but he could take pictures. As he walked out the gate, this voice said to him: 'You can't write about *Menehunes,* but take a picture of me.' So he took what he thought he saw in the tree. He came back with the picture and it looked like in that tree was a chief with a *mahiole* [feather helmet]."

Auntie also tells the story of a policeman who slept during his beat in a church parking lot right next to Mauna ʻAla. As he slept, he dreamed he saw ancient Hawaiians walking around with feather capes on. The next night the female cop who had his beat slept in the same place and had the very same dream, though she knew nothing of his.

"She told him she had a dream that was out of this world," Auntie Namahana relates, "and he said, 'Yeah, you dreamed of all these Hawaiians walking around with capes on.'

"She said: 'How did you know that?'

"'Because I had the same dream,' he said.

"She was scared, but she said it was so beautiful, all those people walking around with capes on.

"Then, in 1977, a young Japanese boy came. He was taking art from the Honolulu Academy of Arts and he wanted to sketch the chapel. So we said sure. He came back a week later with a photograph. He said: 'Something weird happened to me. When I went home that night, I checked my sketch and there was a face in the sketch, and I did not draw a face. So, without you knowing, I came back to take a photograph, and in the photograph was a face in the window of the chapel.'

"Ten years later, the Bishop Estate makes an appointment with me," Auntie Namahana continues. "After 67 years, they finally looked at Charles Reed's will, and in his will he mentions three times: number one, Mauna 'Ala—maintenance, cleaning of the tomb and landscaping. But we never saw any money for 67 years. All his money was going to the Bishop Museum. So, finally we got the money. So I went back and looked at the sketch and said, 'Oh, this in the window, the white man is Charles Reed Bishop. He's looking out the window and he sees nothing is done. He's saying: 'They're not using my trust.'

"This man gave his all. And I know this because he raised my dad. He fed him, he clothed him, he educated him."

Charles Reed Bishop was a New Yorker who moved to Hawai'i in 1846 at the age of 24, and four years later, married one of the most powerful women in the kingdom, Bernice Pauahi Pākī. Bernice was destined to be the last of the Kamehamehas, so she inherited the crown lands (about 9 percent of the total land area in Hawai'i), and when she died, she left a huge trust to educate Hawaiian children. Her husband was involved in both business and government and was the founder of the First Hawaiian Bank. In his wife's honor, he built the Bishop Museum in Honolulu and left monies for various causes, including the maintenance of Mauna 'Ala where he and Bernice are buried (in the Kamehameha crypt).

Auntie Namahana thinks highly of Bishop because he was the adoptive father of her own father. "When my dad was born," she remembers, "Bernice Pauahi wanted to adopt him, but my grandmother said you do not adopt him, but you can take care of him. Then my grandmother died at the age of 28 of consumption, and even though Bernice died too, Charles Reed continued and took care of my dad. My dad was the first student to attend Kamehameha School when it opened. First registered student. My dad had a crooked thumb and they thought it was leprosy. Mr. Bishop did not send him to Kalaupapa [the leprosy settlement on Moloka'i]; he sent him to Japan. My dad lived there five years, and they found out it was not leprosy. He came home when he was 15. Mr. Bishop was a kind, gentle man."

Auntie Namahana doesn't like it when men like Bishop are called *"haole"*—Hawaiian slang for Caucasian. Sometimes the term is used casually with no offense, sometimes it's used as a racial putdown.

"I say, for goodness sake, don't use that word *haole,*" she insists. "I don't like it because a lot of my ancestors were white. I'm Hawaiian, but I'm German and English too. I can't just throw them aside. Eh, those are my *kūpuna* [ancestors], too.

"I say listen to the *haole* sometime. The *haoles* are reading. They know about our history because they read it. When they come and they're so interested in our culture, eh, I want to be there for this person."

"The greatest thing I was ever taught is to love and care for other people. My mother always said love and respect you never go wrong. Because whenever you do this, it's given back to you. In our growing up we were always taught what goes around comes around."

Auntie Namahana is only just beginning to wind up. One hardly need ask her questions—stories and opinions flow easily.

Her *hānai* (adopted) daughter, Malihini Dunn-Keahi, loves all the stories of her adopted mother. "She's the kind of lady where you want to get a pillow and lay on a comfortable couch and just talk story," Malihini says. "I did that with her till four o'clock in the morning the first night that I met her. You listen to her stories till you fall asleep."

One of the best stories Auntie tells occurred in 1994. She insists she's a bit tired of the tale, but she may be the only person in Hawai'i so bored by this infamous incident.

The event was a major coup carried out by a small, silent group of Hawaiians who decided the ancient ways had to be avenged. It was a crime—a robbery—however, many applaud the culprits and actually consider them heroes. But they are anonymous "heroes" because no one knows whodunit. Or at least, no one is talking.

The plot centers around two woven sennit (coconut fiber) baskets, called *kāʻai,* containing the remains of two ancient high chiefs, probably of the 15th or 16th century. It is a story of many complications and sub-plots.

Act I: It began in 1828 when Kamehameha's favorite wife, Queen Kaʻahumanu, destroyed two important Big Island temples after removing all *aliʻi* remains from them. The remains were then reburied in a Big Island cave. Such an act was unthinkably sacrilegious, but Kaʻahumanu no longer believed in the ancient ways. She was a newly converted Calvinist who now abhorred the idea of ancient temples that deified long-dead *aliʻi.*

"She accepted Christianity and these were the old ways that she just wanted to get rid of," Auntie Namahana explains. "Today a lot of Hawaiians get so mad with her, but I'm not mad with her. She did what she thought she had to do. You cannot play two sides—accept Christianity and still go with the old gods."

Act II: Thirty years later, in 1858, King Kamehameha IV decided the ancient *iwi* should be moved from the Big Island cave and taken to Honolulu to be sheltered with their modern *aliʻi* relatives in the mausoleum near ʻIolani Palace. There were those who claimed he would surely die for this; instead, the sea captain who delivered the remains from Big Island to Honolulu died a few days after the delivery. Thus the king was apparently spared.

Act III: In 1865, the *kāʻai* were moved by Kamehameha V to the newly built mausoleum at Mauna ʻAla.

Act IV: In 1918, Prince Jonah Kūhiō, believing himself to be the closest living relative of the *kāʻai,* decided they should go to the Bishop Museum to be studied for their historical significance. The woven basketry, the only type of its kind in Polynesia, was of particular interest. Kūhiō died three years later, before he could retrieve them, and the *kāʻai* remained in a three-foot-long metal museum drawer until 1994.

Act V, the finale: Some time during the night of February 17, 1994, three Hawaiian men entered the Bishop Museum, apparently unstopped by gates, doors and locks, and removed the *kāʻai.* They placed the *kāʻai* in two suitcases and boarded a plane to Kona's airport on the Big Island, where they handed the suitcases over to other Hawaiians who, it's believed, took the *kāʻai* back to the area they supposedly came from in 1828—the majestic and sacred Waipiʻo Valley.

It was a political and religious act—a magnificently executed statement of Hawaiian sovereignty. As bold and as thrilling as it may be, it is not the way Auntie Namahana envisioned the final act. As *kahu* of their relatives, she believes the *kāʻai* should be in Mauna ʻAla. She and other influential Hawaiians had formally agreed with the Bishop Museum that the *kāʻai* would be returned to Mauna ʻAla soon. Little did they know that other Hawaiians plotted against them.

Auntie Namahana does readily admit: "I'm not the *kahu* of the *kāʻai*. I have no jurisdiction. I'm the *kahu* of Mauna ʻAla. I only take care what is in these grounds."

But she soon would have been their *kahu*. "We were going to build a mausoleum above the Kamehameha Tomb to house the *kāʻai*," she says with a doleful sigh. "They are the highest of all these *aliʻi* [due to their age and sacred rank], so they have to be on a higher ground. It would have been really nice to have them situated at Mauna ʻAla where they last were."

The *kāʻai* are not mere historical artifacts, they are significant religious relics of possibly deified ancient chiefs. For a commoner to touch them, not to mention put them in suitcases, is a brazen, blasphemous act—one that could cause death to the perpetrators. Unless the gods agreed with them. Unless the *kāʻai* themselves spoke to them. (One of the perpetrators apparently had an unsettling dream in which he received the message: "The two warriors want to come home." This was months before the heist, before he even knew much about the *kāʻai*.)

Even Auntie Namahana has to admit that the heavens have not rained lead since the theft.

"You know what?" she asks rhetorically. "It wasn't meant to be at Mauna ʻAla. Maybe they really wanted to go back to Waipiʻo. We haven't had any rumbling. There was no storm, there was no flooding. Wherever they are, I just hope they're safe."

Still, she is frustrated with "the audacity" of the culprits. "You do not go and take things like that," she says forcefully. "They do not belong to you. They are for all of us. Those *kāʻai* are for every Hawaiian. We have to take care of them."

As she has done for thirty-some years for their royal relatives. "I'm not here to worship them," she says. "I'm here to take care of them."

CHARLEY KEAU
ARCHAEOLOGIST

Maui's one and only local archaeologist was not the least bit interested in old rocks and ancient ruins when he was first introduced to the subject. That was in 1971, when Kenneth Emory, the dean of Polynesian archaeologists, was on the island, studying Maui's sites. Emory took a liking to Charley Keau and decided to take him under his wing. At the time, Keau (pronounced Kay-ow) thought differently.

"I told him I didn't want to do it," Keau says today. "I thought it was a waste of time—that it should be left alone. Whatever the *ali'i* and the *kūpuna* had left should not be disturbed.

"He told me I <u>was</u> going to do it. He said, 'Charley, if you don't take care of these things, who's going to protect them? What's going to happen to them?'

"My first answer was—to hell with them. I said I'm *hūpō*, which means I'm stupid. I don't know anything.

"Why should we preserve things? The past is very important. Don't go back in the past, but remember the past. Preserve the past, but improve yourself. We have to keep respecting those things that our *kūpuna* had. We still carry today our *aloha* for our temples, even though they're destroyed. Our *aloha* for all these things is still with us, it's not gone, it never will be gone."

"But Dr. Emory saw that I did know much, and there was something in me that he wanted to promote. Because I'm a Hawaiian, the archaeologists accepted me for what I knew about my life style growing up. I told him I never graduated from high school, and I never knew about archaeology. He said he'd teach me."

Maui's mayor asked Keau to work with Emory and his crew, cleaning up the two great *heiau* (temple) near Wailuku town, Halekiʻi and Pihanakalani (also called Piʻihana). Charley was born at the foot of the sand dune where Pihanakalani stands, so he had a personal feeling for the area. Before he knew it, he was hooked, and he wasn't as *hūpō* as he thought.

". . . the old folks always say every land, every stone is valuable because somehow it produces life."

"Somebody told me the *heiau* stones came from Māʻalaea, and that burned me up," he says. "They came from the mouth of ʻĪao Stream—that's what my *kūpuna* told me. I was born and raised right there. I knew I had to get these things straightened out."

He began reading as much as he could find—old archaeological manuscripts and books written by some of the first literate Hawaiians of the 1800s.

"The more I read, the more I became interested, because that's what my mother was telling us. And I never listened to her.

"I kept reading—Kamakau, Fornander, Malo—these were stories the old folks were talking about. I don't think they ever read Kamakau and Fornander. You go to their houses and there's no library, no books, but they tell me the same things that are in the books. That really made me feel so good inside. Hey, this is what my mother said!

"From that time on, I had to do the job."

After the *heiau* work, Emory took Keau to the small village of Maonakala in south Maui, where they spent a few weeks surveying several house sites, a well, a canoe shed, a cooking pit and a fishing shrine. Then, for the next six months, they examined archaeological sites all over the island of Maui.

"That was a big survey—the state historic preservation survey," Keau remembers. "We were out looking for sites that were surveyed in the past, all the way back to 1850-something. It was the first major work done on Maui.

"I became more involved because I thought I could do something for my people. I could do something for the children so our younger generations could learn more about their Hawaiian heritage. I have a lot of *aloha* for that.

"I saw all the artifacts *in situ* on the ground. I started to learn about the scientists' way of understanding the stones. I learned so much from them. I didn't know the scientific words, but I caught on fast. Even when I was working construction jobs, I'd go back to archaeology and work with the Bishop Museum."

He continued crewing on Maui's sites from 1971 until well into the 1980s. Today, though he doesn't do any more digs, he sits on various preservation boards because he's considered a valued Hawaiian historian.

"I just want to be known as a good friend, but they call me a Hawaiian historian. Professional people call me an archaeologist. I don't care whatever name you give me as long as you don't hit me on the head!" Keau jokes.

He is modest about his own contribution to archaeology and is a bit tired of all the fanfare that's come his way over the years.

"They won't let me be—they keep calling me up all the time. It gets monotonous after a time."

He laughs as he says this, but Keau is retired and is no longer interested in being a renowned archaeologist. He likes his quiet life and spends most days helping his daughter and son-in-law run their four-acre botanical garden, a tourist stop in Maui's famous 'Īao Valley.

However, with so many antiquities needing safeguarding, Keau will interrupt his retirement to work for preservation. Wailuku's two *heiau* where Keau started his archaeological career are sad examples. The *heiau* are on the National Register for Historic Places, but that didn't save them from their immediate neighbor—a contractor who was mining the sand dunes they're built on.

"The state called me and asked me to go down and take a look." Keau remembers. "So I went down there and I saw all the tumbling stones that came down from the *[heiau]* walls and I said, 'Oh my God, we gotta stop this.' So now they're doing the restoration work. They're putting it back again.

"It's very, very disturbing. Not just the *heiau*, but the whole dune itself."

Wailuku's two magnificent *heiau* are built high on a dune surrounded by other sand dunes. These huge, old dunes have always protected the town from salty ocean breezes, yet they've received little protection themselves.

In another damaging occurrence, while developing the dunes for housing subdivisions, the state itself did "a mean, cancerous thing," Keau says. "They took a whole mountain down, the sand dune. And that is wrong. They sold a lot of sand. When they started to take about ten feet off the top of the dunes, they started running into all these burials alongside one another. Much of the burials and the archaeological things were lost. The biggest lot of bones [on Maui] is there—from one dune to the next dune, thousands of people buried there."

"I thought I could do something for my people. I could do something for the children so our younger generations could learn about their Hawaiian heritage."

Mistreatment or removal of Hawaiian ancestors' bones is a cultural sacrilege. A person's *mana* supposedly resides in the bones, so bones were always treated with reverence. To dig them up in order to sell the sand they're buried in is anathema to the Hawaiians.

"We believe in taking care of our *kūpuna* bones," Keau explains. "They're part of us; they belong to us. My family, your family, they're part of our people."

Before it's too late, Keau would like to see another place preserved where he worked early in his career—the village of Keoneʻōʻio on La Perouse Bay. The area has never been developed, but it has never been protected, either. These are the villages that Jean-Francois de Galaup de La Perouse, the first European to set foot on Maui, saw when he arrived in 1786. The house sites, temples, fishing shrines, canoe sheds, walls and village streets have never been fully surveyed, and if dirt bikes, fishermen, campers and surfers keep destroying them, they never will be.

"Nobody is maintaining La Perouse, and it's very, very historic," Keau says. "When I go down to La Perouse to monitor the sites, I see the removal of stones from the *heiau* and campsites being built on possible [ancient] house sites. On the village road in 1972 we recorded a large basalt rock with about 200 depressions on its surface for grinding adzes. Right now the four-wheel drives are tearing it up. I don't know when the state is going to do anything about it. Even the [ancient] Pi'ilani Trail is being used by bike riders, motor bike riders, and being destroyed.

"I feel very hurt because I thought I could work with Bishop Museum and work with the state and somehow we would have protection for those sites. These are our one and only. You cannot restore them back to the original the way I've seen them in the early seventies. It's very disturbing to me because we lose all the artifacts. I think it's lack of concern on both county and state."

Keau thinks that Kaho'olawe, a small island uninhabited for decades, is the best area for preservation work in the entire state. Parts of Kaho'olawe have been targets for bombing practice since World War II, but the island was returned to the state in 1993 and people are now trying to decide what to do with it. It is dotted with pristine archaeological sites.

"It's a paradise for archaeologists," Keau marvels. "It's a beautiful place, Kaho'olawe. Preserve that place for our future generations as a school—to learn how we survived in the islands here, one generation to another. I could have a beautiful University of Hawai'i in nature on that island to teach the kids how we lived many years ago.

"You could bring tourists to support that project, but it would be on a guided tour, not a helter-skelter thing. There's a lot of *heiau,* fishing shrines, house sites, quarries, petroglyphs [etchings on rocks], pictographs [paintings on rocks]. So many beautiful things.

"I want it to be left *in situ,* as it is. I don't want restoration. I want stabilization. Stabilize the stones, so they won't roll away. Plant native things around and control the erosion problem."

Keau is not rigid, however, about preserving all things Hawaiian. Special places like Kaho'olawe and La Perouse he wants left alone, but he realizes development and progress must continue throughout much of the state. He agrees that land should be used.

"The old folks told me as a young kid that every land is valuable whether it's dry, rocky, no good—that land is a valuable land," he says.

"Whoever thought Wailea, Kihei, Mākena [desert areas of Maui that are now big resort areas] would be developed as they are today? Because there is no water. You cannot plant fields. But the land was still valuable. Along come the guys with brains—they put in a water line, the land becomes valuable. Who would think?

"But the old folks always say every land, every stone is valuable because somehow it produces life. Put the land into use—let it feed us. *Aloha 'āina* [love of the land] means that. Nobody can save everything, otherwise we wouldn't have a place to be on these islands."

This does not mean Keau wants development to go unchecked. He has seen too many sites obliterated by bulldozers. "It's sad, " he says. "I know about it, but I can't do a damned thing about it."

The resort of Kā'anapali, for instance, is nearly bare of ancient sites, though once there were many—all now bulldozed. Management at one Kā'anapali hotel had plans to reconstruct a Hawaiian village. "I burst out laughing," Keau says. "They had it all there—the villages, the *taro* patches, but they destroyed them. Now they want to build a new one? Kinda stupid.

". . . [Hawaiians] believe in what is shown in front of them —the sky, the earth and the ocean. That's what gives us life."

"It's a shame. We have so much history to share with visitors, so much beautiful things in this *'āina*. But the state and county and federal governments don't protect the sites. 'No more money' are the famous three words we hear time and time again. But, if we don't protect them, we'll lose the sites to development. We'll lose the future of our Hawaiian culture.

"Why should we preserve things? The past is very important. Don't go back in the past, but remember the past. Preserve the past, but improve yourself. We have to keep respecting those things that our *kūpuna* had. We still carry today our *aloha* for our temples, even though they're destroyed. Our *aloha* for all these things is still with us, it's not gone, it never will be gone.

"We Hawaiians were believers of nature. Christians talk about God, the Son and the Holy Spirit; well, the Hawaiians do that too, only they believe in what is shown in front of them—the sky, the earth and the ocean. That's what gives us life.

"I am a Catholic, I'm a strong Catholic. My great-grandparents, I think they were some of the first Catholics on the island of Maui. You can become Catholic or Protestant or whatever religion you belong to, but there's a deep feeling on the inside that says this is part of my life, I came from these roots.

"We knew about pollution, we knew about preservation, we knew about the environment, long before the Westerners forgot about it, because we had to live with what we had here. If we disturb any of the environment, we have no place to run and hide. This is our house."

ACTIVISM

In January of 1893, a group of *haole* businessmen staged a *coup d'etat* on the Hawaiian government, a native monarchy led by Queen Liliʻuokalani. Five years later, in 1898, these businessmen persuaded the United States Congress to annex Hawaiʻi as a U.S. territory. Hawaiians were now Americans. Or so they were told.

In her book *Hawaiʻi's Story,* Queen Liliʻuokalani wrote, in an understatement: "The wishes of my people were not consulted as to this change of government. . . ."

Today, a century later, Hawaiians claim that Liliʻuokalani's government was illegally taken from her, and they want it back. Kekuni Blaisdell, interviewed in this chapter, calls the American government "dominating, exploiting, colonizing." His goal is a separate Hawaiian nation. "Why would anyone want to be dependent?" he asks. "To us there's no sovereignty unless there is independence."

There are dozens of sovereignty groups throughout The Islands, each with different ideas about a new Hawaiian government. Many still want to be affiliated with the U.S., and thus want a nation within a nation. Others, having been raised American, can't imagine another government.

"Sovereignty will happen. Self-governance will happen," says Nona Beamer in this chapter, but, she adds: "I don't advocate separatism at all. I think we can work within the system."

Not all activists are taking on the big issues, however; some, like Kapeka Chandler, are activists for change within their own communities. Chandler raised an astonishing amount of money to build a community center on Kauaʻi, but refused to go to any government for help because, as she says: "We thought the best way would be to do it ourselves." Manifest destiny on the local scene.

It has been a century of despair for what Liliʻuokalani called "a friendly and generous, yet proud-spirited and sensitive race." With their pride returned, they may just prove that the *mana* of their powerful ancestors is still within.

Auntie Nona with hānai *son Kaliko (left) and son Keola (right).*

WINONA BEAMER
HAWAIIAN ADVOCATE AND TEACHER

When we sent our Gods into the mists of the wildwoods so many years ago, they went and waited, while we ran off into a strange world, seeking truths we already had. Our heritage was there all along. It is still there, to build on.

Winona Beamer wrote these poetic words in her book *Nā Hula O Hawai'i* in 1976. All her life she has been encouraging her culture out of the "wildwoods," trying to bring Hawaiian to the forefront in Hawai'i. It has not been easy. And for pioneers like Beamer, the struggle has been a very personal one, exacting a toll on her heart and soul.

One would never guess that this energetic woman has had such a struggle. It appears her life has been a tremendous success. Her triumphs ring like a litany of a life well spent—as a teacher, an entertainer and a champion of the Hawaiian culture.

"I was successful in a Western way. In my Hawaiian way, no. My life wasn't focused on Hawaiian-ness as much as it was on fitting into today's society. I couldn't let my heart lead my life–because we were frowned upon. There was nothing in the Hawaiian culture worth perserving –'lewd and lascivious culture'–that was the Western thought.

This Hawaiian-ness has always been very precious to me all my life, and I never had a chance to live it. There was always a governor in my life, a stopper in the bottle. It has been a real deep-rooted sadness—a lot of hurt that piled up in my life. I'm just beginning to get over it."

Winona Kapuailohiamanonokalani Desha Beamer comes from a Hawaiian family famous for its knowledge of *hula*, chant and music. She composed so many chants and songs herself that she has lost count. She taught *hula* for more than 50 years. Her first student was silent movie screen star Mary Pickford, followed by Hollywood luminaries like Shirley Temple, Mary Astor and Dinah Shore. Her dance troupe performed throughout the 48 Mainland states, including a performance at Carnegie Hall. She choreographed *"Hula* on Ice" for the Radio City Rockettes. She received a Guggenheim Fellowship to Barnard College and she also studied at Columbia University. She worked with Eleanor Roosevelt, teaching underprivileged children in New York City. She taught for 50 years at numerous schools in Hawai'i and initiated the idea of a Hawaiian cultural department in the schools. She was one of only three Hawaiians chosen for a 1983 national commission to study the needs of native Hawaiians. And her two sons, Keola and Kapono, are famous composers and musicians themselves.

Everyone in Hawai'i has heard of the Beamer family.

Auntie Nona, as she is called, coined the word "Hawaiiana" in a 1948 speech to a group of teachers; yet, ironically, she feels she has never been able to live truly as a Hawaiian.

"I was successful in a Western way," she explains. "In my Hawaiian way, no. My life wasn't focused on Hawaiian-ness as much as it was on fitting into today's society. I couldn't let my heart lead my life—because we were frowned upon. There was nothing in the Hawaiian culture worth preserving—'lewd and lascivious culture'—that was the Western thought.

"This Hawaiian-ness has always been very precious to me all my life, and I never had a chance to live it. There was always a governor in my life, a stopper in the bottle. It has been a real deep-rooted sadness—a lot of hurt that piled up in my life. I'm just beginning to get over it."

That sadness has now changed to joy as she has witnessed the uplifting renaissance of her culture—the newfound appreciation people have for Hawaiiana. And, in her own life, she has been inspired by a young Englishman with a penchant for things Hawaiian. Born Simon Charles Trapp on the British Isle of Wight, but called Kaliko by his Hawaiian friends, this young man speaks Hawaiian fluently and chants like a pro. He came into her life in 1992 with an enthusiasm for her culture that sparked an awakening for Auntie Nona herself.

"Now with Kaliko, my Hawaiian-ness is on the upswing," she says. "He's brought a new dimension of enlightenment in my life. Love. Understanding. Belief in the good. He never thinks these old things are trash. My husband used to say:

'Oh, you're always living in the past, living in the past.'"

"I met Kaliko in 1992, and three years later, I awarded him a Beamer Hawaiiana Scholarship, one of seven I award annually [to six Kamehameha High School seniors and to one community member like Kaliko]."

He is now her *hānai* (adopted) son. Auntie Nona wanted to strengthen their bond, so she surprised him one day with her own *hānai* ceremony held in the famous Waipi'o Valley on the Big Island.

"It was my 90-year-old mother's idea—she wanted him to be her *hānai* grandson," Auntie Nona says. "And, my oldest son, Keola, and his wife Moana, assisted in the ceremony."

For Kaliko, the honor was great. He believes his Hawaiian mother "exemplifies what the whole heart is." He says his adopted home "has a spirit that seems to be lacking in the rest of the planet," and hopes that "we'll be able to retain what was so great here before it gets totally erased by foreign influence."

"You have to follow your heart. There's no other way to live. But just now I'm beginning to feel my heart has wings."

"There's a whole new surge of hope in my life," Auntie Nona says. "I'm living joyously now. Kaliko has really made me feel as though my life has had a purpose, and maybe I can still do some good.

"You have to follow your heart. There's no other way to live. But just now I'm beginning to feel my heart has wings."

Certainly, she had known the value of her heritage as a child. It wasn't until her school days in Honolulu that she faced prejudice in a world that did not value hers.

Raised on the Big Island, she was the first grandchild, the *hiapo*. "From early on, I had a special feeling about being that child," she says. "I was with my grandmother [Helen Desha Beamer] much of my childhood. It was like being in school when she came—walking along the tide pools and chanting, turning over rocks and identifying what creatures were there. It was a very special childhood."

Her great-grandmother, Isabella Ka'ili Desha, was also an early influence, particularly in her knowledge of the *hula*, an art Nona was eager to learn.

In her book, Auntie Nona explains the ideals of this ancient dance: "The techniques were designed to take the mind, heart and body of the dancer to high levels. The objective was artistic excellence.

"In *hula,* the dancers became one with everything in nature. They bent, swayed and gestured, moving in countless ways to tell countless stories, most of which had deep meanings. Behind these graceful, expressive, sometimes dignified and sometimes earthy dances, lay years of study, meditation and prayer."

Auntie Nona adds that her own family's beliefs were "based on the beauty of nature, the power of nature, the complexity, the puzzlement, the moods. All the love and the truth and the beauty—those three words go hand in hand. That was our religion."

"In my 50-year career teaching *hula,* I've always told the students, it isn't just what you see and what you hear, it's more importantly what you feel, and the feeling is what translates to the doing. And without that feeling, there's no doing. So you don't transmit it to other people unless something is ignited in your heart. Whether it's good or sad or bad, it's got to start there first. The feelings transcend everything. If you can't communicate a feeling, sit down.

"It's your spirit, it's your soul. It's unlike anybody else. Nobody can tell you, nobody can put it in for you. It's what you're born with. This bubbling up in your heart is your personal expression, your original way of saying things. No two alike. It comes from a place of love and kindness; no matter what kind of vibes you're getting from people, it always surmounts anything sad or bad. There'll be no obstacle, if you keep your love. That's the answer."

Her great-grandmother Isabella expected her great-grandchildren to carry a "bundle of love" with them at all times.

"Great-grandmother said: 'As you carry the bundle of love through life, it may seem to get very heavy sometimes, yet you must not put it down. Keep your *aloha,* no matter how hard that seems.'

"With more love, the bundle gets lighter and then you're sharing it and it gets lighter still. The more you use it, the more it flourishes. It doesn't flourish in darkness, it flourishes in light.

"So, we care about it and we want some good to come out of it, and not neccesarily a six-pack and a Cadillac ."

"Maybe it's like listening to that still small voice—that we have to have time to know ourselves and think inwardly and not to be so concerned with everyday affairs that we forget this place in our hearts that's peaceful and loving and kind."

Ua 'ikea. It is known—look deep within yourself. That was the code taught in the Beamer family. A code that sustained Nona as her values were questioned throughout her life.

Nona was a young girl when her family moved from the Big Island to O'ahu so that the five Beamer children could be educated "properly" at English standard schools, including the Hawaiian Kamehameha Schools.

The Kamehameha Schools, kindergarten through grade 12, were funded in the late 1800s by Hawaiian chiefess Bernice Pauahi Bishop specifically for the education of Hawaiian children. However, somewhere along the line, Kamehameha became permeated with Calvinist thinking, and it was deemed important that Hawaiian children conform to Western ways. Children could not speak Hawaiian in school, and nothing of the Hawaiian culture was taught or encouraged. *Hula* and chanting were definite no-nos.

Little Winona, of course, knew *hula* and chanting well. It didn't occur to her innocent mind that her school would not value her family's teachings.

"I went to a Hawaiian school because I wanted to be Hawaiian. Then not to be allowed to be Hawaiian! Of all things, for a Hawaiian school not to be Hawaiian!" She still can't get over it, though the school is much improved today.

"I started a Hawaiian club at Kamehameha to teach the chant because everything I knew about Hawaiian I learned in the chants. They've always been a real anchor for me. There was not a question in my life that I could not relate to something I learned in the chants."

From her book: "The chants were so haunting, they seemed to flow like clear streams of consciousness from the deep green heart of the forest primeval."

She formed the club to teach her friends both chant and *hula*. When the trustees heard of her club, they invited its members to a trustee tea in one of the school gardens.

"So we walked in chanting," Auntie Nona remembers. "The next day the principal said, 'Wi-i-i-nona, you may pack your bags.' I was expelled.

"I wanted to see the will. I begged to see the will. I couldn't believe the princess [Bernice Pauahi Bishop] would say no Hawaiian spoken, no chanting, no dancing. I couldn't believe a Hawaiian princess would say that."

Did she?

"No, of course not. It says: 'Good industrious men and women.' It says nothing about no language and no chants and no dance and no Hawaiian-ness."

Nona was eventually accepted back in, and, in 1941, as president of her class, was the third-generation Beamer to graduate from Kamehameha Schools.

"Kamehameha had a long road to go before they realized the value in Hawaiian teaching. I was happy to learn Homer, I love Shakespeare; but my basic education was from my family. It wasn't from school."

Ironically, the girl they expelled became the woman they called back years later to teach what they had expelled her for. In the 1960s, when interest in the culture revived, Kamehameha's students began to demand Hawaiiana as part of their curriculum. The school had to call Winona Beamer to teach them.

"The school called and said they would like to have me on their staff," Auntie Nona recalls. "I said, 'Are you sure you have the right Beamer?' I had a cousin teaching at the University of Hawai'i and she was a great teacher. I said, 'You're sure it's not Billie Beamer you want?' I couldn't believe it. They called back the next day and the next day. But they didn't have a Hawaiian department, so I was on half-time for ten years.

"I had kindergarten through 12. Just to give a little smattering of Hawaiiana in every grade level was so minimal, but that was better than nothing at all."

It is more than "a smattering" now. Auntie Nona is retired, but the department she helped start now has a 25-member staff, most of whom she taught when they were children.

She also taught at a Kamehameha experimental school for children with learning problems, a school that's currently one of the best facilities in the state.

"There's really not a problem child. Not in my experience," she says. "The crux of the matter was that the children had to be taught more lovingly. My whole contention was just to teach the child like the child was mine. And when you love the children, they know it and they just respond, and so I never had any problems. That was my style because that was the way I was taught.

"Sometimes I've been out in left field all by myself," she admits. "I've never followed the pack because there's never been a pack to follow. I've always been a loner."

Her opinion was officially sought (then ignored again) in 1982-83, when the federal government initiated a national commission to study the needs and concerns of all Hawaiians. The commission's job: to see if the United States government held some blame in the 1893 *coup d'etat* of Hawai'i's last monarch, Queen Lili'uokalani. According to the report: "Congress then wished to be advised about how to approach and to answer any such possible native Hawaiian claims."

When the three Hawaiian commissioners met with the six Mainland commissioners for the first time in Washington, D.C., Auntie Nona brought a gift book and boxes of flowers for everyone. "This would be an *aloha* from us to them," she says. "They didn't even open the box of flowers, they didn't even open the book. I thought: They're not interested in us at all. They didn't think there was a problem in Hawai'i."

From that poor beginning, there was no return. The nine-month study produced two reports: a majority report from the six in Washington, and a dissenting report from the three Hawaiian commissioners.

Volume II, the minority report, calls Volume I "inaccurate and fatally flawed both in fact and in spirit." In all capital letters, the three Hawaiian commissioners wrote "WE DISAGREE" to the majority report's idea that the U.S. was not accountable, either legally or morally, for the overthrow of the Hawaiian nation.

"We said a wrong had been done," Auntie Nona insists, "and it was the psychological demise of the Hawaiian race. The poor health statistics, the huge population of Hawaiians in prison, overwhelming disease, alcoholism and child abuse and everything that filtered down was the direct result of the psychological demise of the Hawaiians.

"So, we care about it and we want some good to come out of it, and not necessarily a six-pack and a Cadillac. Education is the key. And more programs that can help health and housing. So that's what those two thick volumes boiled down to.

"There was so much distress—going to hear testimonies on all the islands and hearing the Hawaiians cry. It was so hard to take.

"But now the pendulum has swung and things are going to happen for the good. Sovereignty will happen, self-governance will happen. We don't know how it will happen, but it's inevitable, with all indigenous peoples the world over. That's all they want—to be allowed to be themselves. Sovereignty: to have the Hawaiianness back in Hawai'i.

"I don't advocate separatism at all. I think we can work within the system. I'm proud to be an American, but I'm proud to be a Hawaiian first. I think good things will happen. And the students are making it happen. It's not my generation. It's not my parent's generation. It's their generation that's making it happen. They stand up for what they believe and know what is right. We're just standing by saying: 'Go for it, go for it.'

"I'm not out in left field alone anymore."

Kekuni Blaisdell, M.D.
SOVEREIGNTY ADVOCATE

Kekuni Blaisdell's house is filled with his life's passion. Paperwork, documents, letters, videos, even wall hangings and paintings silently proclaim what he is never silent about: the independence and sovereignty of his people. *Kānaka maoli*, he calls his people, not "Hawaiians."

Kekuni Blaisdell is a medical doctor, an internist specializing in hematology, yet few of the papers stacked about his house have anything to do with medicine. Instead, they are about the freedom he believes his people should always have had.

"*Kānaka maoli* was a term our people used to identify themselves as opposed to the foreigners who came," he explains. "Foreigners asked: 'Who are you?' And the answer was: 'We're *kānaka maoli*.' *Kanaka* means human being. *Maoli* means true, real, genuine.

"What the colonizers call us—Hawaiians, Native Hawaiians, Native Americans, Americans—we're not. We're *kānaka maoli*."

"Yes, I'm considered radical in the [sovereignty] movement. But we consider ourselves to be conservative. We want to conserve our people and our lands, our traditions and our language. We cannot let them be wiped out. So to us it's very clear. Difficult. But clear. It's part of the process of strong, distinct self identity. I consider myself to be speaking like my ancestors from our ancestors because of our ancestors."

He speaks his passion with a voice so quiet and tranquil one has to listen intently to hear everything. He makes radical statements with twinkling humor in his eyes. He seems at peace with himself and his vision.

"Yes," he admits, "I'm considered radical in the [sovereignty] movement. But we consider ourselves to be conservative. We want to conserve our people and our lands, our traditions and our language. We cannot let them be wiped out. So to us it's very clear. Difficult. But clear. It's part of the process of strong, distinct self-identity. I consider myself to be speaking like my ancestors from our ancestors because of our ancestors."

Does he truly think it's possible or practical for Hawai'i to separate itself from what he calls "The Continent"?

"Do we remain under the heel of the dominating, exploiting, colonizing United States or do we want to be sovereign?"

"Of course we'll win," he says confidently. "Every day there's evidence of it. Some person I don't know comes up to me and says: 'Ah, kānaka maoli,' or 'Right on, Kekuni,' that indicates he or she knows about and appreciates our struggle.

"It's natural for everybody to be independent. Why would anyone want to be dependent? To us there's no other option. To us there's no sovereignty unless there is independence."

A large tapestry hanging in his living room proclaims: "All peoples have the right to self-determination; by virtue of that right they freely determine their political status and freely pursue their economic, social and cultural development."

"Noble words from 1514," he says, as if everyone is as versed in the politics of struggle as he is. Facing a blank look, he explains: "It's from the United Nations General Assembly Resolution 1514. It's the definition of self-determination in international law.

"So, if we just invoke 1514 and get the colonizer to respect and implement it, we're there. It's a matter of choosing which status we want: do we remain under the heel of the dominating, exploiting, colonizing United States or do we want to be sovereign? History is on our side. Their law is on our side. Of course *kanaka maoli* law is with us. So we just need to get the colonizing oppressor to abide by his own law."

It wasn't until the 1980s that this fire for Hawaiian independence sparked Kekuni's soul. Until then, he was busy on "The Continent," first as a student, then as a practicing physician and professor. As a student, he garnered *cum laude* and *Phi Beta Kappa* honors while studying to be his family's first Western physician. Raised during a time when Hawaiian children were trained for blue-collar jobs, little Kekuni was slated to be an electrician at the Kamehameha School for Boys when a far-thinking Caucasian high school teacher encouraged him to stretch himself. Within a decade he was studying medicine at the University of Chicago, completing an internship at the Johns Hopkins Hospital, doing residencies at Tulane's Charity Hospital and Duke University Hospital, then teaching medicine at his *alma mater,* the University of Chicago. His *curriculum vitae* is three pages long, listing honors and schools and positions he never dreamed possible while growing up "brown," as he puts it. His honors include: 1970 University of Hawai'i School of Medicine Professor of the Year, 1989 Hawai'i Medical Association Physician of the Year, 1990 Living Treasure (of Hawai'i) Award.

During medical school he developed a fascination with his subspecialty, hematology, because: "I love blood. I love blood cells, stained blood cells. Pretty colors. I love to look at them. Blood is easy to acquire. Put a needle in and pull it out, put a drop on a slide, smear it, stain it, look at it. Beautiful."

Dr. Blaisdell ("Please call me Kekuni"), who was born in Honolulu, was called back to Hawai'i in 1966 to help set up the University of Hawai'i's medical school. He chaired the department of medicine for three years, then continued teaching internal medicine.

In 1983, as one of few *kanaka maoli* physicians in Hawai'i, Kekuni was asked to help with the health section of a national report on Native Hawaiians commissioned by the United States Congress. His research stunned him, then changed him forever.

"I discovered that we *kānaka maoli* had the worst health indicators. And I hadn't realized that," Kekuni remembers.

What he discovered: Hawaiians have the shortest life expectancy of any ethnic group in the state, the highest rates of heart disease, stroke, cancer, diabetes, infant mortality, and young Hawaiian males have the highest suicide risk.

"It was striking," he continues. "And then to see that it wasn't confined to health—we had the lowest median family income, the highest rates of incarceration, drop-out for public schools, and for not owning a home. Therefore, it must be something broad, not just health alone. So I began to think about it, and talk to others about it."

A thinking activist, a down-to-earth, practical radical was born. He would never be quite the same doctor/academician again. Studying blood now would include studying his own blood, back to the ancients.

"I began to realize that it goes back to basic feelings about our own identity. Through colonization, we've become ashamed of ourselves. We have been taught that we are a lesser breed," he says. "Therefore, the way to begin to recover is to decolonize ourselves, to identify ourselves as our ancestors, and to use that as the basis for reviving our culture and restoring our nation.

"We're caught in a cultural conflict and have been ever since the first foreigners arrived. The dominant Western culture is based on an economic, capitalistic system which means one puts in so much money and takes out more. One uses the profit for oneself, one's family, one's friends, and, if it means exploiting others and the environment, well, that's what others and the environment are for. It's individualistic, materialistic and exploitative.

"Our culture is the antithesis. Instead of taking, we give. In our tradition, the fisherman catches fish not only for himself, but for everyone in the *ahupua'a* [land section]. The *taro* farmer harvests not only for himself, but for others in the *ahupua'a*. The woodsman up *mauka* [mountainside] cuts firewood and shares. Therefore, the greatest virtue and personal asset is not how much money one has in the bank, but one's relationships. That's the basis for our traditional culture. But we are compelled to abide by Western time [he taps his watch], to get a job, pay taxes, and bind ourselves to a mortgage. If we don't, and we live like our ancestors did by fishing and sharing, we go to jail. So we're caught in the conflict, and too many of our people give up.

"We consider the environment to be sacred. Not to be contaminated, polluted and desecrated, but to be treasured. *'Āina*, our term for land, means that which feeds. The *'āina* feeds us. If we don't take care of it, it won't feed us. We'll perish. The land, the Earth, is our mother.

"If you look up at the mountains, you'll see what Westerners call a mist obscuring the ridge. But to us, it's much more than a mist. It's semen falling from our Sky Father, Wākea, fertilizing, impregnating our Earth Mother, Papa Honua. And out of that mating comes everything in our cosmos. Since we all have the same parents, we're all *'ohana* [family]. And since our parents are living, everything is living.

"Now, we're taught in the colonizer's school that this table, this house is inanimate, but to *kānaka maoli,* everything is living. This table is living. Not only that, but it's conscious. It also communicates. It receives messages and it sends out messages. Everything is alive—the reflections, the shadows, the sounds, the wind, the splash of the waves on the beaches. Everything is alive. And everything is communicating with us. All we need to do is open up our receptors."

He adds that dreams, including daydreams, are "images, thoughts and sounds that float in and out of our consciousness, albeit without our apparent volition, they are real. They influence our thinking, feeling and behavior. *No laila* [therefore], they bear heeding. This is another aspect of the importance of our opening up our receptors to receive messages from all in our cosmos. Because all in our cosmos lives, is conscious and communicates."

How to return to this expansive way of thinking and living?

"Decolonize ourselves," he repeats. "We have to have our own government in order to survive because the health indicators are not only bad, they're getting worse. The figures are in from the 1990 census. The statistics are grimmer. Life expectancy, overall mortality and death rates for heart disease, cancer, stroke and diabetes, and risk factors, such as obesity, hypertension, tobacco and alcohol use are even more alarming than in the 1980s."

"We're caught in a cultural conflict and have been ever since the first foreigners arrived."

When asked why *kānaka maoli* have such shocking statistics, Kekuni barely pauses for breath. There are, he says, five main and interrelated reasons.

"The first one is obvious. A recent estimate is that when Captain James Cook came in 1778 there may have been as many people living here as there are now, that is a million or so. All *piha kānaka maoli,* pure blooded. Living entirely off the land and sea. No imports, self-sufficient, healthy, robust. Cook was amazed. He had never seen such people. He knew that his men introduced syphilis and gonorrhea. We now know tuberculosis also. Rapid depopulation followed.

"At the time of the armed invasion and theft of our homeland by the United States in 1893 and 1898, we were down to 40,000 *kānaka maoli.* Already at that time we were outnumbered by 50,000 foreigners. Just think, if we had been a million strong, I doubt that the United States could have taken us. But we were already weakened by foreign diseases and outnumbered.

"Now the total island population is up to a million, but less than 10,000 *piha kānaka maoli* remain. The projection is that in the year 2044 there will be no more *piha kānaka maoli*. We'll be gone. Extinct. That's genocide, and genocide is an international crime.

"The second reason is exploitation. Foreigners come to our homeland, not to live as we do, not to speak our language, not to share our concepts and values, but to live their way. And their way is to exploit others, to dominate, to take. That is colonialism. The United Nations defines colonialism as foreign domination, exploitation and subjugation. The United Nations also identifies colonialism as a crime, and its official policy is to eradicate colonialism.

"Everything is alive

—the reflections, the shadows,

the sounds, the wind, the splash

of the waves on the beach. . . .

And everything is

communicating with us.

All we need to do is open

up our receptors."

"The United States, knowing this, and knowing that we were on the list for decolonialization when the United Nations was founded in 1945-1946, made sure that we were taken off the list. That's why statehood in 1959 was a fraud. Of course, no one told us. We had to teach ourselves. Most people still don't know about it, and don't believe it when we talk about it. In 1959, the United States held an illegal plebiscite in order to incorporate Hawai'i as the 50th state. The U.S. then reported this to the United Nations so that the United Nations would remove Hawai'i from the list of non-self-governing colonies. We want to be back on that list, to be eligible for decolonization. That's a goal of our movement.

"The third reason is cultural conflict. We're constantly caught in this struggle. I have to decide whether I'm going to go by this clock to do what I have to do to survive, or whether I'm just going to be *kanaka maoli* and do what I feel like doing. That's the *kanaka maoli* way—to do what one feels is proper, *pono*. In fact, if one doesn't feel properly about something, one really shouldn't do it.

"We're constantly caught in this conflict. And too many of our people despair, smoke, sniff drugs, drink booze, beat up on our children, spouses and go to jail. So we have the highest rate of incarceration in the prisons. More than 60 percent of the inmates are *kānaka maoli,* and our people are only 20 percent of the general population. Painful.

"The fourth reason: We have too eagerly embraced harmful foreign ways—drugs, smoking, alcohol, high-speed driving. We have the highest rate of automobile injuries. We eat American junk food. Too much saturated fat and too many calories. We have the highest rate for corpulence. High blood pressure. Too much salt. We have the highest rate of diabetes, and all that goes with it, such as heart and kidney failure, limb amputations. Dreadful. These are harmful foreign ways. They're not our culture. Such self-destructive behavior.

"The last reason is not merely neglect, but malice on the part of the colonial establishment. What some call institutional racism. For example, Queen's Hospital was founded in 1859 by our king, Kamehameha IV, and his wife, Queen Emma. The king went before the legislature and said the number one problem facing our kingdom is the dying off of our people—we must do something about it. Other people have doctors, hospitals, medical care. We don't. This is our country. So that's why the hospital was founded—to treat indigent, sick and disabled Hawaiians.

"In 1909, the *haole* oligarchy amended the hospital's charter to read treatment of 'sick and disabled people' and converted the hospital from a government to a private institution. In 1950, the Territorial Supreme Court terminated the Queen Emma Trust with all of the income from the Queen Emma lands going directly to the hospital. Needy *kānaka maoli* were thereafter deprived of free medical care at the hospital established for them. The hospital is now an integral part of the colonial establishment, a transnational corporation. *Auē* [alas]!"

So how would Dr. Blaisdell, as a physician, prescribe wellness for his people? Return to the old ways, of course.

"Out of the mating of Wākea [Sky Father] and Papa Honua [Earth Mother], came and continues to come everything in our cosmos, and that's why we're all related and why everything is conscious and communicating. That's the basis for wellness—this constant interaction between all life forces. When there's proper interaction, things are *pono* [balanced]; there's appropriate *mana,* special kind of power or energy maintaining this balance. These spiritual inter-relationships are primary. Proper thoughts and actions maintain this *pono,* harmony.

"If there's misfortune, such as ill health, that means loss of *pono* with loss of *mana*. And therefore, diagnosis is a matter of finding out how this has come to be, and treatment is a matter of restoring *pono,* restoring *mana.* That's the underlying basis for wellness, which is more than physical health versus sickness. A health practitioner is one who facilitates this process of maintaining and restoring *pono* and *mana.*

"In the old days, each individual, beginning in childhood, learned how to take care of oneself, to be self-reliant and to maintain *pono* relationships. If sick, one looked within oneself first to see what one had thought or said or done that might be responsible for the imbalance. Then one attempted to correct it. If the illness persisted, then one went to the next level—someone more knowledgeable or skillful, usually an elder within the *'ohana.* If not resolved at that level, and one had the resources to go to the next level, then one went to the *kahuna* [medical expert] at the nearest *heiau ho'ōla* [healing temple].

"Another basic concept is of complementary opposites. That is, just as there is night and day and sun and moon, male and female, hot and cold, there is also right and wrong, health and illness, life and death. *Kānaka maoli* are always aware of this dualism.

"In reality, to us, there is sickness and death. In contrast, modern western society is determined to conquer all disease, and even death! That is not realistic to us *kānaka maoli.*

"Another basic view is timelessness. This is reflected in human anatomy—the concept of *piko 'ekolu* [three body points]. Most people know about the *piko waena* in the middle [the navel]. It connects each of us *in utero* by way of the umbilical cord to our mother. This *piko* represents the contemporary world of one's parents and the *'ohana.* This *piko* covers the *na'au,* the gut, and the gut is the seat of knowledge, learning and wisdom. *Na'au* is also the organ of feeling, emotion. 'Gut feeling' is a very *kanaka* concept. We have the same word for think and feel—*'ike.* We don't distinguish between them.

"We're frequently accused of being emotional. Well, of course, we're emotional. Our basic belief is that we really don't learn anything unless we feel it emotionally. We learn it only when we feel it, and we feel it only when we live it, when we do it.

"The second *piko* is the *piko po'o. Po'o* is the head, and *piko po'o* is the anterior fontanel in the infant, the opening in the skull. It connects the personal spirit, *'uhane* or *wailua,* which is housed in the skull, through this opening with the spiritual realm, beyond all the way back to the beginning of time. So, all of our ancestors in the spiritual world are connected to us through this *piko.*

"Then, there's the *piko ma'i* found between the legs—the genitalia.

And this *piko maʻi* connects us with all of our *mamo,* descendants, after us, forever into the future.

"We have this notion of timelessness—we've always been here, we always will be here; we are not going to go away. Our ancestors are always with us as long as we think of them, talk to them, engage them in our thinking and planning and beliefs and actions. So we can't possibly be lonely; we can't feel insecure.

"How can we lack self-esteem when we're so solidly rooted, anchored with these three *piko?* Not only in the contemporary world, now, but before, and forever. How can we lack confidence?

"How can anyone ask: 'Do you think there's a chance [for sovereignty]? How realistic is this?' With traditional concepts like ours? How can there be any doubt?"

Kapeka Chandler
COMMUNITY ORGANIZER

"I for one don't think that I could describe it *[aloha]*. I think it's in the person. I think you are blessed with it or you aren't. They like to say it's caring and sharing, but I say, no, you folks missed the most important part—loving and caring and sharing. You have to love in order to care and share. To me it's all three."

Seven giant, battered aluminum pots hang from a beam in the Chandler house kitchen on the island of Kaua'i. A couple of other well-used pots as tall as a man's knee sit on the kitchen floor while enormous skillets wait on burners ready to be fired up for lunch. A school cafeteria might have pots this size, not a small family house. However, the fifteen pairs of shoes that crowd the front doorway give the initial clue that this is no small family. Fourteen children were raised under the corrugated tin roof of this simple wooden structure.

The house has the same well-worn, lived-in look as the cooking pots. This is a place used to bare feet thundering back and forth—grown children, grandchildren, aunts, uncles, cousins, nieces, nephews. This is a true Hawaiian household.

And the matriarch of the family loves it that way.

"This house has never been empty. In and out, in and out," says Kapeka Mahuiki Chandler. "I'd go crazy if it was only my husband and I. I have the two youngest children home because they are single. Those who are married don't live here, but they come every weekend or every day, and every weekend I have the grandchildren. Right after school they're here on Friday. They camp out on the *lānai;* they're in here, over there, they're everywhere," she waves her arms to show how full the house becomes. Laughter punctuates her speech instead of commas.

The Chandlers were named Kaua'i's Outstanding Family of 1993. Kapeka herself has the honor of being called a "Living Treasure" by the Kaua'i Museum and by the Catholic Churches of Hawai'i. In 1997, she was honored as "A Woman of Spirit" by a national women's organization, Women of Vision and Action.

Kapeka makes light of such honors and is not sure why they're piling up, but her neighbor, Carol Ann Washburn, says it's simply because: "Everybody loves her. People love to be around her. She has a contagious laugh and she has such a strong spiritual base that she calms people by just being around them."

She is renowned on Kaua'i as a singer and entertainer, particularly of old Hawaiian songs—the "classics," she calls them. However, motherhood Hawaiian style is what she considers her true talent. She and her husband, Francis, have been married since 1951.

"I always say my husband and I had two batches of children because I had six first, then three years after that here comes nine more. One boy died when he was a baby, only 12 days old. Fourteen are living today.

"My way of thinking is: when you're married, you stay at home to clean, cook and take care of the home, husband and yard. When our children came along, God provided with everything needed to raise them. If God gives you, He's gonna take care of 'em. So I never worry.

"Living in the country, we were able to fish in the ocean and the river and hunt in the mountains, so we actually could survive off the land, although my husband had a job. He was a bulldozer operator for the sugar plantation, then he went

"She has such a strong spiritual base that she calms people by just being around them."

into the power plant to work, then he left to work for the county for 16 years in the parks. He retired in 1989.

"Hawaiians are very tightly knit families. My parents [who had 10 children] always had our cousins, cousins, cousins. We all get together, so that even now, as old as we are, we can remember them.

"That's what I'm trying to teach my children: always get together because you can even forget your sister or your brother if you don't get to see them all the time. So they have togetherness. So they can learn that there is love, no matter where they go there is love. And you show love to your family first before you can show it to somebody else."

What Kapeka describes is the Hawaiian concept of ʻohana—family—the strong foundation that is the basis of Hawaiian life. ʻOhana generally percolates on aloha, the Hawaiian ideal of love and compassion.

"I for one don't think that I could describe it [aloha]," she says. "I think it's in the person. I think you are blessed with it or you aren't. They like to say it's caring and sharing, but I say, no, you folks missed the most important part—loving and caring and sharing. You have to love in order to care and share. To me it's all three."

Kapeka extends her sense of ʻohana and aloha beyond family to rally for the community in her volunteer work with the Hawaiian Civic Club and the Hanalei Canoe Club. Since the 1970s, she's been both organizer and cheerleader.

"The Hawaiian Civic Club, you had to be a Hawaiian," she says. "In the canoe club, every race was included. We wanted the children to learn to live with each other because we know there is such a thing as racism. And we wanted them to learn to paddle because that's what our Hawaiian ancestors did. But mostly, for me, my biggest thing was for them to get along with each other. There's maybe close to 100 members in the canoe club now.

"We used to be down there every day [on the beach]. I made sure I was there just so they'd see that somebody was interested. And I always told the parents: 'Don't think we are babysitters. You got to show an interest in them so they want to paddle. You said you were going to back them, you BE there.' But no parents came—they thought they could just bring their kids. They just come and throw the children. Everybody say: 'Hey, how come you here every day?' Well, hey, these kids are not supposed to be here by themselves.

"My husband and I cooked and chaperoned. Somebody had to take over the responsibilities. It didn't bother me at all because I was young. We had a lot of paddlers. I was there just to be an example for them.

"I'm more like an auntie to all, the young children and the young men and women. I'm there to boost their morale. I just show up and I scream. Anywhere they go, wherever they race, I'm the one that's cheering, up and down the beach. I still do. But now I got sick from doing that. Because when I scream, I scream. I want to scream so the children can hear me. Everybody can hear me."

She screamed so much in the hot sun that she had a stroke. She knew she felt sick one day, but hadn't a clue that it was serious.

"I was running up and down screaming, but I didn't feel the sick," she says. "I was pouring ice water on my head. Douse myself and in seconds I'd be dry, it's been that hot.

"I came back from the race to go to a dinner honoring my cousin. She was retiring from the Kaua'i Visitors Bureau. I got sick there. I ate my dinner, which I didn't want to eat, and right there I got upset and vomited into my napkin. The mayor was at the next table; she went and called 911. Before I knew it, the wheelchair was right next to me. I was forced to go to the hospital. They said I had a stroke, but it wasn't bad at all. It was there and gone."

No health problem could deter her from her community work, however. In 1992, after a powerful hurricane named Iniki leveled much of Kaua'i, Kapeka's people skills and organizational talents were truly needed. At first, she was asked to visit the elderly, because, as she says: "The old people needed to talk, but others would go to help them and they'd be silent. Me, they didn't have a hard time relating to. People look up to me."

This proved true when she initiated her next project: raising more than a million dollars through a letter-writing campaign to build a community center in Hanalei. She also received $300,000 more from a Honolulu-based foundation. Raising such an amount is unheard of for a small area on a small island. And it was donated during hard economic times on Kaua'i.

"After Hurricane Iniki, the whole Hanalei area was devastated. The town itself was demolished," Kapeka says. "We thought then that we really needed a place for the community to meet. We never did have a place—we always used people's houses and lawns for luaus and meetings. And after the hurricane we had nothing. People needed someplace to go."

Her friend, Carol Ann Washburn, says: "Because of her, people were willing to step forward. Kapeka energized the fund raising and the whole community."

Kapeka didn't bother seeking government funds because: "Every time you talk to government, it goes on years and years. We thought the best way would be to do it ourselves.

"I knew if people saw me doing it, they'd think it was a good thing because they trusted me. People have to trust you to donate. They put me on a pedestal in this community, so I have to be there for them.

"I care about everybody. I want them to get along, to learn how to live with each other. This [community center] is a place that everyone can use, doesn't matter what nationality. Maybe here we can bridge over our differences."

Kapeka herself is a rare breed: one of the few 100 percent Hawaiians left in Hawai'i, though she doesn't think her pedigree is any big deal.

"I like the mixtures, especially the Hawaiians and the *haoles*," she says. "That makes beautiful children. They're smarter. That is true. We find it true in our family. My daughter's husband is Italian, Indian, English. The children, they are smarter. Smarter than when we were small. Actually it needs the mixture. You have to change.

"Who cares about 100 percent of what? If you come out good, that's what every parent wishes for. First you must be honest, then you must be loving. If you have those tools, you'll get along."

Before the community center was built, everyone was always welcome, and still are today, at the mini community center that has always existed at the Chandler homestead. There the door is always open, with Kapeka usually found sitting on the front *lānai*. When she gives directions to her house, she embodies Kaua'i's laid-back, easy way of living: "Turn right out of the airport and go 45 minutes to the end of the road. Don't worry: there's only one road." A weathered, wooden sign hammered into a huge mango tree at the top of the driveway announces: "Chandler." It has been welcoming visitors in for decades.

"People are amazed that 14 to 20 people can arrive and we'll have food ready for them. It's no big thing," Kapeka says. "I tell everybody: 'What's one more, what's ten more? Doesn't matter.'"

Elaine Kaopuiki
COMMUNITY ACTIVIST

"Hi Auntie! Hi Auntie!" A car full of animated Filipino children drives slowly through a beach park as the kids wave vibrantly from the windows. Elaine Kaopuiki (pronounced Kah-o-poo-iki) looks up from the picnic table where she's sitting and tries to figure out who's waving.

"Trouble is, I can't see them," she admits. "All I can see is a green car. Now who owns a green car?" A few minutes later, another car, this one full of young men in their twenties, drives by honking and waving.

This is Lāna'i—an island where everyone knows everyone. And certainly, everyone knows Elaine Kauwenaole Kaopuiki. Having taught *hula* for 40-some years, she is the island's chief *kumu hula* (*hula* teacher), but today she is almost as well known for her political rabble-rousing. Auntie Elaine has seen her small island change phenomenally since she was born in 1929. She doesn't like some of the changes and she doesn't mind stating her very strong feelings.

"We have to straighten out this mess that we're in today. The overthrow of our queen [in 1893] has never been justified. So they have to remedy that. It might take forever. It may not be my time before we realize the end results. Right now my sovereign right has been interfered with. I lost my birthright. I didn't even realize it until I grew up and learned my Hawaiian history. They never taught us Hawaiian history in school. But now that I know it, you get a little upset."

Lāna'i is an island of extreme contrasts. There is no traffic light, no fast-food joint, no shopping mall. Yet the island is home to two world-class luxury hotels where room rates run into hundreds of dollars nightly. The residents of Lāna'i clean those rooms, but no Lāna'ian could afford to stay in one. Both hotels consistently rank high in listings of the world's best tropical resorts, however, this doesn't create much pride locally. The wealthy tourists attracted to these hotels have little in common with the people who truly love the island—its 2,800 inhabitants.

Auntie Elaine likes to explain how the island used to be. She's well versed in its history and legends, so she'll often begin with the mythical story of Kaululā'au, the mischievous son of a Lahaina (Maui) chief.

In Hawai'i, legend and history are often entangled so that a historical person or event crescendos over the years into mythical proportions; such seems to be the case with Kaululā'au.

It's said he was a wild boy who pulled one too many pranks and was finally expelled from Maui to Lāna'i. Trouble was, Lāna'i was home to numerous bad-natured, foul spirits who killed everyone who set foot on the island. Kaululā'au knew this, of course, but being clever, he was able to kill the spirits before they killed him. With the spirits gone, he returned a triumphant hero to Lahaina, then brought other Maui people back to Lāna'i to set up its first human habitation.

"In that wave of people, that's when my family came," Auntie Elaine says. "The first village on the island of Lāna'i was Keōmuku, and that's where Kaululā'au was. That's where my mother grew up."

Kenneth Emory, the dean of Hawai'i's archaeologists, concurs with Auntie Elaine. He spent months doing research in Lāna'i in 1921, and in his report on the island, he wrote: "All the traditions of real people on Lāna'i date during or since the time of Kaululā'au."

During her mother's time, Auntie Elaine says: "They were very primitive down there [Keōmuku] and they lived very simple. But they had all they needed. They didn't need all these modern things. Much of their livelihoods depended on fishing. They come up the mountain and they hunt goats. The only thing that grew well here was watermelon. My grandmother grew the biggest watermelon ever. The mule would have to carry one at a time."

Lāna'i has scant rainfall, from 10 to 35 inches yearly.

"When they lived in Keōmuku, they never had water," she says. "They had to dig wells to get water. They drank brackish water [combination of fresh and salt waters]. Only one area of the island had water, up in the mountains. But they lived far away from the main stream. If you really wanted fresh water, you had to walk miles. So, my mother learned to live with brackish water all her life.

"My father is from Lahaina. He came here to work as a cowhand. When my mother married my dad, they moved up to Koʻele.

"I was born [at home] where the Koʻele Lodge is standing now. It was a very isolated area then. My mother tells me she was on the floor and my grandmother was in front of her when I came out and I flew right into her apron!

"When my time came, I married a Kaopuiki, which is a famous name for this island. I married one of 16 boys. I married the most handsomest man.

"I was in the era of pineapple. Pineapples came here in 1922. But ranching was here too; it started even before pineapples came.

"It was such a beautiful life. It seemed that we were one big family. There were about two dozen homes, all workers, mostly Hawaiians. English was the primary language. Everybody was threatened—you do not speak any other language but English. My parents spoke fluent

"I can't turn my back on this island."

Hawaiian, but not to me. They were so sure that their jobs would be taken away from them. That's why people of my time growing up don't know how to speak the Hawaiian language."

From his research, Kenneth Emory estimates there were about 3,000 people living on Lānaʻi before Captain Cook came to Hawaiʻi in 1778. The 1920 census counted only 185 people on the island, and of those, 102 were Hawaiians. Now, of Lānaʻi's 2,800 people, Auntie Elaine believes only 300 to 400 are Hawaiian.

"Just a handful of Hawaiians," she laments. "From 3,000 Hawaiians on Lānaʻi, it dwindled down to about 300. There's no full-blooded Hawaiian now. My mother's grandmother had blue eyes. But when you ask her her nationality, and she speaks only Hawaiian, it's pure Hawaiian. How do you say? How can she be pure Hawaiian when she has blue eyes?"

The Dole Company bought much of Lānaʻi in 1922 to grow pineapples, and by 1947, when Castle & Cooke, Inc., bought Dole, most Lānaʻians were working for the island's only large employer, and Lānaʻi became known as "The Pineapple Island." Asian immigrants, particularly Filipinos, moved to Lānaʻi to work the fields, so the island is predominantly Filipino today.

"During the pineapple times, we were all living separately. They didn't want us to mix [the races] so we could get together and fight them. We didn't have a union until 1947/48. During that time we were living solely under the company's sovereignty. They said jump, you jumped. Otherwise, you wouldn't have a job.

"So that's my life on the island of Lānaʻi."

Or, at least it was. The "company store" looks a bit different now, though many Lānaʻi folks don't think the attitude has changed much. Problem was, by the 1980s, pineapple was not a profitable crop, so Castle & Cooke switched gears, plowing under their pineapple fields for golf courses and fancy resorts. One of the golf courses is named "The Experience" and the other "The Challenge." And true it is—the change on Lānaʻi has been a challenging experience.

"I don't mind the change," Auntie Elaine says as she complains about it. "But I say don't forget the people who live here. I think Mr. Murdock's first responsibility is to the people who live here. Then think about the people he would like to bring here."

"If we don't keep up the culture, we would really be in trouble because we would have nothing to hold us to our identity."

As the CEO of Castle & Cooke, David Murdock has been personally involved in Lānaʻi's change. He and Auntie Elaine have squared off numerous times, yet maintain a friendly demeanor. He has bought her quilt work and her feather work and has seen her *hālau (hula* school) perform at his hotels.

Still, Auntie Elaine is frank: "I think he's [Murdock] going to sell the hotels and be on his way because he's getting a difficult time with the people of Lānaʻi. All the things that he wants, when he comes to the public hearings, he gets a difficult time—because we testify, and I'm one of them, testifying against him. I want to be able to live comfortably on my island; I don't want him ruining my island.

"Our people have the minimum kinds of jobs. What do you expect from the hotels—that's the only kind they're going to offer. And now they want us to okay their new subdivision of million-dollar homes. Doesn't matter how much we fight. They've got the money. I'm afraid we might just gel into this community of strangers and we don't fit anywhere.

"I don't resent the hotels. They offer jobs for our young people. But sometimes it's very frustrating. I think they [the resorts] can be very successful if they would only come to the people of Lāna'i and ask how they would like the hotels run. If they came together with the people of Lāna'i. . . ."

When Bill Gates, the CEO of Microsoft Corporation, got married on Lāna'i, he thought he'd have complete privacy, particularly from the press. However, the roads, the beaches, the airport are state property, so reporters did get in. One reporter was arrested on a state road. He sued and won his case.

"The Gates problem? That really hurt," Auntie Elaine says, explaining how it felt to be told she had few rights on her own island. "I felt intimidated. We weren't allowed to walk around the park. We were stopped. When the reporters came, they were arrested. I stayed home. I didn't want to get involved. I was disappointed and angry.

"But when the reporter was arrested, they came to me and asked me how I felt about that. Golly, did I give them an earful—how they think they own this island. Who are they? They think they're God? So he [Murdock] finally said in the newspaper he was sorry. He said he thought he owned the island. He owns about 98 percent.

"I am very vocal in our public meetings. I have to tell them what I think. I sit on the water committee. We're telling them: 'You did this, you did this, you did this.' And they're saying: 'No, we didn't do it.' I get so frustrated. I go home and say I'm going to chuck it all. But, no, I can't. There are a lot of people who come to me in the community. If I don't go to a meeting, they say: 'Auntie, why didn't you go?' Oh golly, then I think I should have gone. So I go back again. I can't give it up. It will always be there.

"Sometimes I think I'll move to Lahaina. My father has *kuleana* [family] lands in Lahaina. But then again, I can't. I can't turn my back on this island. For sure, they'll be making more changes."

Something that never changes for her, something that politics never affects is her involvement in *hula*. She has been Lāna'i's *hula* master for more than four decades. There was no one to teach her *hula* when she was growing up, no way to learn on Lāna'i. Still, she had this drive to dance and eventually teach. She believes it was in her blood.

"Hali'ilehua, my great-grandmother [dead since Elaine was three years old], was also a teacher of *hula*. I feel the energy comes from her to me. Sometimes I really think that she's here. I think it's this energy that got me to take up *hula*.

"I went to Honolulu to gain all this knowledge. I learned from 'Iolani Luahine for many years [reputed to be the greatest dancer of this century]. Oh, she was great, she was great. Very weird woman, but I liked her knowledge. Her type of dancing was very simple. Before she did anything in the morning, she danced in her room. She danced her chants. She'd dance by the window. She'd open the shades and the sun would come in. That way you retain your motions, if you do it every day.

"I love to teach, but I never knew it would bring me this far. In the seventies—wow, the State Foundation on Culture and the Arts was calling me. They wanted me to be a full-fledged teacher on this island of Lāna'i. They paid me! They hired teachers from all over the islands. And I'm the only one for Lāna'i. So the kids were getting free *hula*.

"My *hālau* went to the Smithsonian in 1989. We spent two weeks up there. When they called me from Washington, D.C., I said: 'Are you sure you're talking to the right person? Why me?' They said they thought I was the best of all the others who performed at the Merrie Monarch [a major *hula* competition held annually on the Big Island]. Before they could change their mind, I said yes. I couldn't believe it."

Since the population of Lāna'i is mostly Filipino, the majority of students in Auntie Elaine's *hālau* are not Hawaiian.

"I've had girls who've danced with me since they were little, and now they're 13, 14 years old. And now they don't even look Filipina. They look Hawaiian to me. And when they open their mouths, they don't sound Filipina. Yet they come from parents who speak with that accent. They've become Hawaiian. Most of my *hālau* is Filipina, but I don't care. They want to learn and they wish they were Hawaiians. They have true *aloha*.

"Sometimes our own Hawaiian children, I could choke their necks. I'm there, they know what I am–why don't they come to *hula?* I would even give them free lessons because they're Hawaiian. But the people of different nationalities come.

"If we don't keep up the culture," she continues, looking a bit vexed, "we would really be in trouble because we would have nothing to hold us to our identity. I think we can stem [the culture] from *hula* because it's visible. We're trying to get back our language, get back our lands, trying to get back our dignity. We lost that. If we can start with *hula,* then perhaps the other things can follow."

"And another thing . . ." Auntie Elaine is off and running on another topic. "We have to straighten out this mess that we're in today," she says. "The overthrow of our queen [in 1893] has never been justified. So they have to remedy that.

It might take forever. It may not be my time before we realize the end results. Right now my sovereign right has been interfered with. I lost my birthright. I didn't even realize it until I grew up and learned my Hawaiian history. They never taught us Hawaiian history in school. But now that I know it, you get a little upset.

"We're just chugging along, chugging along. Looking out for ourselves. We have to fight like hell to survive and to be recognized. We have to always be on the alert. But they can't kick me off this island—this is my island."

DANCE, CHANT, GENEALOGY, MUSIC

The Hawaiians had no written language. It was through their chants that they chronicled what was valuable to them—births, deaths, their history, their loves, their lives. Important chants were memorized and handed down from generation to generation, thus their data banks were their prodigious memories. Over the centuries, Hawaiian chants became a complicated and profound art form.

Since the spoken word is transported by breath, and breath is life, then words, the ancients believed, are charged with a powerful *mana* of their own. When they composed their chants, Samuel Kamakau wrote: "Each word had to be studied for its meaning, whether lucky or unlucky, and for its effect."

They had chants for every occasion, but one of the most important was the genealogy chant. A person's lineage gave him his rank and often his profession in society, so remembering the ancestral line was an absolute. Everyone was expected to remember ten generations back. The top *ali'i* could go back even further.

The chant tells the story, and the *hula* sets the story in motion. *Hula* is often called a "sacred dance," yet it is not a form of worship, nor is it a religious ritual. True, there were sacred or religious dances, but *hula* was also danced for successful crops, before battles, at feasts, at the funeral of a chief, for human fertility, and always for entertainment.

Children were selected early for *hula* school. In the *hālau* (school) they were separated from the outside, and in the *hālau* their training was considered religious. They dedicated their lives and their dances to the goddess Laka, patron of the *hula*.

When the missionaries arrived in 1820 they found nothing entertaining or sacred about the dance. Head missionary Hiram Bingham, disturbed that people preferred *hula* to church or school, wrote: ". . . some were disposed to attend our schools and public lectures, others, with greater enthusiasm were wasting their time in learning, practicing, or witnessing the *hula*, or heathen song and dance."

Such Calvinist disapproval drove the *hula* underground, and teachers became clandestine about their schools. Few danced publicly, and those who did had to have a license to do so and had to pay a $10 fee for each performance.

During King David Kalākaua's brief cultural renaissance of the 1880s, *hula* schools were public once more. They performed at his coronation in 1883, then again at his 50th birthday in 1886. Kalākaua loved and encouraged his culture; unfortunately, he died in 1891. The monarchy fell two years later, and with it the culture fell once again.

The *hula* did not recover its popularity until the 1960s and '70s. It was one of the first arts during the recent renaissance to showcase the culture. And with the *hula,* of course, returned the chant.

Hawaiian music starts with the chant, but chants did not employ harmony or melody as tunes sung today do. This type of singing only started in Hawai'i with the introduction of missionary hymns. *Hīmeni,* they were called, and the Hawaiians loved them.

People associate modern Hawaiian music with Waikiki tourist songs like "Tiny Bubbles" and "Lovely Hula Hands," and they are certainly part of Hawaiian musical history. But modern music has progressed in both substance and popularity. In 1975, for instance, only five Hawaiian records were produced; by 1997, 175 new recordings were released—a 3,500% increase. Today Hawaiian music is a multi-million dollar industry featuring falsetto singing, slack key guitar, steel guitar, *'ukulele,* plus the ever-present harmony and sweet melodies made famous by a people who love to sing.

Portrait of ʻIolani Luahine behind Nāʻope.

GEORGE NĀʻOPE
KUMU HULA

"The *hula* is Hawaiʻi. The *hula* is the history of our country. The *hula* is a story itself if it's done right. And the *hula*, to me, is the foundation of life. It teaches us how to live, how to respect, how to share. The *hula*, to me, is the ability to create one's inner feelings and no one else's."

In the days of old Hawaiʻi, children were selected at a young age to devote their lives to the *hula*. Dedicated to Laka, goddess of the *hula*, they lived sequestered for years in their *hālau* under the strict teachings of the *kumu hula* (*hula* master). It was not until graduation, often in their teens, that they were even allowed to mingle with anyone outside their *hālau*. They were not to be tainted by any other influence.

Obviously, *hula* dancers do not live that way anymore. But George Nāʻope's great-grandmother certainly knew of these customs. She had been a "lady in waiting" for Hawaiʻi's last monarch, Queen Liliʻuokalani. She raised George speaking Hawaiian in a very Hawaiian household, and in keeping with the ancient tradition of starting a dancer young, she introduced George to *hula* and chant at age three. As a result, George Lanakilakekiahialii Nāʻope (pronounced Nah-o-pay) is one of Hawaiʻi's most renowned *hula* and chant masters.

None of his siblings learned to dance and chant; George was the selected one.

"In those days," he says of his youth, "no one studied the *hula*." Not openly, anyway, since *hula* was still underground.

George's great-grandmother did not dance, but she sent him next door to study with her close friend, Mary Kanaele, who, as a child, had lived the strict, traditional *hula kapu (hula* restrictions).

"My great-grandmother made me go to the classes. I was learning to chant—four hours every day. Thank God for Sunday," he jokes. "I didn't have a choice—she made me go learn.

"I never thought that one day they would recognize me as one of the masters of the hula."

"I was 12 years old when I began to do the *hula*. I didn't think I would be a dancer. I sat through all those years listening to all the great masters yelling at the different students they had, and I thought, 'Oh boy, thank God I'm not taking the *hula*.' And at 12 years old, I was told: 'It's your turn to dance.' I had watched all those years and had chanted and beat the drums, so I knew all the dances before I even learned to dance.

"I studied with the great masters. But, I never thought I'd be a *kumu hula*. I never thought that one day they would recognize me as one of the masters of the *hula* and a historian of the Hawaiian culture. It's my people and it reflects me. It's my life," he says simply, though his has not been a simple life.

Akoni Akana, one of Nā'ope's former students, thinks an entire book should be written about Uncle George. "No one has lived a life like his," Akana says. "He was contemporary with all the greats in *hula*."

Nā'ope is not only a "great" himself, he is also quite a character. He favors fedoras and fancy, plumed hats and doesn't shy from bright pinks, gold lamé and blinding whites. Nā'ope dresses his slight frame with a flair rarely seen in Hawai'i. But it's not only his apparel that's sharp, his mind is sharp too. When his young grandson asks: "How come you so smart?" Nā'ope quips: "Because I didn't go to school to eat lunch"—a jab at his fellow, often rotund, Hawaiian performers. "You notice?" he asks wryly, "I look anemic on stage next to the rest of them."

Nā'ope has two distinct sides: one, a comedic, crowd-pleasing entertainer; the other, a stern, serious teacher.

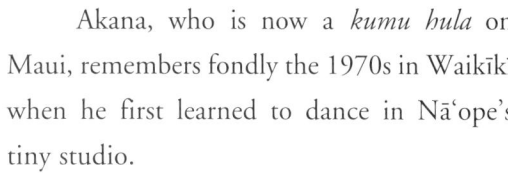

Akana, who is now a *kumu hula* on Maui, remembers fondly the 1970s in Waikīkī when he first learned to dance in Nā'ope's tiny studio.

"Everybody knew he was the guy to learn from. He was the man," Akana says. "He was teaching *kahiko* [ancient *hula* dances]. One of the very few who was teaching *kahiko*. To him, the *hula* was serious. He made the connection to the heart of the *hula* for me. He was tied to it through the religious aspect. I think that's why he was so strict. When he came to class he was mean. He used to whack us on the ankles, scream and swear. It wasn't just fun and entertainment to him—it was serious."

At night, however, Nā'ope was just fun and entertainment. Then he strummed his *'ukulele* and became Uncle George, Hawaiian entertainer.

"He was an entertainer in a tiny bar in Waikīkī, a local bar," Akana says of Nā'ope's Waikīkī days in the 1970s. "In the bar he was one person; in the realm of teaching he was another. I could talk with him in the bar and have fun, then I'd come to class and that relationship was severed. There he was the *kumu*. Strict.

"Uncle was not always the big-time *kumu* master. *Hula* is popular now, but in the '50s, '60s and '70s it wasn't that popular. So people who had the knowledge then weren't given the recognition they deserved. Uncle struggled with nothing for so, so long. He has gone through hard, hard times. Now he's reaping the benefits of his struggles."

Why, of all the people now teaching *hula* and chant, is Nā'ope considered a legend?

"His greatness is twofold," Akana responds: "The wealth of knowledge that he has and his willingness to share that knowledge. Plus, he endured—through very hard times."

"My great-grandmother was friends with all the great *[hula]* masters, and they came to see her quite often," George says of his early years. "They took me under their wings as I got older. So I lived in the right era."

One of these masters was particularly special to him—'Iolani Luahine, a woman considered to be the best *hula* dancer of modern times. She died in 1976, but the stories of her life live on. In a book about her, titled *'Iolani Luahine,* she is described as a wizard, a mystic, an enchantress, a priestess and a dancer of genius. Like George, she was also very funny, and many a wild story is told about her flamboyance and spontaneity.

Right up to the end, when she was dying of cancer, 'Iolani lived her off-the-cuff, invent-each-moment style. On the last night that she spent in her Big Island home, Nā'ope says her friends decided to invite about 30 people for a small party. But, as George remembers: "I knew Auntie 'Io—she only came in that morning [from a Honolulu hospital], but I bet you from the airport to Nāpō'opo'o [her village], she must have invited . . . well, 135 people came.

"When 'Io died, I came here [Big Island]. I've been here ever since. Her house I lived in for ten years.

"His greatness is twofold: the wealth of knowledge that he has and his willingness to share that knowledge."

(said by a student)

"I knew her all my life from when I was little. I would sit hours and hours with her and she would tell me stories. Everybody says: 'You're just like Auntie 'Io.' I wish I was, but I'm not. When our Creator created her, He broke the mold. But I fool around like her and I make fun.

"Auntie was such a great artist. When she danced, I'd get so engrossed in her dancing, I'd be drumming and I'd forget the beat—I'd get into a trance.

"Auntie 'Io never danced a song the same way. She creates as she goes along. As soon as she starts to dance her whole body changes. Everybody sits there in awe. She danced for six presidents; she danced at the White House.

"She lived *hula*. That was her life.

"Every year in the beginning years of the Merrie Monarch *[hula* festival] she'd open Merrie Monarch for me. Every year she'd dance. Birds from the volcano would come into the stadium. The *'io* [hawk] from the volcano. And when I chant they seem to come out too."

DANCE, CHANT, GENEALOGY, MUSIC: George Nāʻope

Her name means "heavenly bird" or bird *(ʻio)* of heaven *(lani)*.

The Merrie Monarch will probably be Nāʻope's greatest legacy. This gathering of *hālau hula* from all over Hawaiʻi has now become the most influential contest in the islands. The media often call it the "Olympics of *Hula*," but it didn't start out to be a contest, and George is still not comfortable with the idea of *hula* people competing.

He founded Merrie Monarch in 1961 because Hilo, the town he then lived in, had no attractions. At the time, he was promoter of activities for the county and the mayor asked him to come up with an idea.

"She said you'd better find something for us to do," he recalls. "So I went to Maui to watch the Whaling Spree because that was the big thing. We spent three days in Lahaina and it was just a drunken brawl. I said, we can't do this, especially in Hilo where everybody go church. I had no idea what I was going to do.

"Comes Monday morning we have a meeting of department heads. The mayor says: 'Oh, by the way, George and Gene went to Maui for the weekend, so they have a plan.' Gene had nothing in mind. I'm thinking, what am I going to do?

"I said: 'We're going to have a King Kalākaua Festival'—off the top of my head."

David Kalākaua was Hawaiʻi's king from 1874 until 1891. A popular monarch, he tried to renew respect for Hawaiian culture, particularly *hula* and chant. He was also known for his love of parties and socializing, thus, he was nicknamed "The Merrie Monarch."

"Kalākaua believed that *hula* is the language of the heart and the heartbeat of the Hawaiian people," Nāʻope says. "He was responsible for reviving the *hula* after it had been lost for about 75 years. He sent couriers all over the islands to seek all the *kumu hula*. He knew they were hiding. He invited them all to his coronation. That brought back all these dances.

"The first three years [at the Merrie Monarch], I had a big show—150 people in the cast. We acted out Kalākaua's coronation. *Hula* came after.

"Then I decided I was going to have *hula*, not as a competition. It didn't start as competition. It was the *kumu hula* themselves that wanted competition.

"The *hālau* came, but nobody knew ancient *hula*. Two *hālau* only can do, out of 26. So we couldn't do a contest. I wrote and gave everybody chants and sent each of these *hālau* a tape [of background chanting and drumming], and then it became a competition. I did that for nine or ten years; after that, I got tired of it. I said from now on you guys are going to do your own thing.

"Now today they're so good."

There are two major categories of *hula*: modern *hula*, called *'auwana*, and the ancient dances, called *kahiko*. Nā'ope is a purist when it comes to *kahiko*.

"As far as I'm concerned, they can stand on their heads in *'auwana*," he says, gesturing elegantly with his ever-present skinny cigarette in hand. "But keep *kahiko* traditional. I'm a stickler for that. The *kahiko* is of the old. *Kahiko* is the history of Hawai'i, the chants. So how can we add anything into it? They abuse it; they change it; they put modern feet movements into the dance. That's not *kahiko*. It must be of the old. You cannot improvise. You cannot take the old and add something to it."

Nā'ope was one of the first to openly teach *kahiko*. He began teaching it in 1942 in an old barbershop in Hilo when he was 13 years old. It wasn't until ten years later that he added modern *hula* to his lessons.

"I was drafted into the Korean War, and I came back in 1952, and that's when I went into the modern *hula*," he says. "Teachers weren't teaching *kahiko*, so you looked weird if you didn't do the things the rest of them were doing. I did teach ancient *hula*, but the emphasis was on modern *hula*."

Back then, he says, "None of the *kumu hula*, or so-called *kumu hula*, were interested in the *hula kahiko*. They learned Tahitian. Then you had "Lovely Hula Hands" and "Beyond the Reef" and "Little Grass Shack." That's modern *hula*, but it's not Hawai'i."

Nā'ope tries to be fair to other teachers and other teaching styles. In fact, he says: "In the *hula*, the first thing you must teach is respect. Number one in the *hula*. First, respect for yourself, because, if you have respect for you, you will have respect for the next person. Rule number two: in the old school it says: *'A'ohe i pau ka 'ike i ka hālau ho'okāhi*—'Think not that all wisdom lies in your school.' So you have no time to criticize the next person. I teach my students, if you see somebody dance and you think it's junk or not right, you *pa'a ka waha*, 'keep your mouth shut' and enjoy it because you know how hard it is.

"Everybody has his own way of teaching. We all have our own style. It's wonderful to take from other teachers. Because every teacher has something that another teacher doesn't have."

Nā'ope, however, remains a strict, old-style teacher because that's the way he was taught. He remembers Lokalia Montgomery, "one of the best teachers of all the teachers I had," as being a true tough nut.

"She was amazing. She was 400-something pounds," he says. "She had an old house with big windows. One day I said: 'Auntie, can I ask you a question? When you dance all the windows don't shake. When I dance all the windows shake.'

She said: 'A very simple answer: You're stupid. You're not good yet, that's why.' So that answered that!

"She'd be chanting while she's typing another chant. 'Okay, here's the next one you learn,' she'd say [pulling it out of the typewriter]. You'd have to copy every one—you write them down yourself. You had to get all the words correct. She'd sit down and make us read them before we dance. She'd tell us the meaning of all these things we'd write down. Then you never forget.

"I do this with my children today. You learn the words first, then you learn the chant and then you learn the dance.

"I speak my mother tongue, and I teach my kids—that's part of their lesson. How else are they going to learn the *hula* if they don't know what the hell they're dancing about? And, I take them to the different places of these songs so they can feel it for next time when they do it. And, in fact, I make them dance it right there—the verse they do for that area—they dance it there, then they can feel, then they can imagine how beautiful it is. And that's the only way they're going to learn. They must learn the language."

He insists they learn the words even in Japan. Nā'ope teaches anyone who wants to learn—"No matter who does it, no matter what part of the world, it's still *hula,* and it's Hawaiian"—and he is particularly popular in Japan, where he has taught since the early 1960s.

"I like their culture, but their culture is also fading. It's so Americanized and Westernized. They're losing their Japanese dancing. I like Japanese dance. Their *kahiko* is almost like ours.

"If you want to teach the culture and keep the hula *alive, you must teach them everything you know. The same way I learned, they must learn."*

"This *hālau* I go to [in Japan] has 5,000 students. There was a big write-up in the paper with my picture in it that said the *hula* is the best thing for older people for exercise. The doctors said it's good for them to keep limber. So now they're doing aerobic things with the *hula!* Oh no!" he jokes, making a funny face. "I was there for the sign-up and 2,000 people signed up to take from my teachers.

"I love to share my culture. The *hula* is the only thing we have left of our own. If you want to teach the culture and keep the *hula* alive, you must teach them everything you know. The same way I learned, they must learn.

"I have children who come from different religions and different races. It doesn't bother me at all. No matter what race or what color, when they dance they're Hawaiian.

"The Japanese study hard and they work hard. This is why I like to teach foreigners. And they don't change the *hula*. They're smart enough to know it's not theirs. But they love it.

"No matter what race or what color, when they dance they're Hawaiian."

"Many of our Hawaiians don't even know our own culture. Many of our Hawaiians are not the best dancers. Hawaiians are great fakers in the *hula* line. You have a bunch of *haoles* in the line dancing, and people say: 'Uncle George, those *haole* girls, they all did wrong.' I say: 'The Hawaiian is the one making wrong.' You have ten girls there, nine going one way, one going the other. Tell me who's wrong—the Hawaiian. But the Hawaiian has a knack where she can just shift the hip movement and get back in line. The *haole* or Japanese, they make one mistake, they worry the whole song, so the whole song is no good. A Hawaiian smiles, and ching-ching, she gets back in. The Hawaiian has the nicest smile, but she is the one making mistake."

Nā'ope has had thousands of students in his five decades of teaching, but of all those, he has only granted teaching diplomas to 12.

"Not that people aren't good dancers," he says. "But that doesn't mean they'd be good teachers. I don't think most are ready for it. [The 12] were ones I felt were sincere in their dancing and did not put money before the dancing."

Nā'ope insists a teacher should never worry about money. When he began teaching in 1942, he charged fifty cents a week. Teachers nowadays charge "$25 twice a week, $45, $60," he complains. "You know, when they took from me, they paid me the first month, and the next 29 years they never paid! I'm the king of the free. It's the only way you're going to be able to teach these people. I don't put money first. I live very comfortably. Every time if I don't have money, here comes the money."

All that's important to him is the purity of *hula*. He's very serious when he says: "The *hula* is Hawai'i. The *hula* is the history of our country. The *hula* is a story itself if it's done right. And the *hula,* to me, is the foundation of life. It teaches us how to live, how to respect, how to share. The *hula,* to me, is the ability to create one's inner feelings and no one else's."

John Lake
CHANTER

Aia ka mana i loko o ka huaʻōlelo.
Ke alo o ke ola, ke alo o ka make.
There is power within the word,
the countenance of life and
the countenance of death.

"Every time a chant is offered, you have to think of the chant as a form of praising—it's a form of prayer. That's first because the spiritual essence, the *mana,* gives us the power to chant. Personal *mana.* The concept of *mana* is the recognition that there is an omnipotent force that's the first source."

"This is a very strong proverb. It literally means that the power of the word can give life and it can give death, the negative," explains John Keola Lake. "There is great *mana* in words."

"Your choice of words is very, very important. In the Hawaiian framework of the heart and soul and the *naʻau* [gut], if our words are negative, it's said we can forgive, but, unfortunately, we cannot forget. Once the word is said, it's said and you can't change it. I can say: 'I'm sorry, I'm sorry; *mea culpa, mea culpa.*' but it has been said. The word is powerful."

Words have been a lifelong *motif* for John Lake. He has been a respected teacher *(kumu)* and a renowned chanter for decades, and both depend upon the spoken word.

Kumu Lake thinks the eminent chanters of old are akin to outstanding poets of any culture. "The great *haku mele* [composers of chants] were eloquent in oratory and styles of chanting and would be able to improvise as they went along," he says.

"The beauty of chant, the styles of chant, the content of chant are just as great as the British writers, the American writers, the Greek tragedies," Lake says. "They have the same topics, they have the same metaphors.

"What makes a good haiku? What makes good poetry or good poets or good writers? It's a sense that they have. It's the same thing in Hawaiian."

Like great poetry, Hawaiian chant often dealt with life's mysteries. Yet the chanter, as the poet, couched his ideas in symbolic language, called *kaona* in Hawaiian. The hidden message within is the true poetic beauty of Hawaiian chant.

"Many times the chanter would disguise the meaning," Lake explains. "The *kaona* have nuances that are hidden and meant only for that particular person or situation."

He cites a famous modern song, called *Hiʻilawe*, written at the turn of the century, that retains the ancient form of *kaona:* "It's about a love affair that should never have taken place. The language is disguised by saying that great flocks of birds flew out of Hiʻilawe, the caverns of Waipiʻo, and flew all the way down to Puna. That's saying that gossip flew all over the place."

The ancients composed chants to record what was important to them—from their personal love lives to their peoples' history. They bragged via chant about a chief's genitals and they praised their gods with sacred chants. *Mele* was a part of every day life.

"It's a form of story telling," Lake explains. "Hawaiians developed so many classifications and categories of chant. *Pule,* praising and prayers, that's one style of chanting; genealogical is another; the laments and the eulogies is another style; birth chants is another style; relaying epic events is another style; procreation chants is another style.

"There's a certain kind of voice and meter and rhythm and tempo you do for each chant style. If I'm chanting within the chant classified as *olioli* my pitch will be in the higher range and the sounds will be in my throat. Then, there's the low-pitched sound and the emotion of the *kanikau,* the death chants. We mean to weep, and therefore, you let your voice weep in that chant.

"I always kid my students; I say: 'We're going to learn the Hawaiian rap, *kepakepa.*' This type of chanting is relegated to epic poetries, to genealogies, histories, and events. You have a short time to do a lot, and therefore, you do it fast. It's like you're swallowing everything and saying it all in one breath. That's the style. [He chants fast on one pitch to demonstrate.]

"Every time a chant is offered, you have to think of the chant as a form of praising—it's a form of prayer. That's first because the spiritual essence, the *mana*, gives us the power to chant. Personal *mana*. The concept of *mana* is the recognition that there is an omnipotent force that's the first source."

What makes a chanter great, Lake says, is: "His vocal power, his control over the nuances that he has in his delivery, his knowledge of the language, his ability to invoke images and emotions like a great orator.

"Chanters [in ancient days] were chosen from their early age. The *kahuna* [chant expert] would watch the young children and listen to the child's voice. Then they were raised with that *kahuna*. Training would take over a 20-year period. There was no pencil and paper or tape recorder, only the memory banks."

"There is great mana *in words. Your choice of words is very, very important."*

Such tough training no longer exists today, but Kumu Lake has taught youngsters both *hula* and chant for years. ("There is no *hula* without chant," he reminds you.)

"When I teach chant," he says, "I tell my students I'll give you the printed material but only when you've mastered it by hearing. You have a hang-up when you have an eye on the paper. You're trying to read it and mimic and you're not listening. When I was a child we didn't have paper, we just had to listen. So those words have hung in my mind after all these years.

"That was part of Hawaiian training: first you watch, you observe, but most important you listen. Before you ask questions, you listen. And you mimic and you mimic and you mimic.

"We sharpen our skills of memory through the art of listening. Our skills of listening and hearing have been lessened by the use of the pen and paper and the tape recorder.

"My students always ask: 'Do you think they [the ancients] would have developed a written language?' Well, we don't know. But, anything put into a physical written form no longer has the *mana* of the *na'au*."

Spoken Hawaiian has always been known as a magical, powerful language. The reason, Lake believes, is that: "Hawaiian language has a preponderance of vowel sounds. We have five vowels and only seven consonants, but they're mostly soft sounds. The hardest sound that we have is a 'k.' In English we have 36 sounds.

"One of the key principles in singing or in chanting is the ability to sustain one's voice, to make it melodious. When you sustain your voice there's an aura of ever-lasting breath, which is called *kō*. In order for the chanter to create this, he saves his breath by not using hard sounds or consonants. That's why in chanting we substitute 'k' with a 't' or with an 'r' so it rolls. We don't say 'n,' we say 'nu.' It's a lighter sound. I sustain and prolong the sounds and don't emphasize the consonant sounds, and therefore, I sustain breath."

"The beauty of chant, the styles of chant, the content of chant are just as great as the British writers, the American writers, the Greek tragedies. They have the same topics, they have the same metaphors."

As he talks, mostly in English, partly in Hawaiian, Kumu Lake chants fragments of *mele*. For him, it seems a natural way of conversation. He has been speaking Hawaiian and practicing chant since his "small kid days" on Maui.

"I had the good fortune to be raised by my grandmother, my mother's mother," he says. "She spoke Hawaiian and she spoke wonderful English. She taught third grade. I had my first *kumu* [of *hula* and chant] when I was five. It was my grandmother's choice. She felt this was culture we should know. You never asked the elder why are we doing this. You just did it. It wasn't until my adult life, I said: 'Thank goodness!' My sisters don't speak Hawaiian; they never learned chant; they don't dance. In my whole family, I'm the only one of my generation that speaks Hawaiian."

Carrying on Hawaiian traditions is his birthright. His middle name, Keolamakaʻāinakalahuiokalaninokamehamehaekolu, means "the life of the common people, a nation of chiefs, during the reign of Kamehameha III." He is the fourth generation son in his family to have this name, a name given to many Hawaiian boys during the era of King Kamehameha III.

Lake believes his name commissions him to "revitalize and preserve the life of the people of Hawai'i—teaching the values that have been lost that everybody should share." And that is why he is a teacher.

He began his teaching career after receiving two master's degrees, one in education, another in Spanish linguistics (besides being fluent in Spanish, he also speaks Maori, can read French and reads and writes Italian). He studied linguistics and education on the Mainland and in Spain, encouraged by a high school teacher who said: "We can't stay in our own world; we become myopic."

But once he had a bit of worldliness on his resume, it was time to come home. In 1962 he began his 31-year career teaching high school boys at St. Louis School in Honolulu. He taught social studies, English and Spanish until 1965, when he introduced the idea of Hawaiian Studies.

"There was no such thing in 1964," he remembers. "In '65 I had my first Hawaiian language classes, then introduced music and dance. So we had young men dancing *hula* in '65 and '66! That was sort of a fluke—no young men were dancing *hula* in the sixties. The football team asked me to teach them Hawaiian *hula*—45 of them. I said: 'You go find 45 girls.' So they did. Started out with a group of 90 kids. They loved it. By 1970, you were a big man on campus if you were in the Hawaiian Club and played football."

From that propitious beginning, he has focused most of his teaching career on Hawaiiana. He continued teaching Hawaiian Studies at St. Louis; he started the Hawaiian program at Chaminade University in the 1970s, teaching there during the summers; he taught *hula* and chant through the Hawaiian Music Foundation in the seventies and eighties; then, after he retired in 1992, he and his cousin opened their own Academy of Arts, Music and Dance. For his dedication to education, he was honored in 1987 as a "Living Treasure of Hawai'i."

He supposedly retired in 1992, but, retirement, he says "is a relative term. When I retired, the first phone call I got was from Chaminade University. 'I'm retiring, Sister,' I said. 'That's why we're calling you,' she said. 'Would you teach. . . ?'" Easily persuaded, he teaches Hawaiian language there every day, yet still considers himself retired.

Retirement has given him the chance to "walk his talk"—given him time to practice Hawaiian ways, rather than just teach them. This new chapter of his life was initiated by a visiting Maori who asked several Hawaiian leaders: "Why are your temples sitting silent? Why are they not used for anything but historical monuments? The temples of New Zealand are used as social and educational centers."

A small group of Lake's peers decided to act on those words by reclaiming the last great temple built in Hawai'i. Their goal was to commemorate its construction (in 1791) with a 200-year anniversary celebration in 1991. That would not be easy to do, however, since most ancient ritual has been lost. The person they looked to for expertise in ritual, chant and protocol was John Lake.

"I was asked to do the research and all the ceremonies and rituals," he explains. "I said: 'That's quite an honor, but give me six months to think about it. You're asking me to do research on research that you know is not available.' There is nothing on what took place that day 200 years ago. We had no idea as to the protocol, customs, rituals and ceremonies. And, it had to be done in chant, of course."

Of course. That's why they asked him.

A tough assignment, but he could not resist the opportunity to be part of such a momentous ceremony.

"So I committed myself to it. The more I got into it, the beauty of the literature started to grow," he reports. "A lot of the chants that I learned as a child started to fit into different categories—oh, these are prayers, oh, these are tributes, oh, these are genealogical chants, oh, these are historical chants. It became such a great influence, I just could not stop.

"From 1988 until 1991 I did almost three years of preparation for this event—how it was done, what were the omens in the skies, what's going to be included. We couldn't do the same thing that was done 200 years ago because that included human sacrifice. But I did come up with ceremonies and rituals, and I also created a new chant commissioned by the elders to commemorate the rededication. It was called *Oli Kinohi Hou,* a new beginning.

"We could not select a text or make it a play, because this wasn't meant to be pageantry. It was meant to capture the past—what literally took place there."

What happened there 200 years ago is quite a story. Kamehameha, a highborn, great warrior from the Big Island, decided in 1791 to capture all the Hawaiian islands and subjugate their chiefs under his rule to make Hawai'i one nation—something never yet accomplished in Hawaiian history. He asked a wise prophet to tell him how to do so, and was advised to build a great temple on Pu'ukoholā (Hill of the Whale) on the Big Island. After it was built, Kamehameha invited all local chiefs to the opening ceremonies. Though his cousin, Keōua Kū'ahu'ula, was a rival for control of the Big Island, and thus might be killed if he came, he was obligated to do so. However, the day before Keōua arrived, he cut off the tip of his penis to make himself a less desirable sacrificial victim.

"He knew what was expected," reports Lake of Keōua's impending death.

"But, in essence, his mutilation was saying: 'You have my body, but you have an imperfect victim.' Mutilating the *ma'i* has tremendous power because of the ability of procreativity."

This mutilation was also a sign that he knew death was coming, and it was—as soon as he arrived, Kamehameha's men killed him. His body was borne up the steps of the *heiau* and he was offered to the gods as a sacrifice.

Keōua ruled the district of Ka'ū on the Big Island, and Ka'ū's people never forgave Kamehameha and never accepted him as their king. So, part of the 1991 ceremony was an acknowledgement of their loss.

"There's an old saying: 'Ka'ū has only one family.' Meaning there's strong intermarriage within that whole society and they're very protective of Ka'ū. To them, Kamehameha was the usurper. He had killed their chief, Keōua," Lake explains.

"We have to mend the past so we that we can move into the future."

"So we had the descendants of Keōua come up in canoes. I greeted them, then people representing Kamehameha and his men walked up and they embraced each other and they gave each other a *honi* [nose touch].

"Our idea was to mend the old wounds and bring everything together. It was called *Ho'oku'ikahi,* coming together in unison as one. We have to mend the past so that we can move into the future."

As *Kahuna Nui* (chief temple priest) of Pu'ukoholā Heiau, the future is Kumu Lake's primary concern. Since the '91 ceremony, he's been holding meetings and workshops at the *heiau* so that the descendants of Hawai'i's chiefs can relearn their past.

"We want people to know the richness that once took place at the *heiau,*" he explains. "It was a place of learning. It could be the social arena, the political arena, the economic arena because it was literally the seat of government. We want to bring that back. In abandoning our old ways, we lost sight of what was valuable.

"There is a prophecy that, if seven generations pass and the seeds are not planted, then the next generation passes away. We're in the seventh generation now of the past 200 years. So, we need to inculcate into our younger generations that there are so many things to be proud of—tremendous riches to be learned and passed on. We must commit ourselves as Hawaiians, be proud of what we have and understand our past, commit ourselves confidently about achieving things.

"And here's a place, literally having a sense of place. Let's reclaim the *heiau* as a living structure."

And so they did, in what he describes as "a magnificent ceremony." On August 17, 1991, as the ceremony's chief chanter, representing a priest of Lono, Kumu Lake stood with eleven family members, chanting on and off all day long. They began the day at 4:30 a.m. by cleansing themselves in the ocean. Then, standing on the steps of the ancient temple in their priestly robes, they greeted 600 canoe paddlers, 2,500 guests from throughout the Pacific and 2,000 visitors who sat in nearby bleachers eager to witness modern history in the making.

"We did the *hui kala,* chants of forgiveness; we did the chant of the opening of new life *[hainaki],* usually done in tribute to Lono; we did a lot of *pule* , we did chants to Kū, Kāne, Lono and Kanaloa [the four main male gods]; we did ʻaumākua chants, place name chants, genealogy chants. We greeted all the chants of the Tongans, Marquesans, Samoans, Maoris. Whatever group came, I had to recognize their birthplace [in chant].

"It was what you call improvisation. We had no script. I guess it was improvisation from the moment it started and the chants fell into place."

Near the end of daylight, as Lake stood in the temple of his ancestors, columns of darkness began to form behind him in the mountains. As he watched in amazement, the darkness moved towards the sea as a red ball of sun began to set with the moon and stars already clear in the sky. This was exactly the scene 200 years ago. In the closing chant he discovered from 1791, this same configuration was described—the columns of darkness, the red setting sun and the moon and stars above the horizon.

"Lo and behold, I turned around and it was happening again—the chant described it 200 years ago," Lake says, still awestruck. "So I thought, I guess this is my cue [to end the ceremony with this chant]. I sounded the *pahu,* the drums. And as soon as I saw it [the sky], my chanters saw it and their volume of chanting picked up and you could hear it in their voices—they were thinking: 'Oh my God, I can't believe this is happening. We're chanting it as it's happening.' The chanters got louder and louder and louder.

"You study for three years, you research the archives, you pull these different chants together, then all of a sudden life is given to the chants because you see them taking place. I didn't expect that to happen. I think our ancestors were guiding things."

EDITH KAWELOHEA MCKINZIE
GENEALOGY EXPERT

Ask Edith McKinzie a simple historical question (Was eighteenth century chiefess Keōpūolani related to Maui chief Kekaulike?) and, without pondering a second, she launches into a detailed genealogy of these two high *aliʻi* who lived centuries ago.

"Kekaulike had plenty of wives, but the most important one was a half sister, Kekuʻiapoiwanui. She had the child Kamehamehanui, and Kamehamehanui had a sister, Kalola, and then they had a brother Kahekili. So the ranking comes from these two brothers and a sister.

"Kalola went to Hawaiʻi and she married the ruling chief of that place, Kalaniʻōpuʻu. With Kalaniʻōpuʻu she had Kīwalaʻo. Kīwalaʻo marries Kamehameha's sister and this is where Keōpūolani comes from. So it comes down from the line of Kalola."

In short, Kekaulike was Keōpūolani's great-grandfather.

"They would apprentice very young to learn chanting. The position was excellent, but you couldn't make mistakes.

They had chants for all kinds of occasions—birth, death, marriage. They had historical chants, love chants, lullaby chants, all kinds of chants.

We need to have more people composing chants today. I've noticed that as long as we had kings and queens ruling, there were always chants being composed."

It takes a special kind of mind to retain the names and relationships of Hawai'i's *ali'i*. It might also be noted that every name mentioned above begins with a "K," as do many Hawaiian names, so confusion is common. Not, however, for Edith Kawelohea McKinzie. Auntie Edith loves the intricacies of genealogy, and as a result, she's one of Hawai'i's top genealogists. She has written two books on *ali'i* genealogy and hopes to produce a third. Her books sell well because genealogy has always been, and still is, important to Hawaiians.

"Hawaiians say they trace their genealogies back to Wākea and Papa [Father Sky and Mother Earth]," Auntie Edith says, "I've never tried to do it. That's the Cosmogonic Period. That's the gods."

Only the highest *ali'i* would claim lineage back to the gods. However, in ancient times, all the *ali'i* class had to know their genealogies at least ten generations back.

"Today, Mormons require their people to do four generations, and that's hard, that's mind boggling. Can you imagine ten?" Auntie Edith asks incredulously. "They were required to do that—ten generations on both sides, mother and father."

Similar to being born into European nobility, Hawaiian chiefs and chiefesses had rank and power established at birth by their lineage. One's status in society and one's job were all according to rank. And rank came from the ancestors.

"The blood line is very important. Your ranking is who you are—you are born into your status," explains Auntie Edith. "Because the society was chiefly, in order for you to hold positions in the government, you had to be a certain rank. The selection for who surrounds the king, who carries out his duties, was done by the ranking. If you wanted to serve the king, then you'd have to know your genealogy.

"Marriages were match-mated for the rank. Ranking comes from the women, from the mother. Your *kapu* [rank] was based on who your mother was."

Connection to the ancestors through an *ali'i* mother was so important that after birth a child's umbilical cord was saved and placed in a temple. The cord, which literally tied the child to the mother, symbolically tied the child to the entire family and to the land the family came from.

"The *piko* [umbilical cord] ties the birth to that particular land," Auntie Edith explains, "because it's connected to the mother. The umbilical cord is important culturally."

Auntie Edith herself wonders why genealogy fascinates her so much. She shrugs when asked, and explains that it's in her blood. "There's someone in my family, maybe two generations before me who did genealogy," she says.

Because of her knowledge, she's called upon to help settle modern land ownership disputes. She has worked part-time for a real estate title company trying to sort out the often complicated land claims of large Hawaiian families. In the past, the *ali'i* could have multiple marriages, thus entwining many families and truly complicating genealogies and land ties.

All these complex genealogies are "fresh in my mind," she says because she taught Hawaiian culture and language at Honolulu Community College, University of Hawai'i, from 1978 until she retired in 1995. "I had to explain genealogy to my students, so I had to know it well," she says.

In ancient times, genealogy chants were recited at introductions when a chief was meeting someone new. They were also chanted at births, relating the history of the family.

"The genealogy chant was a formality of saying who you are," Auntie Edith explains. "Usually when you visit another place you tell them who you are—through chant."

High chiefs had chanters who were trained from youth to compose and memorize these poetic genealogy chants. The recitation of a high *ali'i* genealogy had to be perfect—no slip of the tongue, no improper inflection, no loss of memory allowed. A misstep could mean death for the chanter.

"They would apprentice very young to learn chanting," Auntie Edith says. "The position was excellent, but you couldn't make mistakes.

"They had chants for all kinds of occasions—birth, death, marriage. They had historical chants, love chants, lullaby chants, all kinds of chants.

"We need to have more people composing chants today. I've noticed that as long as we had kings and queens ruling, there were always chants being composed. I think we should do more *mele inoa* [birth chants]. People need to chant why they name their children; a *mele inoa* is like giving instructions—why they're carrying a certain ancestral name, for instance.

"In Hawaiian chant you use certain voice techniques. For instance, in a *kanikau* [death chant] you soften the vowels. Every immediate family member is required to submit a *kanikau*—it's a dirge. When parents die, every child in the family has a little dirge, no matter how young they are, they say farewell to that spirit. You send the spirit away. It's a beautiful concept.

"Hawaiians would chant: 'This flower has faded,' instead of saying *make* [dead], so final. Or they'd say: 'You are going on this one-way path and you cannot come back and you're going alone.' It's the poetry that is so magnificent.

"In the Hawaiian newspapers, there are thousands of *kanikau*." Auntie Edith should know—she's read most of them. She's probably the leading expert on scores of Hawaiian newspapers printed in the state from the 1840s to the 1890s.

It was from these newspapers that she discovered her love of genealogy. In the 1970s, as a senior student in the University of Hawai'i's Hawaiian Studies program, she spent hours in the library reading and translating these old newspapers. She was a rather "senior" senior, almost 50 years old when she enrolled at UH.

"After working for 20-some years for the federal government, I went back to school when I was about 50," she says. "They had just opened the Hawaiian Studies program in 1978, and I was always interested in Hawaiian culture. I got a bachelor's and an MA degree in education, curriculum and instruction."

Though her study of Hawaiian newspapers was for a college class, these century-old papers actually led Auntie Edith into her life's work. While reading through them, she kept finding genealogies—lists of them, chants of them, bits and pieces year after year. In the papers after the 1893 overthrow of the Hawaiian monarchy, the chiefly families were asked to submit their genealogies, so she found a gold mine of information during that era.

Encouraged by her UH teacher, she began putting all these genealogies into book form. Then, at a party she met an editor from Brigham Young University, a Mormon school interested in genealogy—the perfect place to publish her work. The Mormon church has been involved in Hawai'i since the mid 1800s; many Hawaiians are Mormons and many Mainland Mormons have family ties in Hawai'i, thus the interest for this BYU editor. He immediately told her they would print her book and he asked her to write two more.

She researched her books while continuing to teach college; then, when she retired in 1995 with two books published, she found herself back once again poring over old Hawaiian newspapers. Ironically, Honolulu's Bishop Museum had advertised for a Hawaiian language expert to index these newspapers, not knowing that the perfect person for the job had already started the work 20 years earlier.

"I have ten people who work for me in Bishop Museum every Saturday," she says of her work. "They're either translating or indexing. We started with newspapers from 1834. The first two newspapers printed then were religious, printed by American missionaries. That's what they came for, they came to teach religion. I don't have bad things to say about them. Whatever they have done, they have left some wonderful records for us today. I think that when they taught the Hawaiians, they taught them well. The Hawaiians were very educated, especially those who went to Lahainaluna [a school on Maui built in 1831 by missionaries].

"We don't translate into English, it would take us too long. We just tell what's in the article—summarize every article column by column. Then I have someone who checks that the summaries are accurate, then we give it to the indexers.

"We're indexing seven newspapers. Missionary papers first, then Department of Education, then private papers. For a short time the Department of Education handled the newspapers. Some newspapers were run by Hawaiians, but they were short-lived. They didn't have enough money. We had over 100 newspapers [in the 1800s].

"You learn Hawaiian history from studying the hula. From the chants you get into genealogy."

"English language newspapers didn't start until the 1840s. Then they had Portuguese language papers, Chinese and Japanese. But we're not making any comparisons of them. All we want to do is take out what information the Hawaiians had."

The idea is to create a data base, an index, of everything and everybody these newspapers wrote about in the 1800s. Thus, Auntie Edith's work will unearth an abundance of nineteenth century history, adding immeasurably to historians' understanding of a difficult century for the Hawaiian people.

"I want to go right up until 1900. I want to pick up the overthrow [of Queen Lili'uokalani in 1893], so we can get some sort of idea what kind of information was being passed to the people.

"We index the papers in three areas: by subject, by names and by places," Auntie Edith adds. "Everybody wants to know why places, but places are important.

"That means every ship that came in here, every captain, every first mate—we picked up all their names. All of the students who graduated from Lahainaluna—we picked up their names. All the people who visited Hawai'i.

"We have hundreds of chants from the newspapers. We have letters from foreign countries. All the Grimm's Fairy Tales were translated into Hawaiian in the papers. Shakespeare's work too, so the Hawaiians were familiar with Shakespeare.

"Then they tried to get the Hawaiians to write their own stories. So we have many of these stories in the papers. In the 1840s when they set up a legislature, we picked up on all the laws.

"We had to determine how we would identify illustrations. Then I had to make a determination whether to index the ads. They don't index ads in English papers.

"But, we picked up many things from the ads—when the first camera was introduced, when the ships were coming in. What things were being exported. One ad was for a store that bought shark fins for sharks' fin soup. We found out that Bernice Pauahi Bishop's father was the chamberlain for the king. There's no record of her father being chamberlain, but a newspaper ad tells us that.

"Even the state library archivist told me: 'I think you're spinning your wheels' [doing the ads]. She doesn't speak Hawaiian, she doesn't know. When I told our board what we had in those ads, then quickly they changed their minds.

"What I'm shooting for is to put the index on the Library of Congress. Putting it on UH CARL [UH's indexing system] is costing us over $10,000. There are 32 outlets that UH CARL includes, and the Library of Congress is one of them. So they will get a copy."

All this translating and indexing has, of course, been a continuing education for Auntie Edith. Her fascination with her people's culture started early in life and is ongoing into her seventies. She says her earliest education began decades ago as a child studying *hula*.

"I'm not so sure why I'm doing all these Hawaiian kinds of things," she admits. "But I was exposed to Hawaiian things very young because my uncles and aunts lived with us. My father was the eldest, so all his brothers and sisters came to live with us, so I heard them speaking Hawaiian. I understood everything, but I didn't learn to speak it or to write it [until she went to college in the 1970s]. My parents didn't want me to learn Hawaiian. They wanted me to succeed in English. My father was full Hawaiian. My mom was pure Portuguese, but her whole attitude was so Hawaiian.

"My father took me to *hula,* and I learned it very young. I've been at it for a long time. I was in my twenties when I started to teach. Every once in a while I still teach. I haven't given it up. I'm still interested in it because of all these chants I collect. And I like the idea that I can choreograph anything. I hear a certain kind of beat and I don't worry."

DANCE, CHANT, GENEALOGY, MUSIC: Edith McKinzie

Auntie Edith has had several well-known *hula* teachers throughout her life, but the one who impressed her most was the very famous, now deceased, Edith Kanaka'ole.

"I was carried over by her. She was a marvelous person. She made dancing live. I had a couple of teachers that just gave you the words and you memorized them. But with her, you listened and you followed, that's how you got the exact intonation. That's how the older Hawaiians taught. She said the language was the key. She said you put the cart before the horse, if you put the *hula* first—the text was more important. She said the text determines the use of your voice.

"What I like about the *hula* is all the storytelling. Each *hula* is a story. You learn Hawaiian history from studying the *hula*. From the chants you get into genealogy—I knew all the chiefs and who were their children from the chants. From the time of Umi [1500s] we have a record of all the rulers. You get a pretty good idea who these people are from the geneologies.

"You get interested in everything Hawaiian because of *hula.*"

KINDY SPROAT
FALSETTO SINGER

"One *ʻukulele* and one soul can do a lot."
Said by a man who means what
he says and lives by his words,
both spoken and sung.

"When I'm singing a song, I'm singing a story. I think it's important to let people know what the story is about. It touches them. . . . These songs haunt me because they have a message. . . . I like to preserve the story like it is and sing it like it is, like they sang it in the old days."

Clyde "Kindy" Halemaʻumaʻu Sproat is Hawaiʻi's best at what he does—storytelling and singing of old Hawaiian songs. His favorite melodies are songs from the 1800s and early 1900s—songs rarely written down, just handed down on back porches, songs that might be long gone except for the phenomenal memory and committed zeal of Kindy Sproat.

It is his mission and his love.

"These are the songs I grew up with. They make me come alive. The tunes haunt me," he says. "Who knows them? Who sings them? Nobody. So I feel I should preserve them. They're beautiful and they tell beautiful stories. I don't expect any of the young ones to sing and play the songs like I do because they never heard them in their time. I'm just playing and singing what I heard in my time. And I retained all that."

Did he ever. By the time he was in first grade, he knew about 400 songs, both Hawaiian and English. Now he has no idea how many he knows.

He sings because he loves to. For no other reason. When he's alone, he'll sing out loud just to entertain himself. In the middle of a conversation he'll break into song. He's been known to sit upright in bed with an old tune suddenly remembered from his sleep.

He never intended to make a living at it or to become famous for it.

"I don't know about being famous," he answers when asked how fame has altered his life. "I'm just me, you know. Never changed one hair on my head. I'm still the same."

His greatness lies not in his musicianship, as he readily admits: "I just play basic keys. I'm a singer, I'm not a musician. I don't know the first thing about music or music theory. I don't read notes. I just picked it up."

In 1988, the National Endowment for the Arts honored Sproat's importance to Hawai'i's heritage by presenting him with a National Heritage Fellowship Award, an honor given to America's top folk artists.

"I didn't feel I was worthy of such a prestigious award," he says, admitting he didn't want to go to Washington, D.C., for the ceremony. But, he did, and it became a story teller's dream. After the ceremony he swapped tales with fellow honoree Doc Watson.

"The best part of it was Doc Watson. I've been his fan for years," Sproat says. "He's a flat-top guitar picker, one of the best. I have almost every record that he put out. He was getting the award the same year. Being that he was blind and he was sitting next to me, every time I went on stage I took him with me. He is a great, great guy. He and I became such friends. Every night he and I would sit in the corner and he would tell me pig stories or preacher stories. One morning he was telling me a story and the story wasn't finished and they had to take him to catch a plane, so I got on the van and rode with him to the airport to listen to the end of the story."

Sproat is not only a good listener, he's a great storyteller himself. He can tell the same story time and again with the joy of the first telling. In any other state but Hawai'i, Kindy Sproat would be the type of man who "spins yarns." Here it's said he "talks story."

"Have you heard all his stories over the years?" his wife Cheryl is asked. "Yes," she says, without a trace of boredom or exasperation. Clearly, she loves him and knows that he's good at what he does. And, she's been listening since 1976.

He, in turn, calls her "my critic, my traveling companion, my inspiration and my best friend."

Sproat got his start singing and talking story during his "small kid days" in North Kohala on the Big Island of Hawai'i. Back then, in the 1930s and '40s, his family lived an old-time Hawaiian life style. They were the only family in a wild green valley braced by steep cliffs. They were isolated in their paradise—to get in or out, they had to ride their mules two hours to the nearest road.

"It was a four-bedroom house with a huge kitchen and *lānai*. The ocean was about 200 yards from the house. Nice," Sproat says, recalling it with deep sentiment.

"Growing up in the valley, every evening after we got through taking a bath, had our supper, dishes washed, we sat on the porch, that big, long verandah. My mom used to sit on the trunk and put *lau hala* mats down and we kids laid on

the mats. My mom played a four-string banjo. She didn't have an *'ukulele*. I don't know where the banjo came from, but since we had it, she played it.

"When we were singing on that porch I always felt we were singing for the sun before it went over the *pali* [cliff]. And if we sang really good, the next day the sun would be warm and gracious, giving us a long day so we could swim a lot, we could catch *'o'opu* [small gobi fish] and *'ōpae* [shrimp] in the stream. The sun made our day. And if we sang really good, the sun would come a little earlier and stay late.

"We sang all kinds of songs, lots of Hawaiian songs and Mother Goose songs, songs from the first world war, all those we sang. So when I got old enough to go to school, there was hardly any song I didn't know."

When the Sproats' six boys and one girl needed schooling, the family moved to the nearest village, though every summer they'd go back to their valley. In town, little Kindy soaked up more of the songs that he keeps alive today.

"Every evening in the village I took my two sacks and I went around looking for morning glory vines and rattle pod weeds, gathering food for my rabbits. When

I'd go by this place, this lady would call: 'Haole boy, *haole* boy.' I had kind of blondish hair and light skin, and I was about nine," he remembers. "She lived in a vine-covered house with walkways lined with flowers and ponds of water lilies. She only spoke Hawaiian. Every time I'd go by there I'd eat with her. Then, when we got through eating, we'd push back and she'd get her guitar. I couldn't leave—I was just hooked on that. I can still see her singing [he breaks into song]. I learned a lot from her. From all the old fellows.

"My 'ukulele *has been my constant companion. It kept me sane in Vietnam.*"

"At that time people entertained themselves. They played slack key [guitar]. They told stories; they told the stories of a song, mostly in Hawaiian. They'd laugh and sing. [He breaks into a Hawaiian song.] I was glued to that. Every time I heard people singing or the slack key I'd just gravitate and I'd stay there till the last dog was sung.

"The neighborhood saloon was called Ah Hoon's Bar. Every evening the county guys—all the Hawaiians worked for the county—you'd see their horses tied up on the hitch rail and they were in there drinking wine and singing. Some of those old fellows, gruff old guys, but when they pick up that guitar and start to play . . . big, nubby fingers, but, boy, the music they would bring out on the guitar. Then, when they opened their mouths and sang . . . [he sings in falsetto]. I would just stand there. I couldn't move. They were great. Certain songs they'd jump up and dance too. It was a show in itself. Every chance I'd get I'd stop over there; I'd risk getting a beating from my mom for coming home late."

Soon as school was out, though, all these town attractions paled as the whole Sproat family headed straight for their valley.

"The last day of school was always half day. In the morning my dad saddled up all the mules and then we started home," Sproat recalls. "We had two sacks down the front of the mules and each sack had three chickens in it with holes for the chickens' heads to stick out. Live chickens because that was our egg supply. About a dozen chickens we took in there. We had the family cat tied up in a bag and he didn't like it. We had two cows; someone leading the cows with two calves following. We had about five pack mules with all our food and clothes. You should see this line. Jiminy Cricket. Like a big safari.

DANCE, CHANT, GENEALOGY, MUSIC: Kindy Sproat

"Today this is still home to me. When you're born and raised in a place like that . . . when I ride or walk around the valley, boy, the memories that come back. When I sing certain songs they remind me of certain places in the valley. I can still see that scene. It's home."

Years later, after their graceful old homestead was gone, Sproat built a small cabin in its place where he and Cheryl occasionally stay. Little else has changed in the valley, and they still go in by mule.

Sproat left North Kohala when he was drafted into the Army. He did his hitch, then turned around and joined the Air Force for a 20-year career, ending up a tech sergeant. In the military he discovered that his "one soul and one *'ukulele*" could change the mood of everyone within earshot.

"Boy, I kept the peace," he says, laughing. "As long as people sing they never fight. You know young people: they get a little hooch under their hide, they get feisty and they want to fight.

"When I went to Vietnam, I took my *'ukulele*. I tell you, my *'ukulele* has been my constant companion. It kept me sane in Vietnam. At that time I was endless with songs. I sang and sang from midnight to morning. I never drank. Drinking spoils my singing. I cannot drink and sing. Water is what I like.

"When you're in Vietnam you always have these pangs of loneliness because you miss your family. So people just came together. And if they're not singing, they're drinking, and if they're not singing, they're fighting. So I would sing. Music draws people. Music is a great mediator. People get together because of music.

"One time I was in my hooch in Vietnam laying in my bed. I was fast asleep because I had worked the early shift. After midnight someone came and shook me up, said: 'Sproat, we need you at the club right away. Australians just came in and there's Marines up there. They're fixing to have a big fight. They're gonna tear the club apart. We need you.'

"I said: 'I don't know what I can do.' But I went up there and started singing. We sang *Waltzing Matilda* at least 40 times that night. [He starts singing it.] And the Marine Corps—*From the Halls of Montezuma*. [Sings it.] You know, we never had a fight that night."

The power of a song came across loud and clear and blaring on microphones one Vietnamese New Year's Eve. It was then that Sproat's Hawaiian *aloha* sent magic out into the blackest of nights.

As Sproat tells it: "It was the Tet Offensive in '68, when the Communists celebrate the Vietnamese New Year's. The Vietnamese got together on one big push and they were going to push the GIs out of Vietnam. On New Year's night. So we were on alert, and I took my ʻukulele. When it ended we had been through a lot. We were up 40 hours, I'd say. We had a 16-mile perimeter around the air base and it was surrounded by bushes.

"I had all these kids, 17- and 18- and 19-year-old boys, out there in trenches in a bunker with a machine gun. One man per bunker. Jeez. I mean dark. Right in enemy territory.

"I was a tech sergeant and I had to patrol all this. I told my guys, 'Heh, everybody's scared. If you get to the point where you feel you're scared or shaking, don't be ashamed, call me. I'll come up there and sit with you and see what's happening out there.'

"Whoooo. You can't imagine Tet Offensive. I can still see the skies light up at night and the big shells and mortar coming in. Boom. Boom. Boom. This went on for heck knows how long. Everyone was tired.

"We had a place where all the NCOs [noncommissioned officers] met on a hill, just a big bare hill. So when everything quieted down I drove up to the hill and called them up; there were 16 of us, 16 NCOs, 16 Jeeps with drivers and machine gunners. The mood was heavy, really, really heavy. We wished everybody a happy New Year. Then I got my ʻukulele out of the bag and I played and sang *Auld Lang Syne*.

"While I was singing the guys grabbed their microphones from their Jeeps and put the microphones right in front of me, and that went right into the big headquarters underground. They keyed it up and I didn't care. I gave it my all. I sang my heart out. I never sang it like that before and I don't think I'll ever sing it like that again.

"When it was finished and they unkeyed the mikes, there was a dead silence. The chattering on the radio went on for 24 hours, never stopped. Wasn't a second went by someone wasn't sending a message on that radio. But when they unkeyed the mike, there was a dead silence, then someone came on from headquarters and said: 'Amen. Sing it again.' So I did, and they put it out on the loudspeakers.

"You could feel each guy's spirit, the mood was so heavy. There was nothing that compared to that—just the feeling on New Year's on a hill in Vietnam."

It was in his early military training days when he was still stationed in Honolulu that Sproat discovered he could sing falsetto, a high-pitched, rolling style of singing that's very popular in Hawaiian music.

"I'd be laying in my barracks at night in the dark and I'd hear this guitar playing and this falsetto voice," he remembers. "You don't know how heavy my heart was just listening to this music . . . ah, that's home."

He soon discovered which soldier was singing, then found himself going over to hear him sing every chance he could.

"Right after that I graduated from basic and I became an MP. I kept thinking if he could sing falsetto, so could I. So I went to the PX and I bought a *'ukulele*. My place of patrol was on the jeep, patrolling the national cemetery at Punchbowl. So after dark I'd drive up on that high lookout looking down on the cemetery and I'd practice my falsetto. Just makes me smile when I think of it—here I had this captive audience down there. They had to listen to me, they couldn't get away. And I sang and I sang. [He breaks into a falsetto song.] There are some songs that only the falsetto can bring to life."

Today, he's so well-known for his falsetto that there's an annual falsetto contest on the Big Island named after him. The contest wasn't his idea, but he truly enjoys seeing new talent. He's not a judge, but the winner does get to shake the master's hand.

In 1995, Sproat was finally convinced to do an album (called "Clyde Halema'uma'u Sproat Sings . . .").

"They'd been after me for years and years to do one, but I thought it wasn't necessary," he says. "I always had the feeling that these were old, obsolete songs that nobody wanted to hear anymore. When I sang these songs the Hawaiians used to say: 'Hey, brah, that song is all *limu* [moss] already. Nobody want to hear it.'

"There are some songs that only the falsetto can bring to life."

"The old songs were not the thing. It wasn't cool to be Hawaiian. Just in the last ten years I saw more Hawaiian songs brought out than I saw in my whole life [due to the Hawaiian renaissance]."

The old songs Sproat loves are different from most songs written today because they tell a story and the story often has a hidden meaning *(kaona)*. For instance, in one song, a Hawaiian cowboy and his girlfriend promise to be faithful when he has to leave for two years. But . . .

"Two years is a long time," Sproat explains. "When he went back he saw a dried *lei* on the porch. He said: 'That is not the *lei* I gave to her.' And then he saw that somebody else's boots were where his ought to be, so he left his honeysuckle *lei* at her doorstep just to let her know he'd been there. His honeysuckles were all drooped just like his heart was. As he was riding home, all he could think about was how he wanted once more to return to the scene and pluck that flower.

"It has a sexual connotation—once more pluck that flower.

"People say: 'Oh, that's bad.'

"I say: 'That's telling it right.' That's the *kaona*. Instead of saying: 'Oh, I want to have sex with that lady again.' Hawaiians had no swear words in their language. They inferred a lot with beautiful words, and they told it like it was."

Sproat insists that songs be sung with all the verses because: "When I'm singing a song, I'm singing a story. I think it's important to let people know what the story is about. It touches them. You cannot leave out a portion.

"These songs haunt me because they have a message. I don't write my own songs. I listen to what somebody else wrote, and that's what I like. I sing the songs like I heard it, exactly like I heard it. I like to preserve the story like it is and sing it like it is, like they sang it in the old days."

Still, he insists that everyone's presentation of a song be their own.

"You should never try to sing like somebody else. Every person is an individual. I think what really counts is your expression, your personal feeling.

"When you hear a song and you learn it and you know it, you take it down and strain it through your heart. You just listen with your heart. Open the ears of your heart and you can hear something good all the time."

This attitude plus his talent have made him famous both in Hawai'i and on the Mainland. He didn't seek this fame, but the organizer of national folk festivals discovered him in Hawai'i and kept pestering Sproat until he agreed to attend an upcoming festival in Ohio.

"Joe Wilson seemed like just an old hayseed with a pot belly and a worn-out sleeve, with a deep Southern accent. I didn't know who he was. He's the head of the National Council for Traditional Arts in Washington D.C., and I just thought he was an old bean picker. He was a friendly guy.

"He said: 'How'd you like to go to Ohio?'

"I said: 'What for?'

"He said: 'They have a national folk festival in Ohio and I want you to go there.'

"I said: 'Joe, I just built a cabin in the valley and the farthest I'm going to go is to that cabin and back. I don't want to go to Ohio.'

"Every day he kept bugging me. He said: 'We need you to go to Ohio.'

"I said: 'No, Joe, I don't want to go anywhere.'

"We got down to when he was going to get on the airplane [to return to the Mainland] and he said: 'You know, Kindy, you're a stingy son of a bitch.'

"I said: 'Whoa, Joe, what's all this about?'

"He said: 'You know I'm a folklorist. I listen to you and you're one of the greatest in Hawai'i, and I've heard a lot of people, and you are great. You have so much to tell the people but you're a stingy son of a bitch and you don't want to share it.'

"I said: 'Okay, Joe. You struck a chord there. What can I say?'

"Six weeks later I was in Ohio."

He has now done these festivals for years. Been all over the country and even played at Carnegie Hall.

"What I love is when you meet people," he says characteristically. "I mean you don't know beans about them or their culture, but as soon as you strike a note and start singing and playing, there is a bond. Music is a glue that bonds people together."

ARTS AND CRAFTS

Art in the ancient days was utilitarian rather than "art for art's sake." Hawaiian artwork was found in *kapa* cloth designs, in wooden serving bowls, in intricate weaving for mats, in body tattoos, in carved musical instruments. The work was excellent, especially considering Hawaiian tools were stone—there is no metal found naturally in the Hawaiian Islands. Adzes and chisels were made from basalt and trachyte rock. Bamboo and bone were also utilized as needles, knives and chisels.

The bark cloth *(kapa)* that women pounded for clothes and bedding was the finest such cloth made in the Pacific. Each two-inch strip of bark could be pounded out to about six inches of "cloth," then that six inches was overlapped against another six-inch piece. In other Pacific islands, the overlapped section was an obvious seam; in Hawai'i, it was put together so flawlessly that no seam showed. Some of their *kapa* was as fine and thin as lace.

The colors used to dye *kapa* were also unmatched anywhere else. Browns and blacks were commonly used throughout Oceania, but Hawaiian women found the appropriate berries and flowers and roots to make yellows, greens, lavenders pinks and blues.

Oddly, the ancients didn't paint or draw with any of these colorful dyes. They were not interested in depicting portraits or nature scenes; their artwork was either utilitarian or religious, never done to wile away a day or create a masterpiece.

They did etch symbolic petroglyphs and paint primitive pictographs on rocks and beds of lava. In fact, nowhere else in the Pacific are there such large areas covered with so many petroglyphs as there are on the Big Island's lava beds. Yet, no one understands why they were made.

Most Oceanic art was created for religion or ritual, and that is true in Hawaiian sculpture. Wooden or stone *ki'i* (carved images) represented gods or spiritual concepts. An image of Kūkā'ilimoku, Kamehameha's guardian war god, was always carried into battle with the great warrior chief.

Generally, though, the *kiʻi* were found in temples.

Hawaiʻi's *kiʻi* are lauded as the best. Other Polynesian images lack the emotional intensity found in *kiʻi*. They're human figures, not animal, and they're carved with exaggerated features showing emotions, energy and a sense of movement to such an extent that the form becomes abstract.

Feather work: once again, nowhere else in the Pacific was an art so beautifully developed. Women wore feather *lei* around their necks; and feather standards, called *kāhili,* were the symbol of royalty. Only the nobility, the *aliʻi,* wore Hawaiʻi's famous capes, cloaks and helmets.

Captain Cook was apparently dazzled by the continual arrival of chiefs to his ship, all of them bedecked in splendid feathers. He was so impressed by the workmanship and design of the capes and cloaks that he bought several and was gifted with more to take back to England. Kamehameha I, then a young warrior, traded a cloak for nine of Cook's iron daggers.

Red signified royalty in Polynesia, but in Hawaiʻi, the royal color was yellow, because yellow feathers were rare. Kamehameha was the only person known to have a cloak made entirely of yellow feathers. It took about 80,000 birds and nearly a half-million feathers to make the famous cloak. Today, it is occasionally displayed at the Bishop Museum.

Weaving was an every day, ongoing art done by women. They used leaves from the *hala (pandanus)* tree for ordinary floor and sleeping mats; for more skillful, refined weaving, they used a sedge called *makaloa*. They did weave some baskets, but basketry was not highly developed in Hawaiʻi.

The simple art of stringing flowers together beautifully has been done all over the world, but it's best known in Hawaiʻi as *lei* making. A *lei* is not just a pretty adornment, it is a gift of *aloha.*

Flowers, leaves, bark, feathers, wood, stone. It was through nature that the ancients evolved all these arts.

PUANANI VAN DORPE
KAPA CLOTH MAKER

"I have seen Pua in Chicago examining *kapa* at the Field Museum, and I watched her start to cry," says Bob Van Dorpe. He is speaking of his wife, Puanani, who is the leading authority on *kapa,* Hawai'i's ancient bark cloth. "Some of the *kapa* was so fine, and done with such a high degree of excellence that she was moved by looking at it. She knows what went into it—she knows the labor."

As he speaks, there is a constant, primal beat, beat, beat, beat, beat in the background. His wife of four decades is doing what she does every day and has done nearly every day since her early forties—beating fibers like those that clothed her ancestors.

After eight, ten, eleven hours a day of steady beating, Pua's right arm aches, her back hurts, her shoulders burn, the foot she sits on all day is cramped and sore. Still, unconcerned about her pains and driven by an inner mission, she gets up the next morning and starts the cadence again. Beat, beat,

"The work was done almost exclusively by the women and that intrigues me. I want the world to know what that Hawaiian woman did and what she went through to produce the ultimate art piece in fiber arts. When I work, I feel like that Hawaiian woman, back in time. The more I discover [about *kapa*], the more I discover them—my ancestors. You're just so proud, you're just so honored to touch their work. All Hawaiian women share their honor, but they are the masters. Believe me, I could never do what they did. I'm just trying to follow in their footsteps."

beat, tap, tap, tap, her wooden mallet pounds down on tissue-thin fibers laid against a large wooden anvil.

No one writes banner headlines about a woman who sits in solitude beating an ancient craft back into existence. But Pua Van Dorpe certainly deserves the recognition. She has almost singlehandedly brought the craft of making *kapa* back from death. Others have made and researched *kapa,* but no one else in modern Hawai'i has dedicated her life to it. Before she began researching and experimenting, no one knew much about making *kapa.* And, when she began, neither did Pua.

"Nobody knew how to tell me how to make it. *Kūpunas* to teach you—none whatsoever," she says simply. "The craft had been dead for at least a hundred years when I picked it up."

Samuel Kamakau wrote in 1870: "All are dead who knew how to make coverings and loincloths and skirts and adornments and all that made the wearers look dignified and proud and distinguished."

"To know that you're doing something that your ancestors did on a daily basis—I guess that's what really motivates me: to bring life to what our ancestors did."

"Here was something that was lost in Hawai'i," Bob reiterates. "People talked about it, and people even got their doctorates writing about it, and the only muscles that they used relative to their knowledge was in their jaws. They did not heft one of the tools. They didn't know how to make it. Doing it was lost to the culture. We needed somebody who would dedicate her life to it, which Pua has done."

She has done so because she considers it her mission. She feels she was "selected" for this lifelong, seven-day-a-week task.

"I'm very proud I was selected. I think I had to be. This was not my quest," she says. "I can't get away from it now. I'm only happy when I beat *kapa.* I find myself very lucky to be able to do this—to love it, to have that desire to do it."

"If she goes with me to Honolulu," reports Bob, "by the second day she's impossible. She hasn't beaten and she has to get back to her work."

Her husband never begrudges her time spent on *kapa;* in fact, he is her biggest supporter.

"This woman is absolutely amazing," he says proudly. "Most people think it's a nice little hobby, but it's not. It's a very intense thing that she pursues with all of her abilities. She's been declared a 'Living Hawaiian Treasure' [in 1990]. Her work is absolutely fantastic. She's kept a record of everything she's done, step by step."

Bob and their long-time friend and neighbor, Herb Kāne, actually got Pua involved in the pursuit. In the early 1970s, the Van Dorpes were living in Fiji, where Bob was the project director developing a Fijian cultural center. Pua wasn't doing much more than playing golf, so both men encouraged her to investigate *kapa,* called *masi* in Fijian.

"She's like a *hānai* sister to me," explains Kāne. "I told her, as long as you're here, this is something the Hawaiians did also. The Hawaiian technique is much more polished, much more complex [than the Fijian], but the Fijians do have the same basic process. I said: 'Why don't you take the time and learn it?' Then I went away. I didn't realize how difficult it might be for her to do it."

No one writes banner headlines about a woman who sits in solitude beating an ancient craft back into existence.

The difficulty started immediately.

"I went to this small island of Vatulele in the Fijian Islands where the women just beat *masi,*" Pua recalls. "When I went there my thoughts were: 'Well, okay, I'm just going to do this for Bob and Herb and I'm going to please them. It's only going to be five days.' And I took my daughter with me; she was about five years old. I thought I was going to be on this lovely boat and just pampered. It turned out to be a small boat—bananas, pigs.

"Got there. Went through all the Fijian ceremonies accepting me because they had never taught anyone else how to make their *masi.* The only reason I was accepted was that one of the chief's nephews was working with my husband building the Fiji Cultural Center.

"A Fijian woman sat on the left-hand side of me, teaching, and I went through the motions—I started to beat. But I was more observing at the time. What I did learn is the reverence that they take in making their *masi.* It's their living; all they do is make *masi.* I didn't realize, at the time, that this was going to be my entire life too.

"There was no running water there [on Vatulele], no showers, no stores where you buy food. Using the outdoor bathroom was a big, big shock. At night they all gathered around in the living room, pitch black with kerosene lamps. The unity that happened around that lamp . . . they were all talking in their native tongue, and I said, 'Gee how lovely. This must have happened in my ancestor's time—where they talk story about their day.'

"When I got back home [in Fiji], I went to my bedroom. I locked myself in that bedroom for two days and went through cultural shock. I literally locked myself in for two days. Came out and started to try and remember what I had learned. And then it dawned on me—wait a minute—I understood from Herb and my husband that nobody was doing the Hawaiian *kapa*. The Fijians were teaching me how *masi* is made, not *kapa*.

"I used to dream at night and something would come. The next morning, I'd think: 'Try this, try that.'"

"I had played golf every single day for six years. I had not gone to Bob's culture center. I was not interested. I was interested in my golf. But I quit and I started to try and remember what the Fijian ladies had taught me. I never touched a golf club again."

After working with *masi* for about five or six months, Pua returned to Hawai'i to study her own culture's bark cloth.

"I went to the Bishop Museum [in Honolulu] and I looked hands-on at Hawaiian *kapa* and I realized it was something totally different. This was tissue-paper thin, soft, seamless. I could not do what I saw in Fiji because they're totally different; Hawaiian *kapa* is much more complex.

"I said, 'Well, I'm going to try.' So then I started to experiment. Then the quest began. I gathered everything I could think of, then I found out there wasn't a whole lot. It was disappointing, depressing."

"She was astonished to see how much finer Hawaiian *kapa* was than Fijian or anything else in the South Pacific," says Herb Kāne, "and how much more varied it was in its processes and design and textures and thinness. She started asking: 'How was this made?' And no one could answer her. She gathered all the accounts about *kapa* written by Europeans in the 1800s. They wrote about what they had seen, but none of these accounts had been tested. So she, with Bob helping her, set up a program of putting each one of these accounts to careful scientific tests."

"When I first started, frankly I didn't even know what the *wauke* plant looked like," Pua remembers.

The *wauke,* or paper mulberry plant, is tall and thin, and its bark provides two- to three-inch-wide strips of fiber. Other plants, like the *māmaki,* were also used, but *wauke* was the best. From these two- to three-inch strips, the ancients fashioned astonishingly elegant clothing and bed covers. Some of the thinnest, most expert *kapa* had the quality of lace.

The Hawaiians also had the most diversity of colors and dyes. While most islands are known for their blacks and browns, the Hawaiians had indigos, purples, yellows, greens, reds, and they even had pastels—pinks and light blues. They also used natural mordants to fix those dyes, mordants so good that colors still remain in the old pieces today.

"They always strived for excellence," says Pua of her ancestors. "I got really devoted to the craft as I discovered the unbelievable artistry of their work—how intricate and difficult the work really was. It is much more than just moving fibers."

In 1778, Captain James King, who was on Captain Cook's voyage, agreed. He wrote: "Their cloth . . . is painted in a variety of patterns, with a comprehensiveness and regularity of design that bespeaks infinite taste and fancy."

It was the women who beat the *kapa,* and that was part of the attraction for Pua. They worked in an enclosed area that was devoted strictly to *kapa* making. Since it's more like paper than cloth, a piece of *kapa* could not be washed, and *kapa* made into everyday clothing would generally last only a month, so the beating of *kapa* was ongoing, day after day.

"The work was done almost exclusively by the women and that intrigues me. I want the world to know what that Hawaiian woman did and what she went through to produce the ultimate art piece in the fiber arts. When I work, I feel like that Hawaiian woman, back in time.

"The more I discover [about *kapa],* the more I discover them—my ancestors. You're just so proud, you're just so honored to touch their work. All Hawaiian women share their honor, but they are the masters. Believe me, I could never do what they did. I'm just trying to follow in their footsteps.

"I'm still researching. I'm still doing new experiments, a lot of it with dyes. I'm still moving fibers and I guess I'll never be satisfied. I will not stop. It will take the rest of my life. And I love it."

One *kilohana* (bed cover) Pua worked on took 500 hours of beating. That was the large piece she wore wrapped around herself for the beatification ceremonies in Brussels for Father Damien de Veuster. Damien was the priest who devoted his life to the leprosy patients living on the island of Molokaʻi in the late 1800s. He died and was buried there, but 47 years later, his body was returned to Belgium, much to the dismay of the people he served in Hawaiʻi.

For his beatification towards sainthood in 1995, it was decided that his right hand should be returned to Molokaʻi. Pua was asked to make two pieces of *kapa* to cover the hand.

For her, the honor was great. As a child, she had been taught by Sacred Heart priests, the same sect that Damien belonged to, and as she says reverently: "Now here I am the one to wrap his hand." She flew to Brussels with a black and a white *kapa* cloth, and during the ceremony, was asked to wrap the reliquary.

Generally, she is not in the limelight like that. Her solitary work usually takes her no farther than her own country home on the Big Island. But there was one other occasion when her *kapa* skills pulled her to the forefront. This was in 1989 when she organized a group of women to make 1,018 *kapa* cloths to rebury the remains of 1,018 ancestors who had been dug up during construction of a new hotel on Maui. Once the remains were unearthed, the Hawaiians battled to have the hotel site moved off the cemetery grounds and to have the remains reinterred.

Pua spent a day at the burial grounds, and the next morning when she woke up, she knew immediately: "I had to do it. These were my ancestors. I had to do what I could for them. It was my duty. There was no one else to do it."

However, there was no way she could do it alone. So, she gathered ten women and taught them to beat—which they did for ten hours a day for four months. For her team, she accepted only women with Hawaiian in their genes. "I knew they could do it—it's in their blood," she explains. "It's their past."

Many men, particularly those involved in the *hula,* wanted to help, but Pua was firm: "No men. This has always been work reserved for women."

Even her husband, who knows so much about the craft, has never beat *kapa* himself.

"I've never picked up a tool and struck a piece of bast [woody fiber]," he admits.

"I wouldn't let him," Pua says firmly. "This is only for women."

Pua decided to treat all the bodies as if they were *aliʻi*. She took her group of women to an ancient *heiau* on Molokaʻi, a *heiau* she knew was reserved in ancient times for making *kapa* for the *ali'i*. After it was cleared of the brush growing on and around it, the *heiau* was opened for eight hours for Pua's team—eight hours of work, beating *kapa* in the hot sun.

When the cloth was ready, she had it all dyed black, a color reserved for *ali'i*, by soaking it in the black, muddy earth of Maui's *taro* fields. Once the women's work was done, the *kapa* was handed over to the men, who wrapped the remains.

Though the ten women working with her were dedicated to their project, Pua knew: "None of them could devote their entire lives to it, and that's what I would want. You have to live for *kapa*." As a result, she has only had two apprentices over the years, including her daughter KaPua.

She hopes, however, that her years of research will be used by future *kapa* makers. When she dies, her files will be given to the Bishop Estate, Kamehameha Schools.

"The research is ongoing. It will be my lifetime and then some. The experimentation is very hard. I think my Hawaiian ancestors were scientists, botanists, chemists."

Those who follow her will have the benefit of reams and reams of records and files. Pua has recorded all her experiments over the years, and most of her work has been purely experimental.

As Bob says: "She has notebooks tucked in corners. She stops every ten or fifteen minutes when she thinks she wants to record something because everything is an experiment. There are more experiments that have been failures than have been successes. That's because there was nobody she knew who was 250 years old that she could ask about it."

"My whole quest, my whole love is the research—how did they do it?" Pua asks dramatically. "The research is ongoing. It will be my lifetime and then some. The experimentation is very hard. I think my Hawaiian ancestors were scientists, botanists, chemists.

"There's so much to *kapa* making. It's not something that you hit, hit, hit and make a *kapa*. Every *kapa* is different. The research is never ending."

Her records show years of working the whole process: from stripping the bark off the trees, to soaking it in the ocean, to drying and bleaching it in the sun, to soaking it again in fresh stream water, and, of course, beating it between all the steps.

At first, Pua had no idea how long to soak the bark, how many days to dry it in the sun, how far she could stretch the bark by beating it. She did know, however, that she could never cut corners and do something "modern."

"You do it ancient and it never fails," she says. "You start doing modern and it never works. Everything I do is ancient. The dyes, everything."

The dying is a separate technology of its own—"another art form," as Pua says. Even though she has a whole filing cabinet full of her dying experiments, she claims she has hardly scratched the surface in learning to make and use the dyes.

Then there is the design work. In the final stages, the ancients pressed designs into the cloth, designs that were complicated and very artistic.

In 20 years she has unlocked 14 different techniques in making 14 different types of *kapa*. To make her *kapa* look exactly like that of the ancients, she studies pieces of museum *kapa* under a microscope and compares it to her own, continually refining her own until she can barely tell a difference between the old and the new.

One technique, an experiment with *māmaki* fiber, took her nine years to perfect. She says her heart nearly stopped when, under the magnified scrutiny of the microscope, her modern sample matched the fibers of the old. Such are the quiet victories celebrated in the Van Dorpe household.

Most of the time, the work is repetitive—the constant beat, beat, beat of a woman obsessed. Like her ancestors, she sits in a private outdoor enclosure, an extension to her home devoted strictly to *kapa*.

When she sits down to start a day's work, she first acknowledges the *'aumākua* (ancestral patrons) of *kapa*, Lauhiki and La'ahana. As she works, she faces the small altar dedicated to them and asks for their help.

"Because so much is unknown, I ask for help every day." She believes strongly that: "The path is guided. I know they're helping me. Before I beat I have a prayer—I ask [for help] every day before I start. I used to dream at night and something would come. The next morning, I'd think: 'Try this, try that.'"

Does she get bored sitting in the same position, listening to the same rhythm of her own beating hour after hour for twenty-some years?

"No," she answers firmly. "My mind is right here [on the work]. This takes all my mind. It is a lot of work. But the finished product is very rewarding. To know that you're doing something that your ancestors did on a daily basis—I guess that's what really motivates me: to bring life to what our ancestors did."

By bringing *kapa* back to life, Pua Van Dorpe has become the living link between the ancestral time and today.

"It's not easy," she says. "But it's my heritage. I can't not do it."

MARIE McDONALD
LEI MAKER AND AUTHOR

"Be careful what you name your children," the Hawaiians of old would admonish. "They will live up to it, even when they don't know."

That is certainly the case with Marie Emelia Leilehua McDonald. As a child, she didn't know the story of her name and often wondered why she had such an ordinary Hawaiian name as Leilehua, which refers to a common *lei* made of flowers from the *'ōhia-lehua* tree.

"There were so many people called Lei and so many called Lehua," Mrs. McDonald says, remembering how she complained to her mother about her name. "Then I found out my name is not just a wreath of *lehua* blossoms."

As a young teenager she left Moloka'i, where she was raised, to attend Honolulu's Kamehameha School for native Hawaiian children. "Everybody there had all these wonderful Hawaiian names," she recalls. "So, when I went home, I asked my mom: 'Why did you give me this very commonplace

"It [the *lei*] appeared in the fields with the farmer when he invoked the blessing of the gods upon his fields and crops; it was a necessary ornament for the dancer; it was worn by the nursing mother; it was used in the healing rites of the *kahuna lapa'au*, the healing priest. It was the mark of chiefly rank. It was offered to the gods. It was a symbol of love and lovemaking. It belonged to the festivals and it brightened up the routine of daily life as well. Children made them. Men and women made them. Gods and goddesses favored them. The poets sang their praises."

name?' When she told me the story, I felt so much bigger and better than all those kids in Honolulu.

"She told me I was half of a set of twins and shortly after we were born, my twin brother died. So my great-grandmother gave me this name, and the meaning of it is 'the strong child.' Throughout my life I've felt I'm two, not one, because I don't have my brother. And I'm bigger in stature than all the girls in my family. And I feel I've been gifted with twice as many gifts. I am the strong child."

Years later, Leilehua took on an even more profound meaning for her when a Hawaiian man she'd never met approached her as she was making a *lei* during a demonstration in a county park. He asked her in Hawaiian what her name was. She just happened to be making a *lehua lei* at the time, and when she told him her name, he responded prophetically: "Leilehua poetically means *lei* expert."

Mrs. McDonald is, in fact, Hawai'i's foremost *lei* authority. She spent seven years researching and writing her book, *Ka Lei,* published in 1978 and still the premier work on the subject. For her dedication to her art, she received a National Heritage Fellowship Award in 1990 from the National Endowment for the Arts, an award recognizing her contribution to Hawaiian culture. Then, in 1992, she was named a "Living Hawaiian Treasure."

"Just living up to my name—that's what I'm doing," she says with a laugh, and, as a matter of fact, the *lei* made of red *lehua* flowers is her favorite. "My *tūtū* [grandmother] knew what she was doing. She gave me the right name."

How can one say much about a necklace of flowers? How can one write an entire book about flower/shell/nut/seed/bone *lei?*

Marie McDonald has no trouble doing either. *Ka Lei* is 180 pages of photos, legends, personal stories and research on the whys, the hows, the mythology, the traditions, the history of this very Hawaiian tradition. Just a few of her anecdotes prove how a body ornament can become a truly rich custom.

• Never give a pregnant woman a tied *lei.* Hawaiians believe that the fetus might strangle.

• A *lei hala* (made from the *pandanus* tree's fruit) should never be given to a campaigning politician—that could signal defeat.

• The leathery-leafed, shiny green *maile lei* is a favorite of the gods. It's believed that if you smell *maile* where you don't see it, that area is the site of an ancient temple.

• Since the red *lehua* flower is sacred to Pele, goddess of the volcanoes, the *lei lehua* is often tossed into the volcano's smoking cauldron as an offering to Pele. However, picking the blossoms en route to the crater might bring rain, so it's best to make the *lei* on site.

• *Tī* leaf *lei* were worn to cleanse and to ward off evil spirits. The *kāhuna* (priests) wore them for ritual and for healing work.

• *Lei* of the beach morning glory vine *(pōhuehue)* supposedly has magical, bewitching powers. Surfers beat the ocean with these *lei* to incite big waves. Fisherman beat the sea with them to scare fish into their nets.

• A sick person would wear a seaweed *lei (lei limu kala)* into the ocean, and, as the *lei* floated off, so might the person's ills.

When the culture was thriving, in ancient time, the *lei* was ubiquitous. In her book, she writes: "It appeared in the fields with the farmer when he invoked the blessing of the gods upon his fields and crops; it was a necessary ornament for the dancer; it was worn by the nursing mother; it was used in the healing rites of the *kahuna lapaʻau,* the healing priest. It was the mark of chiefly rank. It was offered to the gods. It was a symbol of love and lovemaking. It belonged to the festivals and it brightened up the routine of daily life as well. Children made them. Men and women made them. Gods and goddesses favored them. The poets sang their praises."

Of her own time, she writes: "My recollections of how the *lei* has influenced my life are not unique stories. Anyone who has been born or has grown up or has come to live in Hawaiʻi is influenced by the *lei* in much the same manner as I and can probably tell countless more stories. And this is the real significance of the *lei*. It has universal appeal."

In giving a *lei,* one shows respect and love for someone else. "It isn't just a means of ornamenting the body. More important, we make a *lei* and present it to honor our fellow man," Mrs. McDonald says. "You do it with care, and care, to me, is high regard for the person for whom you're making it."

"I told [deceased national journalist] Charles Kuralt that one of the reasons we present *lei* is to honor accomplishment. He said to me: 'My first time in Honolulu, I didn't do anything great, I was just passing through. I was a nobody, but they gave me a *lei.*' And I said: 'No, you were somebody. No one is a nobody!'"

One does need to present the appropriate *lei,* however. As an example of the wrong *lei* at the wrong time, Mrs. McDonald tells this story on herself: "I went to visit my mother in the hospital during the last days of her life, and I had all these plumeria *lei* that were given to me, so I took them to her thinking she would enjoy them. Oh, she sent me out of there fast. She said: 'Get out of here. Get out of here.' She ordered me to get rid of the *lei,* so I took off the *lei* and I went back and she said: 'I said stay out of here.' I still smelled like plumeria. My brother Dick said: 'Stupid. It's *make* man flower.'"

Since the plumeria flower can grow in dry, poor soil, it's often found in cemeteries, and thus it's called "*make* man's *lei*"—dead man's *lei*.

"You look at the older cemeteries and you find they have a lot of plumeria trees," Mrs. McDonald notes. "Hawaiians made *lei* with the flowers and gave them to the dead. They didn't have embalming in country places like Keʻanae or Hāna or Kaʻū. You had to go too far to get them embalmed. So, if the body was left for viewing, the scent of death was disguised with sweet-smelling flowers, and one they used most often was plumeria."

Hawaiʻi is known as the land of *lei,* but, in fact, *lei* have always been a worldwide tradition.

"The whole idea of the *lei* probably originated on the Asian continent," Mrs. McDonald says. "There are many southern Asian people that still do *lei* of some kind—the Indians, the Thais. Evidence of floral *lei* were found in the tomb of King Tut.

"The Greeks had *lei*. They made *lei* for their heads and gave *lei* to honor some kind of accomplishment. They presented *lei* at the Olympic games. They gave their great statesmen *lei* of olive or laurel. And the olive and laurel *lei* are very much like our *maile lei,* so there is a connection there.

"As people settled the Pacific, they took the idea with them and at each point the *lei* changed a little bit, so by the time it came to Hawaiʻi, like so many of the other arts and crafts of the Pacific Island people, the Hawaiians fully developed the idea of the *lei*.

"In studying some of the other Pacific islands, I found that they may have maybe one or two, maybe three different methods of *lei* making. Hawaiians had six. One of the reasons could be that Hawaiʻi has higher islands with mountains, [thus] a greater variety of plants. On a low, flat coral island, an atoll, you wouldn't have many flowers. We have the conditions to grow a lot of different plants."

As a result: "It's Hawaiʻi that has made the *lei* world renowned. So if you mention *lei,* you don't think of these other places, you think of Hawai'i."

Still, Mrs. McDonald worries that this very local tradition may lose its Hawaiian distinction if Hawaiian resources are not cultivated and protected.

"Can you imagine being greeted at Honolulu airport with a fresh orchid *lei* made in Singapore or Thailand?" she asks as an example. "We may have revived our arts in the past 30 years, but we've done little to protect the raw materials needed to perform them. For instance, we import gourds to make *hula* drums, *lau hala* for plaiting, feathers, *kukui* nuts, even flowers for *lei*. The list of endangered plants includes a number of *lei* plants. If we are to survive as a culture, we have to nurture our cultural practices and protect our environment."

She wants to save endangered endemic plants, but that doesn't mean Mrs. McDonald shuns the use of introduced plants for *lei* making. The ancient Hawaiians made *lei* with whatever was available, and so do good *lei* makers today.

"I do not resist using introduced materials," Mrs. McDonald says. "I think that is a sign of your creativity. I do consider *lei* making an art; I don't consider it some mundane ordinary thing, not the way we make *lei*. If you are creative, you would use any introduced material, and that has been our history.

"We make a lei *and present it to honor our fellow man."*

"When archaeologists and historians dig up and study the fossils of our time a few thousand years hence, they will be able to tell the difference between us and our forebears. We would have each left definite, different marks on our cultural patterns by creatively using new and different materials.

"When Hawaiians select materials for *lei,* first of all they select them for fragrance, and, secondly, they select them for color, then movement. The *lei* is used to ornament the dance. In the dance there's movement, so if you wear a *lei* that moves, it tends to attract attention. If it laid still, you probably wouldn't look at the expression on the dancer's face. But because it moves, it attracts you.

"*Lei hala* [fruitlets from the *pandanus* or *hala* plant] was one of those frequently used in the dance. In my research, I found there is more written about the *hala lei* than any other *lei*. It has nice fragrance and the fragrance lingers, especially on bare skin. Just like *maile*. Even if you take a bath you can smell it, if it was worn next to your skin. It has oils in the leaves that stick to the skin. *Maile* smells better after it's been worn on the skin.

"When dancers gathered in the wilds, they were very careful in gathering material because those things they gathered were *kino lau* or another form of their patron [goddess Laka]. So they wouldn't stomp all over the plants or tear up the forest, knowing that this was another form of the patron, the being they were honoring with their dance. They would collect only what they needed.

"I do consider lei *making an art; I don't consider it some mundane ordinary thing, not the way we make* lei."

"Before the collection they would offer prayers and receive permission to pick the materials. Then they had a whole ceremony in getting ready to perform. Every time they put on certain apparel there was a chant that went with it."

In one sentence in her book, Mrs. McDonald describes the importance of the *lei* to the *hula:* "Through the *lei*, the dancer is inspired to perform magnificently for the *lei* is *kino lau* [a form] of Laka herself."

A very special, quite profound, ancient *lei* is the *lei niho palaoa*, a hook-shaped pendant carved from a sperm whale tooth attached to thin braids of human hair. It is not just any human hair; it is hair made from the ancestors of the person wearing it.

In her book, McDonald writes: "It was worn as a mark of social rank, and passed on to bind one generation to another and still another to insure one's heritage and one's all-important family ties. It is believed that the tongue-shaped pendant represented the authority of the ruling class."

From her childhood, she remembers: "The first time I saw one of these I was 14. I said: 'What, they used human hair? Ugh. How cannibalistic, how savage.'

"Maybe at 14 you don't quite understand, since my education up to this point, and even until I was in college, was completely Westernized, lacking any or little knowledge of my cultural heritage.

"But the hair in these awesome *lei* was not just anybody's hair. The hair came from people in the family. The number of strands increased with a new generation in that family. They kept something from all these generations and wore it. After I learned that, then I felt quite differently. It is a token of kinship.

"It is believed that the women wore the bigger *lei,* many more coils of human hair and bigger tongue-shaped pendants."

Today most *lei niho palaoa* are found only in museums, and Mrs. McDonald has only once found one for sale. She didn't buy it because: "I wouldn't wear one if I wasn't connected [to the family]."

People often ask her how to make a flower *lei* "last," and she has a hard time keeping herself from flippantly answering: "Bronze it."

She explains: "It really bothers me because that's not the reason for the *lei*— that it should last forever. What should last is the thought, the reason for giving that *lei,* the thought that went into it. Words can be beautiful, but sometimes 'I love you' is not enough. If you say it with something as beautiful as a *lei,* you know there's a lot of power in that."

ELIZABETH LEE
LAU HALA WEAVER

"I do put my love in my work because this is what comes from my heart and I want to share it. If you don't give what you have from your heart, sharing all what you have, it don't mean anything."

Elizabeth Lee started out more than 50 years ago weaving hats that sold for 20 cents a piece. Today, she sells her best *lau hala* hats for $600 to $1,000. She is one of the last, and best, of a very scarce breed—the *lau hala* weavers of Kona Coast on the island of Hawai'i, commonly called the Big Island.

One of her apprentices, Lynne Hanks, a younger weaver who lives on Maui, says it is an honor to work with someone with such talent and character.

"At first, I didn't realize how lucky I was that Auntie Elizabeth asked me to apprentice with her," Hanks says. "She is the best. By far the best. She's very humble, so you couldn't get her to say that, but her work is just phenomenal. The hat she wears—no one does that anymore. It's very fine weaving. It's an Elizabeth Lee hat—it's a coveted item like Stetsons and Baileys and Panama hats. Like an antique, it will only increase in value.

"And now I've found out what an incredible person she is too. I learn so much more than weaving from her. She's so open. Every hat she makes is a piece of love. She doesn't just whip these things out. Every piece comes from her heart."

"I do put my love in my work because this is what comes from my heart and I want to share it," says Auntie Elizabeth. "If you don't give what you have from your heart, sharing all what you have, it don't mean anything."

She is one of the last, and best, of a very scarce breed.

Lau hala weaving was an important craft in old Hawai'i. *Lau hala* are the leaves (three to four feet long), of the *hala* tree, called screw-pine in English (genus *Pandanus*). The *hala* tree was so important in Polynesia that it's believed the Tahitians brought it to Hawai'i when they settled here. They used *lau hala* to make baskets, to thatch houses, to make floor mats and sleeping mats, and to make sails for voyaging canoes.

With the introduction of Western items like beds, carpets and canvas, this time-consuming craft fell in importance and some of the old techniques were lost. For instance, it's no longer known how to weave sails that won't tear in ocean winds, sails that can endure a long sailing voyage.

Hat weaving, though it too nearly died out, has held on with a tiny toehold thanks to old-timers like Auntie Elizabeth. "Who else is going to do it?" she asks rhetorically. "Especially now. I like to perpetuate our culture because it's important for our young people to learn all this. We have the Western, we have our culture and we really don't know where we're standing. I feel myself that I am responsible to share this art with the young people.

"I can't take it with me. To be honest with you, that's why a lot of our artwork has been lost. I remember way back, I can hear them saying: 'I'm going to teach you this thing, but don't you teach someone else because this is ours—our pattern, my pattern, my style of hat.' And look what we have today: we have not much left.

"I find there's so much hunger out there of young people who want to learn. I like to teach as many people as I can."

Even she, however, gave it up for a while. It no longer seemed vital in the world she grew into. Elizabeth had made hats since she was a child of six, but, by the 1950s, the effort seemed too much for too little money. The sugar and pineapple plantations had once bought *lau hala* hats for their workers, but now factory-made hats could be had cheaper and quicker.

"After World War II, the *lau hala* hat was not needed because money was coming in so good," she says. "You worked, you had 50 cents an hour, four bucks a day. People got lazy. They didn't want to do hard work. They think *lau hala* is

trash. They didn't think it was valued. So no one was weaving. Myself, I wasn't weaving because it wasn't in demand.

"In the 1960s, I thought I should go back and start weaving for my family. I started thinking, if I wasn't going to do this, I was going to lose it. Good thing I didn't lose my [hat] molds and my mother's strippers."

During that decade she was "discovered" by the State Foundation on Culture and the Arts, an organization trying to revive interest in things Hawaiian. Since then, Auntie Elizabeth has become one of the most famous *lau hala* weavers in the state.

"I was nobody at one time," she says of her current fame. "The *lau hala* brought me where I am today. I'm very thankful for it. I thank the Lord—for all I have today, He has given. He's given me the desire and strength and the inspiration. I'm thankful that I could share this knowledge. I didn't realize it was something important until now.

"I never had much education. When we first went to school [she and her brother], we were quite frightened because we didn't know how to speak English. We were too shy and afraid. It was hard. Those who knew how to speak English, the Western language, would feel they were better than we were. In those days none of the Hawaiian kids spoke English, we spoke pidgin. No one could help us at home—we taught our parents to speak pidgin. We were like country jacks."

Until she went to school, Elizabeth spoke only Hawaiian, then amongst her classmates she learned pidgin, and in school she was taught English. Pidgin in Hawai'i developed when numerous races, all speaking their own languages, came to work the sugar plantations in the late 1800s and early 1900s. It is a compilation of words from several languages, mostly English, with its own grammar and syntax.

"Now through my *lau hala,* I'm brave enough to go out and speak the best I can," she says.

Auntie Elizabeth came from a family of 14 siblings. Her father was a lawyer and a judge, but, as babies, she and one brother were adopted by her father's cousins, people who weren't as well off, though that never mattered to Elizabeth. *Hānai* (adopted) children are common in Hawai'i.

"I'm really thankful for what happened—my adopted parents took me and raised me. My aunt [her adopted mother] couldn't get any children. My parents were having too many children. So they asked my Dad. They shared what they had. At the time people got together and took care of each other's children. There was no separation. Hawaiians were like a family. There was a lot more closeness, there was more love and discipline. There was no 'This is my child and you don't touch my child.' We don't have the closeness today that we had before.

"I feel it was an advantage for me. We were raised very natural, not with everything on a silver platter. We worked for what we had. Our dad was a very important man in the district, served in the legislature, served on the judge's bench. He was an attorney. They were much more comfortable than us, but we didn't think about that.

"We were raised very Hawaiian. We were taught to economize. There was no wasting. Like water—you had to be very careful using the water because we depended on catchment from the rain.

"In those days we never had any doctor bills. My mother knew what kind of medicine for a cough or a cold or for a fever or chicken pox. If we had fever blisters, she would know what herbs to get.

"We had *taro* and sweet potatoes and that was what we were raised on. There was nothing from the store like canned goods. We ate the *taro* shoots and the stem and the green leaves. There was a lot of vitamins in there, which we didn't know. We just ate it because that's all we had to eat. We had the same food every day.

"Papa would go out hunting wild pig. And in those days the land was so free for everybody to go; there was nobody to come and say private property.

"Fish and seaweed, we ate anything from the ocean. In those days, when they throw a net, there was so much fish. One or two throws is enough for the family. We just take what we need, and throw back the rest. No waste. Today you can't get enough, even two throws.

"During the week we pull *taro*, and the weekend we start preparing to cook *taro*. Saturday we spend just pounding the *poi*, at least half the day. We had like competition. My brother has the advantage of pounding the *poi* with our papa and I'm with our mama. We each have our big pounding boards. My brother and dad have the big one. We pound the *taro* and smack the stone on our hand and you hear the pop in the *poi*. And it's fun. Just to hear the sound in the *poi,* who makes the loudest sound, who makes the smoothest *poi,* who makes the biggest *pūkele* [amount]."

Her *hānai* mother taught little Elizabeth and her brother to weave. After working in the *taro* fields during the day, the whole family would sit and weave at night.

"We didn't think why in those days. We just did it. It was part of our livelihood. It wasn't considered a woman's art," she explains. "It was considered a family art. At age six I remember my mother putting me to work. In those days there were two things: farming and weaving. My mama would weave mats just for sleeping. Then there were mats we would walk on or weave on. Only time you could go back into the bedroom was when it was time to sleep. Every one of us had our own little mat on top of a big mat. When we get up in the morning we roll it up and put it away. No beds, sleep directly on the floor. Sleeping on the floor was good for the body, makes your bones get stronger. Sleeping on something soft, they don't believe in that, because you get too relaxed and your body gets too soft, doesn't make your body strong. They had their own imaginations.

"I'm thankful that I could share this knowledge. I didn't realize it was something important until now."

"The hats were very important in those days for the plantations. They didn't have the hats of today, they depended on *lau hala* hats. You can't believe this—it was 20 cents a hat. We would be out in the field in the daytime and at night we would be weaving. Maybe we would make half a hat a night. We didn't make it as our job. *Taro* was much more important than the *lau hala* hat.

"My mama would get the crown first and put it on the block, and at six and a half years old, I would start from that. The difficult part is adding, splicing in those little pieces.

"You know how kids are, you want to play. But when Mama talks to you, you better listen, and she'd tell you, 'If you're not going to work now, there's no food on the table.' So, we have to change our attitude, and go back to work—whether it's digging the hole to plant the *taro* or peel the sweet potatoes or weaving."

The work of weaving and prepping the *lau hala* leaves has not changed since ancient times. The leaves are taken off the ground or from the tree when they're brown. Some will already have rot or mildew and most will be dirty and buggy. And, to make matters tougher, the leaves are ridged with very sharp thorns that must be stripped off.

"It's hard work," Auntie Elizabeth readily admits. "It's a lot of work before doing the weaving—stripping it, taking the thorns off, selecting the best."

Her student, Lynne Hanks, is more graphic in her description: "The first day she taught me to prep the *lau hala*, I looked like I'd been in a cat fight. Those thorns are vicious. She makes it look easy but it takes a lot of practice. She's a master weaver. Like she said, this is nasty work. Hard nasty work."

"During the picking of the leaves there's lots of cockroaches, lizards, spiders. They come with the *lau hala*," Auntie Elizabeth laughs.

"You gather the *lau hala*, you cut the stem, take the tip off. You have to size the *lau hala*. This piece is not good," she says, picking up a few pieces to demonstrate. "You see all those spots there? This is water rot inside of it. The *lau hala* is old. This part here is mildew. This crack here is dry rot. I will not use this for a hat. If you're working it, it will be breaking. This type of *lau hala* is a waste of time because it is already rot. This one is beautiful *lau hala*.

"Some people like dark *lau hala,* but they forget that the *lau hala* is waterlogged and that's what turns the color.

"I normally wipe the leaves down with water and disinfectant because of all the accumulation of bugs and dirt that's under the tree. Then we start rolling it up. We soften it up with a knife [she smoothes it over a knife to demonstrate]. Of course in the old days the Hawaiians didn't have knives, but they used bones, pieces of wood. After that, we strip it [into narrow, long strips for weaving].

"Lot of people they say they like the *lau hala* that grows down at the beach. I don't believe it. It's not my favorite. The *lau hala* at the beach grows in the salt air all through the life of the leaves. That much salt air is built in the *lau hala*. The doctor says salt is no good for you. And to me, it's no good for the plant either. It could be used—I don't say don't use it, I do use—but it's not the best *lau hala*.

"Kona has the best *lau hala*. In all the years I've worked, I still say I like to work with the Kona *lau hala*. It's because it's sun dried. Hilo is too wet. The *lau hala* gets so logged with rain. And the *lau hala* there is not as strong as in Kona."

Auntie Elizabeth signs the inside of every hat she makes. She also includes her phone number and the date she made the hat.

Her best hats, the $600 to $1,000 tightly woven types, take her two weeks to finish, from prepping to weaving. What she calls "regular street hats"—the $60 to $100 ones—she can weave in an hour and a half.

"It all depends on what size weave," she says. "If it's a Kona hat, the short brimmed hat, I make five or six hats a day—that's when I'm concentrating, that's when I get all the crowns made and put them all on a block and put my whole time on it. It all depends on how large and how fine. The finer and more intricate weave takes about two days, eight, ten hours a day. It takes time. You need a lot of patience.

"Some people, they don't see the workmanship in the hat because they've not tried it, and a lot of people think it's straw—something you just pick up and weave. Those who know about crafts will appreciate it. At one time, people think it's just a hat. But this generation is trying to appreciate the artwork. It's a piece of art."

CANOE

It was the ancient, sea-faring canoes that originally brought the Polynesians to Hawai'i, and it is the canoe that has symbolically brought modern Hawaiians back to their culture.

In their 80- to 100-foot canoes, the ancients discovered island after island by voyaging across huge distances on the largest body of water on Earth, the Pacific Ocean. Their ocean exploration occurred while the Europeans still thought the Earth was flat.

Once they discovered all the Pacific islands, the Polynesians apparently ended their long-distance traveling. Centuries ago they stopped building the long canoes; they needed only smaller fishing and war canoes. Then, when Europeans began arriving in the late 1700s, they introduced modern ships with navigational instruments, so a return to traditional deep-sea canoe voyaging was never even considered. Until . . .

The 1970s when the revival of the canoe created the greatest story in modern Hawai'i. As Jo-Anne Sterling says in this chapter: "To understand the Hawaiian renaissance, you must understand the *Hōkūle'a*."

Hōkūle'a was a replica of the ancient double-hulled canoes. Initially, it was built to prove a scientific point: that the early Polynesians were capable of navigating from Tahiti to Hawai'i, a month-long voyage. At the time, many anthropologists argued that the early people were too primitive to be so accomplished; that, instead, they had merely drifted, or accidentally bumped into Hawai'i.

Hōkūle'a's first journey disproved this notion. But there was more to *Hōkūle'a* than scientific discovery. To the Hawaiians, she represented a great culture now nearly obliterated. With her birthing voyages in the 1970s came an emotional rebirth of that culture.

Jo-Anne Sterling believes: "The conception of *Hōkūle'a* was the cause of all the Hawaiian renaissance. . . . It all came about because of that canoe."

Jo-Anne Kahanamoku Sterling
Leon Paoa Sterling

Feather Worker, Hōkūle'a Crew

"I'm not a *kupuna*," Jo-Anne Kahanamoku Sterling says with characteristic bluntness. "It's not vanity; I'm still on my journey. My concept of *kupuna* is someone who is learned. It is a time of mastery. So when I say I'm still on my journey, I'm still in the learning process.

"Maybe I'm making too much of it, but why is the terminology used in the first place?" she asks rhetorically. "It was never used as freely when I was growing up. Perhaps today it's more out of respect."

"Identity," Leon Paoa Sterling answers succinctly, then adds with humor: "I have to add that to my resume: I'm a *kupuna*. I'm now *makule* [aged, old], and I know all.

"But you don't," he says, turning serious, "because every day the sun rises, every day is a new day. Every day you find something new. If you don't grasp what was given that day or during that hour or during that minute, if you lose it, then you erase it, because you won't find it again, because a new

". . . Being able to be one with the universe. Being able to experience infinity, which I have on the canoe. I cannot describe the emotion. It's like a tremendous connection between you and the universe, a feeling of oneness—very serene, very contented."

Jo-Anne

"Every day the sun rises, every day is a new day. Every day you find something new. If you don't grasp what was given that day or during that hour or during that minute, if you lose it, then you erase it, because you won't find it again, because a new day is arising. For someone to say 'I am all of what is' is wrong, because the sun rises the next day—there's a new day, a new dawn, a new sunset."

Leon

day is arising. For someone to say 'I am all of what is' is wrong, because the sun rises the next day—there's a new day, a new dawn, a new sunset."

Kūpuna or not, the Sterlings do understand why others tag themselves with titles.

"You have to remember the renaissance of the early 1970s when the revival of the Hawaiian culture began," Jo-Anne explains. "When the renaissance started, everybody started putting labels on everybody.

"All of a sudden you had this newfound Hawaiian-ness in all the Hawaiians. It was an elation of joy and self-gratification to attach oneself to a culture which for years suffered a degree of suppression. What emerged out of this is that our history and our language are now being taught. Also, Hawaiian men became involved in cultural things—dance, building canoes, writing songs. We all became Hawaiian again."

Jo-Anne Kahanamoku Sterling found her own "Hawaiian-ness" and identity through various modes over the years, but one of the most important has been via the art of feather work. She is renowned island-wide for her skill in an ancient medium she perpetuates with very few others.

In the past, feather capes, helmets and standards signified the chiefly class, so feather workers held important status in society. "It really was one of the most prestigious art forms—then and now," Jo-Anne says.

"The mere beauty of those objects like the capes and cloaks—my God, to think that centuries ago they developed those things," she marvels. "There was no metal here, no precious gems, so feathers became very prestigious objects. Chiefs that went into battle wore their cloaks as a form of identification."

Jo-Anne was initially attracted by the color, design and quality of the originals she saw in museums. "How could they put these things together? So tiny as they are," she still wonders. "Today I don't see that quality, not even in my own work."

The feathers used in ancient times came from small native birds found only in Hawai'i. Their feathers were painstakingly sewn on rope or cord backings. Now, with many of these native species endangered or extinct, today's feather workers use plumage from more common birds like pheasant, chicken, goose and peacock.

Few others do this tedious work. "It's for the serious minded," she says. "Feather work is an attitude. It's not for everybody. You can't afford to be distracted. I can't do my feather work when my husband is home. I have to be completely by myself. I get lost in the whole thing. It's really a mind set."

Jo-Anne's husband (and fourth cousin) has a mind set about his own work too. Leon is a man of the sea—captain, longshoreman, crewman, fisherman, merchant marine—whatever job it takes to keep him on the water.

"I grew up on Oʻahu, Molokaʻi and the Big Island," Leon says. "Life basically has been very close to the ocean, mostly on it. Being in the water. Daily. If I don't see the water, I don't feel right. The *kai moana*. *Kai* is water. *Moana* is ocean. A place where you cannot see an island. My home is the water and any vessel I'm on. To see land is the end, or a big stop sign."

"The water is better for him. The land energy screws him up," agrees Jo-Anne with a laugh.

Apparently, the ocean is his heritage—his ancestors were as dedicated as he is. Leon's middle name is Paoa, and, like Leon, the early Paoas were seamen and navigators. Leon finds descendants of these early Paoas on island after island as he sails around the Pacific.

"We somewhat live yesterday in combination with today."

"In Rarotonga [one of the Cook Islands], there's a special place where they say the canoes left to migrate to New Zealand," Leon says. "It is sacred, and there are stones to depict the canoes, seven canoes, that left. One of those canoes was navigated by a Paoa.

"When I was in New Zealand there was this elderly woman that greeted us and she noticed a whale's tooth I had around my neck and inscribed in this whale's tooth was the name Paoa. And she asked me, 'Where did you get that name?' And I said, 'It is my name.' And she said, 'It is my name also.' This New Zealand Maori. She said, 'I have to go to Auckland, I'll come back.' And she returned two days later, and what she returned with was a genealogy [of Paoas] pertaining to canoes with the name of the navigator and or captain [all Paoas] and it went back 87 generations."

In Tahiti Leon even found another Leon Paoa, but this Leon had fallen from his dignified heritage—the Tahitian owned a pool hall.

Jo-Anne's people, the Kahanamokus, were watermen of a different sort—her father and his six brothers were well-known surfers in the early 1900s. The most famous of them, her uncle Duke Paoa Kahanamoku was a swimming star in four

Olympics and held all the top Olympic swimming records until 1924 when Johnny Weissmuller of Tarzan fame beat his record by one second in the 100-meter freestyle. Jo-Anne's father, Sam Alapai Kahanamoku, was a freestyle sprinter in the Paris Olympics of 1924.

Today, their personal family histories merge in importance with their cultural history. Since the Hawaiian renaissance, Hawai'i's past has become an integral part of its present, and this has changed the lives of the Sterlings. Since the early 1970s, they have become leaders in this movement towards cultural integrity.

"We somewhat live yesterday in combination with today," is how Jo-Anne puts it. Hawaiians, she says, want to honor and respect their past, yet they do have to live in the present world.

"The water, the cleansing, the purification. It has been my journey."

"We can't go back," Jo-Anne says, but they're both emphatic that the culture can go forward. They renewed their own roots and sailed forward during the 1970s via the *Hōkūle'a*.

"The canoe is the most important artifact in the Pacific Ocean. It was the mode of travel, of migration," Jo-Anne says. "I still believe that the conception of *Hōkūle'a* was the cause of all the Hawaiian renaissance. Men were not dancing prior to the 1970s, songs were not being written, language was not in the schools, history was never in the schools. Every aspect, I don't care whether it's food or dance or songs or whatever, it all came about because of that canoe. It brought out the dormant, the things that were asleep for a long while, and made it very, very exciting."

It certainly was for the Sterlings. After *Hōkūle'a's* triumphant return from Tahiti in 1976, they crewed a six-month tour that sailed throughout the Hawaiian Islands to introduce the canoe to its proud and inquisitive people.

"I always refer to the canoe as an ancestral spaceship. It brought back those kinds of feelings," Jo-Anne remembers. "We took the canoe all over the place. The people were so amazed to see it."

The Sterlings and two other men sailed from island to island, picking up fresh crew members as they went, giving new people a chance to learn the old ways of sailing. And in each port, they were greeted by thousands of the thrilled and curious who came to see how their ancestors had done it.

"We sailed the canoe from port to port, and she supported us," Jo-Anne says. "We did it about six months. People brought food, people donated money, people invited us into their homes. None of us had any money. Leon had to fly back and forth. He was the only one working. He'd run back to Kona to go work and come back during the weekdays."

Being one of the few crew members adept at sea, Leon's expertise was needed in the beginning. Most of the early crews were brand new.

"We have a lot of mileage on this canoe," Jo-Anne says of herself and Leon. "Thousands and thousands of miles, sailing throughout the Pacific. By 1980, you had to qualify to be on the canoe. We had to work on the canoe in dry dock, repair it, go on day sails. We had to know everything about that canoe, from the bottom up. We had extensive training, and had to know the dos and don'ts of the other island traditions. We were very strict as to our behavior, attitudes, team playing."

Leon has captained numerous voyages throughout the years, beginning during the 1977 educational tour. And Jo-Anne has been one of his crew members several times.

"Word got out—this guy knows something about sailing, about the ocean, he knows how to handle the canoe," Leon explains of his role on *Hōkūle'a*. "I don't consider myself captain—*kāpena* they call you in Hawaiian. My nickname on the canoe was 'Asshole.'"

"Leon, let's not get into that," Jo-Anne groans, covering her face. "He's a very complex, very indepth person. He's usually very quiet."

But he's on a roll. He can't resist: "Hard ass and s-o-b. You name it. Because I won't play. I don't have time to play. If I'm in charge of that canoe, it's my job to ensure that everyone is safe, that the vessel is safe, that the vessel is in tune with what she has to deal with."

Jo-Anne: "Can I interrupt? Just to understand what he is talking about. First of all, the canoe is a double hull, it's not a luxury canoe, it's a working canoe. You're in adverse conditions. Conditions on board are not like some liner. You need to be alert at all times. You need to be doing your job. I think that's what he's getting at—this kind of concern—because something can happen in a split second and you need to react."

Leon cites the example of the time a crew member fell over board in the dark of night: "He had to go to the bathroom. We're sailing from Rarotonga to New Zealand. Navigator Nainoa Thompson is on his platform, checking out the stars and giving us a course to steer. Kimo says, 'Eh, I gotta go bathroom.' So he puts on a safety harness, which is priority. Nainoa says, 'Hike out.' So he did, he hiked out and the safety harness broke. Kimo ended up in the water. So, all the safety equipment was deployed. Nainoa says, 'I go in.' I said, 'You ain't going no place.' He didn't listen to me. He grabbed a surfboard, he jumped in the water. Now we can't see the navigator. I said, 'What the fuck is this? Navigator's gone, first mate is gone. Good God.'"

Luckily, both were retrieved unhurt, but it left Leon wondering: "So who's gonna follow orders? If you're captain and they still don't follow orders, it's still your butt."

Jo-Anne agrees: "The chain of command on the canoe wasn't embedded into the crew members."

"Only because they have never been to sea," Leon says. "They have no concept of what it takes to be out there. Be out there three days and they're asking you: 'Where's land?' You tell 'em: 'It's another 30 days before you see land.'"

Jo-Anne adds: "Everyone that was on the canoe, they had to understand that the immediate environment was that canoe. So you're dealing with the elements, and the only way you can survive on that ocean is to put yourself into that realm. Do you feel that I'm wrong on that?"

Leon: "No. You have to be focused. With *Hōkūle'a*, your body, your mind, your physical being has to be there. Maybe that's why I get upset, maybe that's why people call me s.o.b. But the end result is that we get there safely, everybody's still on board and we've reached the goal, which would be another landfall."

Jo-Anne: "A lot of people miss the boat when they get on. They bring on their land energies with them. They get on board with their hang-ups and they travel for 30-some days before they reach land, never really experiencing that immediate environment.

"What I'm saying is, leaving those kinds of energies behind opens up tremendous observation of where you are. Just letting yourself go with the wind and the canoe and whatever. The silence of the night, the viewing of the stars, the sound of the ocean between the two hulls, the sound and creaking of the boom or the wind.

"Being able to be one with the universe. Being able to experience infinity, which I have on the canoe. I cannot describe the emotion. It's like a tremendous connection between you and the universe, a feeling of oneness —very serene, very contented. Understanding the elements surrounding you. I'm always seeking out."

Leon: "She has a tendency to talk to the vessel. Constantly. [Jo-Anne laughs.] I'd say: 'Ma, quiet.' She's getting goofy."

Jo-Anne: "It's almost a love that describes my feeling of the canoe. It's my culture, it's something I can attach myself to."

Leon: "Ma, attach?—You don't let go!"

Jo-Anne: "They're always going 'ding' when we're on the canoe."

Leon: "Ding. Round two."

Jo-Anne: "You know damned well, once we're on the canoe we're divorced. I respect him as an officer. There's no dope, sex or any of these things. Drinking was never allowed—there was a very high respect for this canoe. He is my superior on the canoe. So when he and I were on together, maybe once in a while we may sneak a kiss, but other than that, it's the respect of his position. We need to maintain ourselves."

"As far as husband and wife—that was out of the picture. Period. As long as you're out at sea," Leon agrees.

But did they argue like husband and wife?

"No. Never. That's a no-no," Leon says seriously. "But Jo-Anne's always starting something—conversation going back and forth—and some of the crew members don't quite understand our relationship.

"Sometimes she'd get nervous, maybe looking up at the rigging, thinking something was wrong with it, and she'd come up to me and ask: 'Daddy, how about this, how about that?' And I'd say: 'Don't worry about it, it's all right.' It's just her concern. She's a worry wart. She's always looking out after the canoe like it's her own personal boat."

As her captain, Leon has only high praise for her. "She's right up there with the guys—not afraid of work, always willing to jump in on anything that needs to be done. She's strong physically and mentally."

Doing something together as important as the *Hōkūle'a* bonded them as a couple and changed them as individuals. Leon was able to show Jo-Anne firsthand why life on the ocean is so vital to him and this, he feels, strengthened their relationship. For him, the voyages stretched his imagination, giving him "a better awareness of what the ancients did—gave me more respect for them and how strong they were."

For Jo-Anne, mere words about the *Hōkūle'a* can't compare to her strong emotions about it. "I've always said to Leon, the *Hōkūle'a* has her own *mana*. She gives me a quieting sense of being. She changed my life for the better, for the best. The water, the cleansing, the purification. It has been my journey."

It was and still is a journey deep into a culture that means so much to them.

"Everything that connects to the culture is very important," Jo-Anne insists. "Without the culture, you would not have a people."

"You're lost," Leon agrees. "You're nothing. You're zero."

Jo–Anne: "The *Hōkūle'a* was like a new beginning for everybody."

Painting of Hōkūleʻa *by Herb Kāne*

HERB KĀNE
ARTIST AND HISTORIAN

In 1970, Herb Kawainui Kāne left a successful career as a graphic artist in Chicago to begin a new life in the land of his ancestors. Within 14 years he was so renowned in Hawai'i he was named one of the state's "Living Treasures."

He was in his forties when he made this leap of life styles, not an easy age to begin anew. But he has cut off the past and faced the unknown several times over the years—when he "gets tired of one room and steps into another room and slams the door," as he puts it.

"I've gone through several of these in my lifetime. The first was leaving advertising [design and artwork], and the second was leaving my clients on the Mainland and moving back here. The third was closing the door on design consulting work [designing Pacific hotels and cultural centers].

"I had to slam the door and that meant turning down offers of work at a time when the bank account was getting thin again.

"The canoe I perceived as lying at the heart of the old culture—it was the central object at the heart of the web of the culture. Almost everything in the culture could be related to the canoe in some way. Certainly Polynesians would not have come into existence without it."

This has always created dislocations and financial difficulties, but it has enriched my life. Although I'm not a wealthy man, I feel my life has been enriched more than if I had stayed the owner of a small commercial art studio in Chicago."

That is an understatement. In his past two decades in Hawai'i, Kāne (pronounced Kah-neh) has become renowned as a fine artist, mostly as an oil painter. His work is seldom found in art galleries; usually every painting has a buyer before it's completed. He keeps a computerized data base of his work, but he's so prolific that even he doesn't know how many paintings he's done over the years.

"Not all my paintings are on the data base," he explains, "and I've never sat down and actually counted those that are on it."

In addition, he has created the artwork for six postage stamps for the United States, 18 for the Marshall Islands, four for French Polynesia and another six for the Federated States of Micronesia. He also sculpts, has written three books and numerous magazine articles, and he is a very knowledgeable, self-taught historian. Combining his love of both history and art, he paints what he loves—Hawai'i's past.

From his earliest days, Kāne was drawn to draw. "I just developed the itch," he says, "and the more I scratched it, the more it itched." During his childhood in the 1930s, his family lived both in Wisconsin, the birthplace of his mother, and the Big Island of Hawai'i, the home of his father. Many of his paintings are from his own early history—memories of a slower time in Hawai'i—his "small kid days," as childhood is called in Hawai'i.

Kāne continued to pursue his itch in college and graduated with a master's degree from the Art Institute of Chicago. He began working as a commercial artist in Chicago, but after "it got to be a bore," he switched to free-lance story illustration for magazines and books.

"There wasn't enough soul in advertising," he explains. "There's only so much you can do with dog food or tractors or whatever comes along. The end came when I won a Jolly Green Giant campaign, and for a year, did drawings and paintings of that big green fairy until I could no longer suffer it."

His dream was to be a fine arts painter, and the journey to that end brought him deep into his own Hawaiian culture. In the early 1970s, paralleling Hawai'i's cultural rebirth, Kāne was beginning his own renaissance. While still in Chicago, he had begun researching Polynesian canoe designs and became so passionate about canoes that "I found myself turning down good assignments to pursue my obsession."

He was researching, of course, to pursue his other obsession: painting. Eventually, he had a series of paintings of 14 Polynesian canoes that so impressed

Hawai'i's State Foundation on Culture and the Arts that it purchased them, and, ever since, they have rotated on the walls of different state buildings. Still today, "various departments fight over them," Kāne says.

These canoe paintings would soon evolve into the real thing for their painter. "It was the sailing canoe that brought me home," Kāne says simply.

Settling in Honolulu, he met others who shared his passion, and together they formed the Polynesian Voyaging Society. Their purpose was to build a 60-foot replica of an ancient Hawaiian canoe.

"As an artist, in order to paint people of another time, one must develop an empathy with them."

As the canoe's designer, Kāne was given the task of naming it, and, in the tradition of the ancients, he dreamed the name one night after seeing the star *Hōkūle'a* in the heavens. "In my dream it grew brighter and brighter and it woke me up," he says. In English, *Hōkūle'a* is Arcturus, the zenith star over Hawai'i, a star used by the Polynesians as a crucial navigational aid.

Though the canoe was initially built to prove a scientific point (that the early Polynesians were capable navigators), Kāne became more interested in the cultural impact of the canoe on Hawai'i.

"What intrigued me was to see, if by building this canoe and putting it to active use and taking it out on a cruise throughout the Hawaiian islands, introducing it to the Hawaiian people, training Hawaiians to sail it, if this would not stimulate shock waves or ripple effect throughout the culture—in music and dance and the crafts. And we know it did.

"The canoe I perceived as lying at the heart of the old culture—it was the central object at the heart of the web of the culture. Almost everything in the culture could be related to the canoe in some way. Certainly Polynesians would not have come into existence without it."

Kāne began to understand that quite literally. After years of research, a light bulb flashed in his head one day—that the canoe not only shaped the culture, but also shaped its people.

"It came to me all in a rush," he says. "I staggered across my studio to my typewriter."

In an article he later wrote for the *National Geographic* magazine, Kāne explained his idea—his theory about why Polynesians are bigger, with more muscle and fat, than other tropical peoples: "When a chief began a voyage of exploration to find new land for his people, he would choose as companions men with powerful muscles, stamina and ample fat to sustain them in times of hunger and to insulate them against the energy-sapping and eventually deadly exposure to wind and spray. He would bring women who seemed capable of bearing children of that type."

In a 1991 documentary about Kāne, called *Children of the Long Canoes,* he adds: "So the canoes could have had a shaping influence on those who shaped them, making us truly the children of the long canoes."

Kāne skippered the *Hōkūle'a*'s first voyages, sailing inter-island throughout Hawai'i, training crews on every island and introducing *Hōkūle'a* to its people. This "first voyage" lasted five months, off and on, mostly weekends.

"I was very surprised and really gratified that the Hawaiians accepted it. There was always a possibility in my mind [that they might not]—they are also modern people today. Had they not accepted it, I wouldn't have let the canoe go to Tahiti. We proved the scientific point anyway. I was convinced halfway through the inter-island voyage that the canoe would make it to Tahiti and back without any problem. The waters between the Hawaiian Islands are rougher than anything between here and Tahiti. So we had ample time to test the canoe's performance."

"I'm trying to divine the original world of the Hawaiians."

Kāne never crewed any of the numerous voyages to Tahiti or back. He chose to step from the limelight and go back to his artwork. Besides his commitment to painting, he had another reason: "I had put a lot of my own money into the canoe and was pretty much broke."

The *Hōkūle'a* is still very active, but Kāne has not been involved for years. He moved from Honolulu to a quieter, country life on the Big Island—a place, he says, "I could get more solitude."

Though the canoe now took a back seat in his life, Hawaiian history remained a vital interest for both his own curiosity and his paintings. He became "intrigued by the detective work that is involved in research." He was becoming quite famous for his Hawaiian historical paintings, and it was important to him that they be accurate.

Others might overlook details that Kāne finds significant. For instance, in his book *Voyages,* he explains how he drew the scene of Captain Cook's death at Kealakekua Bay on Big Island: "Geologists believe that this coastline has subsided 28 inches in the last 200 years. The rock from which Cook fell is now submerged, but one may still locate it and study it through a diver's mask."

He did just that in order to paint the rock correctly; then he went a step beyond—by following the moon phases backwards, he estimated what the tide would be at 8 a.m. on February 14, 1779.

"With this data," he writes, "the water line could be depicted on the rock with some confidence."

In another painting, this one of a chief sliding down a lava rock runway on a wooden sled, he realized nobody really knew how the ancients played this sport (called *hōlua).*

In *Voyages* he writes: "Conventional wisdom holds that the sleds moved on a slippery surface of layers of grass or broad leaves of *tī* and banana, but within living memory no one had actually tested this. . . . I decided to make the test myself."

He found the remnants of a huge *hōlua* slide, constructed a wooden sled after one he'd seen in the Bishop Museum in Honolulu, walked 3,000 feet up the great rock slide, padded it with grass and leaves, then threw himself down on the sled. The sled ground to a quick halt, while his body continued to crash forward in hilarious, but painful failure.

Next try, he decided to pad a section of the lava slide with woven *lau hala* mats, something that would be plentiful in ancient times.

"Terminal velocity!" he writes of his next ride. "But in that same instant I saw that I really hadn't prepared for the experiment being such a success. It was a thrilling ride so long as the mats held out, but then I shot over the last strip of matting. The bare rocks gripped the sled, I was briefly airborne, then on the rocks myself—lava rocks with lots of sharp edges. Later, while applying peroxide and Band-Aids, I was consoled by the thought that data derived from experiment was, in the absence of historical knowledge, acceptable."

Philosophical about his various methods of research, he maintains: "If you take the trouble to turn over every stone, you may find things that change your whole attitude about what you had originally set out to do, and change the visual appearance of it. That's interesting and exciting and it's fun: to turn that last corner and find something that no one has ever found before. You feel like you're breaking new ground."

He finds this type of accuracy critical because: "My paintings are going to go on speaking to people long after I'm gone, so I feel a certain obligation to make sure that what I say is as truthful as I can find it to be. If my work contributes to our comprehension of Hawai'i's past, that will ultimately become the greatest reward.

"Every culture romanticizes about its past. Hawaiians are no exceptions. You have Hawaiians who talk about the old days as some kind of utopia. What I try to do is avoid that kind of thing, because by stripping away those layers of fancy that obscure the past, when you get down to what really happened, what people were really thinking about, it's always more interesting, and always much more rewarding because you know you're getting close to the kernel of truth that lies in the center of every legend."

The rewards for expressing truth are sometimes sweet and simple. For instance, once, after Kāne created a painting of a great war temple, such a reward came from a young Hawaiian man.

"He had always looked at *heiau* as piles of rocks, but when he saw the painting and saw how I reconstructed the *heiau* with the rock work as it once was, with structures on the platform with people in a ceremony, then he said he could never look at it as a pile of rocks again. So I changed his vision. I feel good about that."

Kāne had, of course, painted that *heiau* rock by rock only after detailed study of it. In his book, he explains: "I studied the site with archaeologists from all angles and from the air. Then I took a sleeping bag and spent two days and nights, studying the path of the sun, the cloud shadow, the moon light, and only then did I receive the answers to my questions, only then was I able to pick up a pencil and begin to design the paintings."

Kāne adheres to an elementary rule he learned as a young Navy man from a Chinese painter in Shanghai. "He told me, in order to paint a tiger you have to be a tiger; in order to paint a flower you have to be a flower.

"As an artist, in order to paint people of another time, one must develop an empathy with them. [Historian] Barbara Tuchman once said the difficulty of empathy is the major obstacle for the historian. Her point is, that without empathy, it's not possible to really approach the essence of the historic period."

Studying ancient Hawaiian culture, he found it "similar to so many primal cultures, yet so different from today's culture."

He explains: "I discovered a people whose premises, logic and attitudes were based on an entirely different world view than my own."

For example: "The European attitude had conceived of a supernatural sphere separate and apart from and hierarchically above the natural sphere, and man had a role halfway in between, below the gods and angels, but above the beasts.

"Polynesians did not share the European vision. To them, all spirits were a part of nature and ancestral to nature. So, if you can grasp a world view with no concept of the supernatural, then you're beginning to grasp the Polynesians.

"The major spirits were their natural ancestors, as well as the progenitors of everything in the universe; hence humankind was related by ancestry to everything else. Religious thought was so inseparable from life that no separate word for religion was needed.

"Polynesians saw themselves as the living edge of a much greater multitude of ancestors who, as ancestral spirits, linked the living to a continuum going back to the first humans, to the major spirits and thence to the ultimate male and female spirits that created the universe. The living and the spirits shared a universe in which there was no supernatural because all was natural."

His study of cultures leads Kāne to believe that neither the modern nor the primal world is better or higher than the other, just different. He does know, however, that once a primal culture comes into contact with the modern, there is no going back—except, perhaps, in his own paintings.

By putting paint on canvas, Kāne goes back to a time that he not only loves, but feels a duty to cultivate. Combining his creative imagination and his historical knowledge, he has become a keeper of his own "primary" culture. That, he has come to realize, is an essential reason for his work.

"I'm trying to divine the original world of the Hawaiians. In that way I'm different than artists today who want to express their personalities. I want to express the personality of the subject. It's more like method acting—allowing oneself to be completely subjugated by the role and let the role take over the personality of the actor.

"I'm in opposition to the mainstream of art today as it's taught in the universities, which is that art should be a highly personal thing—highly distinctive to the personality and expressive of the inner self. If the artist is concerned about his personality being expressed, there is no way he is ever going to be able to express the essence of the subject.

"The matter of style and technique is something that an artist should not worry about. Artists worry about that an awful lot—that their style is consonant with what is hot in New York last week. That's a needless worry because no two hands set the paint down with the brush the same way."

Since his school days at the Art Institute of Chicago, he has been told that the type of art he prefers is not real "art," it is mere illustration. Yet realism, or representational art, is all he ever wanted to do.

"Representational art goes way back," he says. "Much of what we know of the past we get from artists who have documented their time and place, their people, their culture."

Just as he is doing.

Next Generation

It's not my generation. It's not my parent's generation. It's their generation that's making it happen. They stand up for what they believe and know what is right. We're just standing by saying: 'Go for it, go for it.'

Nona Beamer is justifiably proud of the generation following hers. They came into their teens and early adulthood as Hawai'i began embracing the cultural renaissance of all things Hawaiian. Speaking the language was suddenly "cool," as was learning the *hula*, the chants, the ancient art of wayfaring.

It is this generation that has insisted on Hawaiian Studies programs at the university level, on Hawaiian history being taught at all levels. This generation is building canoes and investigating the ancient religion and researching the rituals of the past. And, perhaps most importantly, this generation is insisting on the return of sovereign rights.

It is no accident that the two men in this chapter, representing their generation, have been involved in the revival of the canoe, the most significant and symbolic event in modern Hawai'i. By building canoes, they have sailed back into their heritage, making themselves once again "the people of the long canoe."

NAINOA THOMPSON
NAVIGATOR

Nainoa Thompson is a genuine Hawaiian hero, a treasure to his state and his people before he was 30 years old.

The reason is simple, yet the story is complex: Thompson is the first Hawaiian in centuries to become a deep-sea navigator, the most important job in the ancient days of Polynesian voyaging.

The story dates back to the early 1970s when a small group of people built the double-hulled canoe *Hōkūle'a* and sailed off to Tahiti, where their ancestors had come from hundreds of years before.

This initial effort by a few has evolved into "an enormous human endeavor," Thompson says. "Twenty years of work by thousands of people. I need to be very clear that I'm only one of those thousands. All of us have strived in this modern day for something that is very important: to bring some dignity and pride back to our people."

"[Navigation] is a commitment that comes from, I don't know, someplace that's very deep inside, I think from the spirit and soul of those who take on this challenge. It has something to do with pride, not in a vain way, but in a way that you represent not just yourself, but your family and the dignity of your culture. You have to make that kind of commitment and endure suffering to take command and guide canoes in the way of the ancestors."

Frankly though, without Nainoa Thompson it could not have been done. Obviously, someone has to know how to reach the destination—that's the navigator's job. Thompson is the one who took on the early task of learning the lost art of navigation—sailing the ocean with no guidance from modern instruments. He studied science and math, astronomy and oceanography, then coupled his book learning with hundreds of hours examining the stars in the Bishop Museum's planetarium in Honolulu. He accomplished this quietly, just for his own knowledge, having no idea of the cultural explosion he was helping instigate.

He has never been comfortable with the hero moniker, though numerous honors have been heaped upon him over the years.

"I'm wrestling with it," he says, looking pained. "It's certainly against my nature. I'm a very private person. It gets confusing at times, and I don't like that confusion. I like to be as clear as I possibly can.

"On the other hand, when people ask you [to lecture or teach or show them the stars], especially when the schools ask you, I try to respond. But I gotta strike a balance between the need to maintain who I am and my own personal sense of integrity with meeting the needs of others."

Thompson often finds this balance by going out alone at night on the ocean in his funky little motorboat near his Honolulu home.

"I get out there, under the stars, everything's so big, everything seems infinitely so far away, it makes your thoughts big, it makes your visions large. It's a good place to think, it's a good place to be," he says. "As I look at the whole universe and the wideness of the ocean it kind of dissolves some of the crampness of society, especially O'ahu."

When *Hōkūle'a* sailed its initial trip from Hawai'i to Tahiti and back in 1976, it was the first deep-sea canoe voyage in hundreds of years. Thompson crewed on the second leg back to Hawai'i. He had been involved, building the canoe, since 1974, when he was 20 years old, but he was not yet a navigator. There was not a single navigator left in all of Polynesia, so the Hawaiians brought in a Micronesian navigator named Mau Piailug from the island of Satawal.

"I never thought that I would navigate," Thompson says. "I just wanted to learn about it. I thought navigation was too complicated, too mythical. It was nothing about the real world—it was too far back in the past. I didn't have the confidence to do it."

Two people changed his mind: the first being Mau Piailug.

"He came to help us in 1975. He was a magical person. He's not of our world," Thompson says. "He was so powerful in my perception that I wouldn't

NEXT GENERATION: Nainoa Thompson

even talk to him in 1975. I'd just be around to listen to what he had to say. I really placed Mau someplace else—a different time, a different world, a different ability. He is so in tune with everything. He's so phenomenal."

There wasn't a serious need for a Hawaiian navigator anyway. No one expected *Hōkūle'a* to sail more than the one voyage to Tahiti. She was constructed to prove a scientific point, nothing beyond that.

"But the canoe was so powerful that everybody wanted to sail, so the canoe kept sailing [mostly short trips in Hawaiian waters]," Thompson says.

Then something happened in 1978 that changed Thompson's life: a friend drowned when *Hōkūle'a* capsized.

"It was just going to be a learning experience. Mau wasn't there. I would navigate the best I could, knowing that I knew very little," Thompson remembers. "But the canoe swamped and we lost Eddie Aikau. It was a very emotional time, and that's when I recognized that we could never turn our backs on doing the voyage to Tahiti, because that's what Eddie's dream was about. He believed so much in *Hōkūle'a* and its power. I couldn't just let his loss be for nothing. That was very personal. I didn't talk about it. But that's when navigation became my whole life."

"There is a whole other journey that goes on, and that's internal. It's one that tests you to do things you can't do in your normal life. Much of navigation is this internal journey."

And so he set out to learn with a renewed purpose. Yet to do it right, he realized the Hawaiians needed Mau Piailug. Thompson went to Satawal to talk with Piailug, beginning an apprenticeship and friendship that continues today.

"He is the one, that single rare individual, who came forward to help us regain our past," Thompson says, very much in awe. "He revived voyaging, not just in Hawai'i, but in all the Pacific. I talk a lot about his greatness, but the thing I respect most is his kindness. He virtually took 20 years of his life—he brought all of his experiences and gave to us freely. You cannot measure that kind of value.

"Mau is one of five traditional navigators left on Earth. You would consider him a global treasure. He started when he was one year old and was sailing at age five.

"The knowledge that Mau has is so vast. We are like children compared to what he knows. When I was having a difficult time learning how to read the waves—the ocean's so complicated—he said, 'You're too old already.' I was too old to learn certain things that you can only learn when you're a child."

Thompson supplemented experiential learning with his science and math background and with his training in the planetarium, and Piailug never objected to the academics.

"He recognized we didn't have the time to learn the way he did—there was so much to learn," Thompson says. "All the science did was ground me in making sense of the natural world; the real learning came on the canoe by actually observing him. It was a very profound time for me.

"Don't look with your eyes.

Let that go.

Look inside to find the answers."

"The ocean is a very humbling place. It's been the best classroom of my life. Navigation is a rare, special experience and it's not that easy for me to articulate it," Thompson says, and then he does so poetically.

"Navigation is about observing your natural world. It's about recognizing and understanding your natural environment in its totality, purely out of a need to survive. You've got to understand everything in the heavens, the atmosphere, the weather, down to the ocean, to the crew, to yourself. And integrate all that into a system where you can use the natural elements to guide you.

"Navigation would be easy if the weather stayed the same—you could follow certain stars and bump into islands. But the weather is never the same; it always changes. And navigators need to adjust to the change. You can't position yourself by the stars alone.

"You only know where you are on the ocean by memorizing where you came from. That means you have to memorize how fast you're going, in what direction, for how long. We don't have a watch, we don't have a magnetic compass. It's all what you read in the ocean. That requires navigators to be watching and observing and memorizing that course for whatever length it takes to sail the sea. We've been at sea for 43 days.

"It's interesting, when you finish a voyage, the crew will talk about all these events that took place on the canoe. A lot of them, I wasn't there. Your mind is out on your job. Your job is to observe and make critical decisions to guide the canoe.

"We use about 200 stars to navigate by. They're our best friends, they never change. The moon is used in the daytime, also at night. It's a very important friend in navigation.

"The navigational day begins with the rise of the sun. It gives you a known bearing. The sun and stars are fixed in the sky to some degree and they are things you can count on, but sometimes you can't use them, so you have to use the ocean waves. And they're always changing with the wind.

"At sunset you repeat the process of looking at how the sun cuts through clouds, the colors and the movements of the clouds. The colors of the clouds tell about the weather.

"Navigators on average, sleep only two or three hours a day for 30 days—in 15 to 20 minute catnaps. You navigate as long as you can think. As soon as you're exhausted mentally, you lie down. You only rest until your mind is clear. When I first start to dream, I get up. Mau told me that he can lie down and close his eyes, but inside he never sleeps.

"You've got to always be observing nature. The navigator cannot lie down too long or he won't know where he's going.

"Navigation that I've spoken of so far is more external: it's what you see; it's looking at stars, infinite and far away; it's looking at small waves that are very close. Taking this information and making it into knowledge is one thing. Being able to navigate is another. There is a whole other journey that goes on, and that's internal. It's one that tests you to do things you can't do in your normal life. Much of navigation is this internal journey.

"It's a commitment that comes from, I don't know, someplace that's very deep inside, I think from the spirit and soul of those who take on this challenge. It has something to do with pride, not in a vain way, but in a way that you represent not just yourself, but your family and the dignity of your culture. You have to make that kind of commitment and endure suffering to take command and guide canoes in the way of the ancestors."

Thompson glimpsed his own internal journey on the 1980 voyage to Tahiti, the first time he was head navigator. In the toughest possible place, the doldrums near the Equator, he went beyond his five physical senses into what he calls the sixth sense—the spiritual.

"This was one of the more powerful experiences I've had on the canoe—one of those special moments when you step out of the bounds of your normal consciousness—outside your normal existence into another place," Thompson says.

"When you go into the doldrums, that area near the equator called the max cloud line, it's the cloudiest place on earth. You are blind as a navigator—you can't see heavenly bodies.

"The ocean reflects the character of the sky. When the sky is gray, the ocean is gray. But on a black night, the ocean is black. You cannot even see on the canoe, let alone see the stars, see the moon or even the ocean waves. You're blind.

"Mau said, very profound, I'll never forget this: 'Don't look with your eyes, look inside.' He said, this is how you stand, this is how you feel the canoe as the waves pass through. To read the ocean waves, that's hard. That's when you step from science to art.

"I just feared the doldrums. I didn't know how in the world I was going to get through this band of clouds, because I didn't have the skill to navigate without seeing the stars and the sun. I come from science and math; I had overtrained in studying the stars and the celestial stuff. I didn't have the time to study the waves with Mau. I just didn't have the time.

"So when I get into the doldrums, what in the world am I going to do? And I was fairly young—I was 25 years old. I wasn't mature enough to deal with all this pressure. Not finding a balance where I could be relaxed, and you need to be relaxed to be able to sustain yourself.

"You have to be alert without being too intense, because to be able to endure, you've gotta relax, and that's hard out there. If you get intense and you don't relax, you get fatigued and you can't endure. You get too tired to think.

"We sailed down and you could just see this wall of clouds. I did not want to go in. We saw it before we got to it—100 percent cloud cover, solid rain, no wind at all. The drops were just vertical. Wiping the rain off your face. It's still daylight. Worrying about when the sun's going down. And the sun went down, but the wind came back. But the problem is, from where? When you're in cloudy conditions, that's when the wind is going to be the most unreliable. It changes a lot. Plenty wind. It's taking you someplace and you don't know where. But off we sailed.

"And I wasn't mature enough to tell the crew: I don't know. So I faked it and hid it, and I was trying to read the ocean waves in all this rain and in all this changing wind. I was a wreck. I was pacing around. I was getting very intense, looking for things you couldn't see.

"Mau was with me, but I couldn't talk to him. That was the agreement. I knew if he had to step in, it would have taken away from his success as a teacher. If I succeeded in navigation, he succeeded as a teacher. It would be his honor, if, when he sailed with me, he would never have to say anything to me, and I knew that. I never wanted him to have to correct me.

"It was getting very intense and I was extremely tired. I was so exhausted, I turned to the rail and I locked my elbows on the rail and tried to get rest standing up. In doing that, in all this rain and all this cold, I felt this really warm sensation and my mind got very clear. And I could feel the moon. I knew the moon was up, but I didn't know where it was because I couldn't see it. But somehow I could tell the direction.

"Does that make sense?

"In the fatigue, my best guess is that you let go. Like Mau says: 'Don't look with your eyes. Let that go. Look inside to find the answers.' At that point, when I leaned on my elbows, I was really giving up. And in giving up, it was like letting go, and letting go allowed this other experience.

"I turned to Buddy [the steersman] and I said: 'Go this way.' A lot of confidence, not knowing why. I knew, but I didn't know how I knew. We kept sailing and sailing and I could track the moon in my mind.

"Then there was like a gift—a hole opened up in the sky and the moon was right there.

"Take it for what it's worth."

"Our goal was to recapture our traditions, to make our people feel proud of those traditions and therefore proud about themselves."

While his personal journey was evolving, a parallel journey was happening for all of Hawai'i—a cultural explosion that wouldn't stop at one canoe. Going deeper into their past, the Hawaiians decided to build another canoe, but unlike *Hōkūle'a*, which is made of modern materials, the new canoe, named *Hawai'iloa,* would be hulled out of two giant logs, constructed of native materials and built in traditional ways. It was an enormous project.

"It was intended to find out what is the whole human effort to put on a voyage in the old way," Thompson explains. "Our goal was to recapture our traditions, to make our people feel proud of those traditions and therefore proud about themselves."

There were compromises from the start, however, one of the greatest being that there were no native *koa* trees large enough in all of Hawai'i to make two hulls.

Thompson reports that after searching for nine months: "We ended up seeing that our *koa* ecosystem is very unhealthy. About 90 percent of the original *koa* when Captain Cook was here [1778] is gone. And for our project we had no logs."

The Tlingit and Haida Indians of Alaska came to their rescue, offering two 200-foot spruce trees, weighing 100,000 pounds each, one of them 418 years old.

"It was painful to see them fall," Thompson recalls, "but it was a promise—we would give them a new life as a voyaging canoe."

With the search for native materials to build Hawai'iloa, the importance of the environment began to evolve as part of the picture. As Thompson says: "We were struck, from the very beginning, that the ancient Hawaiians were here 2,000 years, and maybe they built 50 canoes a year for survival—that's 100,000 canoes—and today we cannot even build one completely from native materials."

It bothered Thompson that Hawai'i had to go to Alaska for trees, even though the Alaskans were gracious and assured him they had plenty. A wise Hawaiian elder counseled him that his feelings were valid and gave him an answer to cope. "You walked away on your land," said the elder, speaking of the futile search for large *koa*. "Before you cut down somebody else's trees, go plant your own."

And so the canoes sailed into the arena of environmental education. With school kids as helpers, they planted 11,000 *koa* seedlings—a mini forest that will someday be grand.

With this venture into education, Thompson and his fellow members of the Polynesian Voyaging Society began to ponder: "Where are we going to go with our work? What's the best use of these canoes now? What can a group of voyaging people do to contribute to the health of Hawai'i?"

The answer was education.

"The canoes are great platforms of learning," says Thompson. "The next step is to get the canoes into the classrooms and develop a whole brand-new way of looking at education. Not just hands-on, but rather, I think education needs to be directly geared to the relevant issues that students are going to face in their future. We need to get our youth on the canoes and relate voyaging to a whole spectrum of broad issues."

Some of these issues are those most critical in Hawai'i: environment, health and self-esteem.

"We can't take our experiences and give them to somebody else," Thompson realizes, "but we can teach what we value. And what we value is this place we call home. We want to protect it. We want it to be clean and healthy.

"Hawai'i has a special environment, so in isolation. If the quality of our land

and sea is not healthy, neither is our life style. We've got to take care of our land, and we've got to take care of our people."

He points to several social problems: the terrible Hawaiian health statistics, the high rate of incarceration in prisons, the poverty level of so many.

"Look at all indigenous peoples," he says. "Hawai'i is not unique with health or economic issues or the numbers in prison. Something's wrong.

"The loss of culture, loss of beliefs—you end up feeling second-rate in your homeland. I think there's a strong connection between self-esteem and physical health, and sometimes we define that as spirit.

"That's what's very important about these canoes—the intent is to make people stronger. The pride the canoes generate is a part, maybe a fraction, of that healing process.

"The canoe is really a vessel of healing."

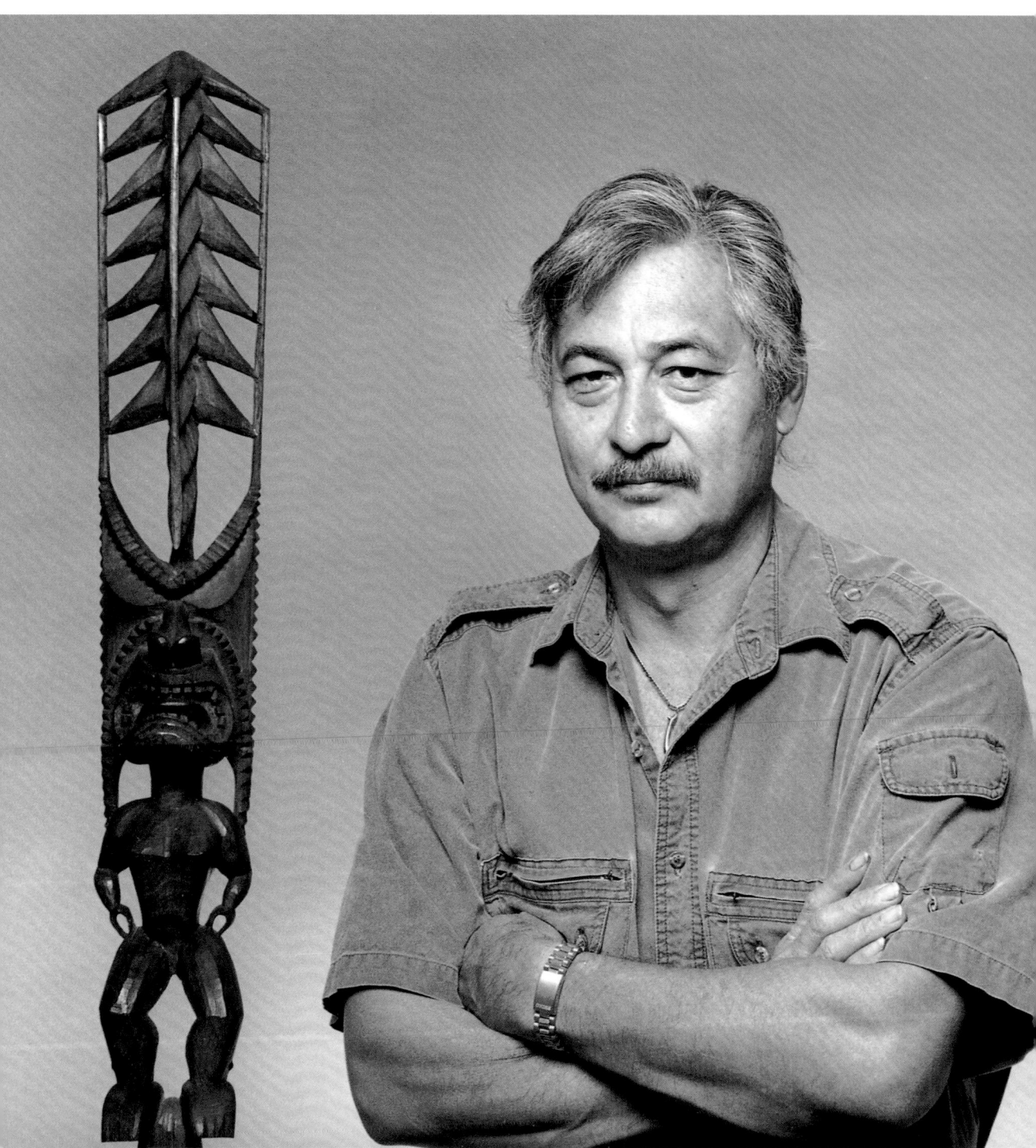

KEOLA SEQUEIRA
WOOD CARVER AND CANOE MAKER

Keola Sequeira is one of Hawai'i's best wood carvers, yet he does not just carve wood. Sequeira has taken his craft into the higher realms of art and spirit. Over the past three decades, as he chipped and carved layers and layers of wood, he also unfolded subtler layers that he believes are the secrets of his ancestors. It is through these secrets that he has begun to understand his art. And, as he does so, he believes he receives the wisdom of the ancients.

Huna is the secret lore of ancient Hawai'i and *kāhuna* are those who know *huna*. In olden days, an apprentice would study 20 to 30 years with the *kahuna;* today, there are no such masters left, but Sequeira says the ancients teach him in spirit and in dreams and through pieces of their work that still remain.

For instance, he has found rotting old canoes hidden in caves in remote areas of Maui, and as he studies these canoes, they come alive for him with information.

"This deeper knowledge, this *huna*, has to come from the ancient pieces. I don't have a *kahuna kālai wa'a* [canoe master] that I can speak to today; but they don't have to speak to you in words, they can speak to you in what they did.

In dreams I pick up knowledge too. I get so intense into it I can dream about it, and, if I have questions, in dreams answers will come to me. They talk to you in dreams, then they talk to you when you're actually making it. The spirits are with you, guiding you, all the time."

"I spent hours in the museums studying the ancient canoes," Sequeira says. "And any time I hear about canoes in caves, I go study them. I've seen canoes in caves that Bishop Museum thought were junk, but I saw through different eyes. I could see things in there—I could write a whole thesis on one board. These things could speak to me—these things told me what part of the tree the wood came from, why it's carved that way, why the certain thickness, why the certain shape, on and on—I could see all that.

"This deeper knowledge, this *huna,* has to come from the ancient pieces. I don't have a *kahuna kālai waʻa* [canoe master] that I can speak to today; but they don't have to speak to you in words, they can speak to you in what they did.

"In dreams I pick up knowledge too. I get so intense into it I can dream about it, and, if I have questions, in dreams answers will come to me. They talk to you in dreams, then they talk to you when you're actually making it. The spirits are with you, guiding you, all the time."

Sequeira has dedicated his life to wood carving. It is his way of perpetuating Hawaiian culture. He is known for two very different types of wood work—building canoes and sculpting *kiʻi* (tiki-like images).

Whatever he is building or sculpting, he always knows: "It is not done through you alone. If I try to carve without spirit, without my spiritual helpers, then the job goes really hard, it doesn't come off right."

The *kiʻi* are themselves like little spirits, probably because many of them represent Hawaiian gods. Sequeira began carving them in 1970, drawn to them, he says, because: "I found out that the highest form of wood sculpting in the Pacific Triangle was the *kiʻi,* the Hawaiian images. The more you study them, the more you understand this to be true."

Sequeira felt a responsibility to bring these *kiʻi* back. "There are only about 70 [originals] that survived," he says. "There was a great need for somebody to research them.

"Nobody really knows what they mean, what they stood for. There are a few Hawaiian images that are carved to look like a person, but the rest are abstract. Some people interpret them as being ugly. Why? Because they don't understand.

"Joseph Campbell says in his book *The Power of Myth* that a true artist, a true poet, has the ability to leave this plane of existence or reality, move their mind and spirit into a another plane of reality and see what is there, and then bring it back and interpret it. The Hawaiian *kahuna kālai kiʻi* [master wood carvers] definitely had that ability.

"The *kiʻi* are abstracts. But what this abstract is saying, there again that's the *huna,* that's the secret. Once you understand what it's trying to say, then you see the beauty in it.

"Nobody has tried to interpret these images," Sequeira admits. However, he does so himself as he replicates the ancient *ki'i* in his garage-studio. Sometimes, as he's copying an old image, he doesn't understand the symbolism, but he has found that, "When you carve it, it starts to reveal the secrets behind it."

To explain this *huna,* Sequeira points to a wooden statue of the god Lono that he has carved. It's a fierce-looking statue with a very tall headdress.

"When you carve it, it starts to reveal the secrets behind it."

"Lono is the spirit of peace, of agriculture, of healing." Sequeira says. "But why does he look so fierce? The nostrils are flared because he is breathing in. As you bring in air, your body creates energy. As that energy is projected or used, the mouth becomes open. It looks fierce because Lono is not something to be taken lightly—if the spirit of Lono does not help man, then man is going to do poorly in agriculture. So his mouth is expressing this energy, this breath, this *mana* of life that Lono gives out."

Lono's eyes are large and are carved on the side of his head. "That's saying, that because of his larger eyes, Lono observes more than we see and from all angles," Sequeira theorizes.

The *ki'i* have been misunderstood since the first foreigners came to Hawai'i. Since then, the images have been called "idols," and that rankles Sequeira.

"Because of Christianity, the Hawaiians were labeled idol worshipers," he says. "But what is Lono? What is Kū [god of war]? They're both spirits that concern themselves with mankind. If you acknowledge them, then they will help you.

"The Hawaiians knew that the image was not the spirit, it was a receptacle. Catholics do the same thing. They pray to Mother Mary on the altar. That's a focal point instead of facing a blank wall. Well, the Hawaiians are doing the same thing.

"My wife and I are not Christians. We respect Christianity, but we do not worship in that way. We worship in the beliefs of our forefathers. I pray to the gods who were here for who knows how long. These are the ones who help me—when I pray to them, I get answers, I get guidance.

"I was Christian up to maybe my late twenties and it was unfulfilling.

After that I started slowly moving into the ancient religion, working more with nature spirits. This is the only time I found results. The spirits will guide you, they'll show you where to put your energies to get the job done.

"If it worked for the Hawaiians for thousands of years, it still works today. Let the Christians have Jesus, I'll stay with what I have."

> "I designed this canoe to be just like a fish's body, to be part of nature. So, as the canoe goes through the water it is not fighting, but is becoming part of nature."

With his guides directing him, Sequeira built his first canoe in 1974—a giant leap for someone who, at the time, was not a builder. He and a few friends put together $80—seed money for a dream.

"We were not boat builders," he admits of this early group of visionaries. "Basically, I'm a wood carver, but that didn't stop us. What we didn't know, we'd find out."

Their first project, a 42.5-foot canoe, called the *Moʻolele,* eventually cost $11,000 to finish. The initial challenge for Sequeira's group, however, was not just money. None of them knew how to design a Hawaiian canoe as the ancients had built them.

"All we had was a French drawing [a simple line drawing of a Hawaiian canoe sketched in 1839 by a French artist named Paris], and that didn't show the details," Sequeira says. "So we were pretty much on our own in 1974. There were no *kāhuna kālai waʻa* to talk to. Because I was the one in charge, I had to literally put my spirit into the different parts of the canoe. I would actually move myself into the different parts, feel everything that was going around me, feel all the stresses, what this thing was supposed to do, and then design it accordingly. Then, if I got stuck, I had dreams where I could see myself or somebody else working in the shop making these parts, and I would wake up and go out there and say: 'Now I know how to make this part!' And that's how we did it. Took us one year."

Sequeira calls canoe design "functional art." A canoe is a "sculptural form that functions in the ocean," he explains. Of the second canoe he built, the 62-foot *Moʻokiha,* he says: "We didn't build a 62-foot hull, we built a 62-foot sculpture. Every part of the canoe was thought out as a sculpture."

His dilemma is to make replicas of the old canoes, remaining as true as he can to original designs, while still being a modern builder.

"Actually, I've taken the best in the design of the old and I'm incorporating it with the best that we have today. Some Hawaiians think you're not a Hawaiian unless you're wearing a *malo* and you're tromping around in a *taro* patch. I'm saying, no, you have to know the essence of what is good from the past and take it into the twenty-first century with the best technologies of today. I'm showing it can be done. You can incorporate the best of these two worlds. And I'm showing it in three dimensions—in the canoes.

"*Moʻokiha* [the 62-foot canoe] is designed to be the Hawaiian double-hulled canoe of the next century. I took the ancient design and I'm applying it to today's building techniques, not dissimilar from what the old *kāhuna kālai waʻa* would have done. They put aside their stone tools as soon as metal tools came along."

He can cite many innovations that the *kāhuna* of old designed as they traveled throughout the Pacific. For example, when the Tahitians came to Hawaiʻi centuries ago, their canoe crossbeams (*ʻiako*) were straight, but in the higher Hawaiian swells they needed to redesign crossbeams that were curved. Their end pieces (*manu*) in the calm waters of the South Pacific were long, but here, in Hawaiʻi's rough waters, they needed blunter ends.

"The channels here would tear the old *manu* design apart," Sequeira explains. "Ours is the roughest water to sail in in the Pacific Triangle.

"I've come up with even more innovations than what our ancient *kāhuna* did, but still in keeping and still maintaining the Hawaiian designs."

The most astonishing innovation he borrowed from ancient Sumeria and ancient Egypt, yet he firmly believes the Hawaiians had this knowledge too. One night, as his wife, Apela, tells the story, after studying a book on Egyptian mathematics: "He jumps out of bed and goes into the workshop and starts going like crazy with geometry and mathematics. And about three days later, after he gets bored with the math, he wants to go to three dimension because that's how he works, and he started making these model hulls."

Sequeira built hulls following a "phi" design that relates to nature. Phi, according to the Egyptians and Sumerians, is a ratio formula of 1.618 that the Egyptians used to build the Great Pyramids. Sequeira's excitement grew as he learned that this same formula was utilized throughout ancient civilizations because it is based on a formula found throughout nature.

"The king's chamber [in the Great Pyramid] is built directly in proportion to the phi formula—height, width, length," Sequeira says. "The sarcophagus where they put his body, that is in exact proportion to the phi formula. The human body proportions are made according to the phi formula. A flower opens up according to the phi formula. The Greek Parthenon temple was built according to the phi formula. This goes on and on.

"When I looked at this, I wondered if this thing could be applied to canoes. So I took the formula and started working geometrically. Took me a few days, but I finally got it. I found out where that curve came in. And lo and behold, the curve came in perfectly. It had a V where you wanted a V. The proportions of the V, if you make it too deep, the canoe will have too deep a draft; if you make it too wide, it's not going to go to windward very well. The phi formula brought all of those lines right into perspective. The phi formula just fit to a 't.'

"What is beautiful about this, is that a fish's body is designed to this, it fits into the phi formula. So I designed this canoe to be just like a fish's body, to be part of nature. So, as the canoe goes through the water it is not fighting, but is becoming part of nature.

"There again, this goes back to the *huna*. I believe I found a formula that our ancestors knew and I'm bringing it into reality again.

"I'm gonna get put down for that maybe, and they're gonna say there's no place in Hawaiian history that this shows up. Well, Hawaiians didn't have a written history and a lot of the old chants didn't survive. That kind of *huna* was probably never released anyway; it was only passed down. We can only see it in the end result which is the shape. And I believe I've stumbled on something that was that shape."

His wife, Apela, who has a Ph.D. in philosophy from Harvard, always cautions her husband in the excitement of his discoveries. "When your teachers aren't living teachers, you have to be sure that out of your drive and your need and your desire for the knowledge that you're not fantasizing," she warns even as she encourages him. "How do you know that you got it right—that this is not just your fantasy of changing it this way or that way? There might be some fragment of old knowledge that in 20 years or 50 years or 100 years will be a key that somebody needs for really important life-sustaining purposes; and, if we lie or distort or make up or fantasize on that, it won't be there for them." Apela, who is an Oneida Indian, holds fast to the Indian concern for seven generations ahead. Still, she shares her husband's enthusiasm for the phi formula.

"We're talking ancient knowledge and it's almost basic knowledge," Sequeira explains. "And I think a lot of this knowledge was shared by all these old cultures. I think there would have been a lot of voyaging to other places and I think a lot of this knowledge was spread around.

"There's not enough information that I could find in Hawai'i, so I had to go into other cultures. But you have to be very careful about how you apply this to our society, because you can contaminate the Hawaiian society very easily that way. But this is knowledge based on nature, and the Hawaiians were great observers of nature. That's why I think I'm not too far off in left field when I take a concept from Egypt and apply it."

What Sequeira is doing is what the *kāhuna* of old might do. "*Kahuna* was like the Ph.D. level," he explains. "You had fifty guys working on a canoe, but there's only one who is the *kahuna kālai waʻa*—who is directing the whole work. The blueprint is in his mind."

Sequeira is willing to stick his neck out and call himself a *kahuna,* a title no longer freely used. Since the early missionary days, the term has been distorted, implying that these teachers practiced black magic.

He was hesitant at first to use the term, but Apela convinced him that someone has to take on this important role. And like the *kāhuna* of old, he has studied his craft for more than three decades.

"Today, you can probably count on your hands anybody who professes to be *kahuna,*" Sequeira admits. "We were talking about this a few years ago, and I said I was still afraid to use it [the title], but Apela said, 'If you don't use it, then your culture will die. You have to bring back the *huna* system.' So okay, I'll be that bouncing board and I'll take the flack so that maybe the next generation will have an easier time. And that's why I feel I can assume that title.

"We're in a time of regaining our knowledge. So much of it is lost and we're just trying to bring it back."

"We had to go back to the past to create the future."

Nainoa Thompson

Glossary

A
    ahupua'a - land division, an area usually stretching in a pie-shaped wedge from the tip of the mountaintop to the base at the sea

    'āina - land, earth

    akua - god or goddess

    alanui - road

    ali'i - chief, chiefess

    aloha - love, compassion, greeting of hello and goodbye with affection

    'anā'anā - sorcery, usually means black magic of some kind

    'aumakua (**'aumākua** plural) - personal family gods, either deified ancestors or animal spirit guides

    'auwana - modern style of *hula*

    auē (also **auwē**) - oh dear, alas

    'awa - plant native to the Pacific islands from which a slightly narcotic drink is made (from the roots); *'awa* is drunk at most rituals

E
    'ehā - four

    'ekāhi - one

    'ekolu - three

    'elima or **lima** - five

    'elua - two

H
    hā - to breathe

    haku mele - composer, poet

    hala - also called *pandanus* or screw pine; native tree in Hawai'i, other Pacific islands, Australia and southern Asia; leaves of the *hala* are used to weave mats, hats, baskets

    hālau hula - *hula* school

    hānai - adopted

    haole - white person, foreigner

    heiau - temple

    heiau ho'ōla - temple for healing the sick

    hiapo - first-born child

    hōlua - sled used on grassy slopes

    honi - to kiss, to touch noses in greeting

    ho'oponopono - mediation process used within families to clear wrongs

    hula - native Hawaiian dance

huna - metaphysical, hidden, secret

hūpō - stupid

I

ʻiako - outrigger canoe boom

ʻike - to see, know, feel, understand

ʻio - endemic Hawaiian hawk

iwi - bone

K

ka poʻe kahiko - the people of old, the ancients

kāʻai - sennit container used to store the remains of a chief

kahiko - ancient *hula*

kāhili - feather standard, a symbol of royalty

kahu - caretaker, pastor

kahuna (**kāhuna** plural) - priest or expert in any profession

kahuna lāʻau lapaʻau - expert in herbal medicine

kahuna kālai waʻa - expert canoe maker

kai - sea water

kala - to release; *limu kala* is a type of seaweed used to release sickness or troubles

kamaʻāina - Lit., "child of the land;" Hawaiʻi born

kanaka (**kānaka** plural) - human being, man

kanaka maoli - Hawaiian, native person

kanikau - death chant, dirge

kaona - hidden, deeper meaning

kapa (also **tapa**) - cloth made from bark, usually from *wauke* or *māmaki* plant; all ancient clothing and bedding were made from *kapa*

kāpena - captain

kapu - taboo, prohibited

keiki - child

kepakepa - conversational, fast, rhythmic style of chant

kiʻi - image, statue, usually of a god

kilohana - bed cover

kino lau - earthly manifestation of a god

kīpuka - oasis of greenery in midst of lava flow, generally on higher ground

ko - to hold a note for several beats in chanting

kukui - tree native to Hawaiʻi, Polynesia and southern Asia; also called candlenut tree; oil in the nut was used for lighting and as a lubricant

kuleana - responsibility, authority, right, claim

kumu - teacher

kumu hula - *hula* teacher

kupuna (kūpuna plural) - elder

L
lāʻau - plant; medicine; medical
lāʻau lapaʻau - herbal medicine
lānai - porch
lani - heaven, sky
lau hala - leaf of the *hala* tree (also *pandanus* tree)
lehua - flower of the *ʻōhiʻa* tree
lei - traditional garland, necklace of flowers, shells, leaves, bone, feathers
limu - seaweed
loʻi - *taro* patch
lōkāhi - harmony, unity, accord
lomilomi - Hawaiian massage
lūʻau - young *taro* top; Hawaiian feast

M
mahalo - thank you
mahiole - helmet
Māhea-lani - night of the full moon
maʻi - genitals
maile - native shrub with shiny, fragrant leaves
maka - eye
make - to die
makua - parent
makule - old, aged
mālama - to take care of
malo - loincloth worn by men
māmaki - small native tree; its bark was used to make *kapa*
mamo - descendant
mana - divine power
manō - shark
manu - end pieces of a canoe
maoli - native, true, real, genuine
mauka - towards the mountain, inland
mele - song or chant
mele inoa - birth chant
Menehune - legendary race of small people who worked at night
moana - ocean
moepuʻu - someone who kills himself to "sleep with the chief" when his chief dies
muʻumuʻu - woman's long dress

N na‘au - gut, intestines

niho palaoa - whale's tooth pendant hung on necklace of human hair

O ‘ohana - family

‘ōhi‘a lehua - native Hawaiian tree with red flowers sacred to Pele

‘ōlena - tumeric

oli - chant not accompanied by *hula*

olonā - endemic shrub; strong rope is made from the inner bark

‘o‘opu - general name for small gobi-like fish

‘ōpae - general name for shrimp

P pahu - drum

pali - cliff, precipice

pau - finished

piha - full-blooded

piko - navel

pōhuehue - beach morning glory

poi - paste pounded from *taro* root

pono - goodness, uprightness, balanced

po‘o - head

pule - prayer

T taro or kalo - Hawaiian staple food, both root and leaves are eaten

tī - woody plant in the lily family

tūtū - familiar name children call their grandparents

U ‘uhane – soul, spirit

‘ukulele - Lit., "leaping flea;" popular instrument in Hawai‘i; brought by the Portuguese in 1879

W waena - middle

wailua - spirit

wauke - paper mulberry tree; inner bark used to make the best *kapa*

ACKNOWLEGEMENTS

I'd like to acknowledge and thank the 24 people I interviewed for being generous with both their time and their knowledge. They took a chance that I'd write them right, and I'm grateful for their confidence.

Mahalo nui loa . . .

To Steve Brinkman, my photographic partner, for his wonderful photos and for three years of a very easy working relationship. To his partner, Susan Hiraoka, for her patient, enduring interest in the project.

To Rita Goldman, visionary editor and friend, a woman of words and wit who had fun catching my mistakes.

To Jill Engledow—this time you edit me. Thanks for enjoying the Hawaiiana you already knew so much about.

To Tamara Lester of Yellowbird Graphics for designing the cover we always wanted.

To Eddie Pu for being our radiant cover portrait—a true picture of Hawaiian *aloha*.

To Pamela Beverly for her interior design.

To Patt Narrowe for adding the finishing design touches in her clear, precise way.

To David Ulrich for his darkroom magic and his artistic advice.

To Lori Sablas and Donna Wendt who extended themselves with great enthusiasm for the book.

To the following friends who helped me contact *kūpuna* to interview: Akoni Akana, Patti Cook, Cathy Davenport, Malihini Dunn-Keahi, Lynn Hanks, Dick Nelson, Carol Ann Washburn, Elaine Wender, Celeste Wohl. Without them as liaisons, I would not have been able to reach some of the elders.

To Joie Detre, Pam Haggerty, Ka Pua'ala, Nerita Machado, Glenna Wilde and Maka'ala Yates for sharing their experiences with their *kūpuna* friends.

To Roger Jellinek and Eden-Lee Murray: the introductions I dedicate to you—you were right to insist on them.

To Marian Harden, Al Lagunero, Holly Richards and Vicky Schulte for their generosity.

And, certainly not last: to Ken Schmitt and Chris Recor for faithfully listening to unfinished chapters, and to Helga Fiederer, JJ Jasinski, Cathy Davenport, Lono Hunter, Marko Polo Cunningham, Jose Benitez, Judy Edwards, Jim Hedani, Cam Camara, Beth Marcil, Jon Woodhouse, Dave Baker, Kenny Redstone—the Hike Maui *'ohana*—for their moral and financial support during the three years it took to complete the book.

. . . mj harden

MJ HARDEN

After traveling the globe for years as a freelance travel writer, MJ settled on Maui where she has written a travel guide to Maui, published a feature magazine for Maui residents, started an arts and cultural magazine for Maui's cultural center, and written a medical magazine for Maui's hospital. As a journalist, she has researched and written about the Hawaiian culture since the early 1980s.

STEVE BRINKMAN

After graduating from Art Center College of Design in photography, Steve moved back to Hawai'i where he had previously earned his undergrad degree. In 1984 he opened a photo studio in Wailuku, Maui, where he still is today. Steve generally works with commercial clients, and has been published both nationally and internationally.